ARABIC
VOCABULARY

FOR ENGLISH SPEAKERS

ENGLISH ARABIC

The most useful words
To expand your lexicon and sharpen
your language skills

9000 words

Egyptian Arabic vocabulary for English speakers - 9000 words
By Andrey Taranov

T&P Books vocabularies are intended for helping you learn, memorize and review foreign words. The dictionary is divided into themes, covering all major spheres of everyday activities, business, science, culture, etc.

The process of learning words using T&P Books' theme-based dictionaries gives you the following advantages:

- Correctly grouped source information predetermines success at subsequent stages of word memorization
- Availability of words derived from the same root allowing memorization of word units (rather than separate words)
- Small units of words facilitate the process of establishing associative links needed for consolidation of vocabulary
- Level of language knowledge can be estimated by the number of learned words

T&P Books Publishing
www.tpbooks.com

ISBN: 978-1-78716-695-0

This book is also available in E-book formats.
Please visit www.tpbooks.com or the major online bookstores.

EGYPTIAN ARABIC VOCABULARY
for English speakers

T&P Books vocabularies are intended to help you learn, memorize, and review foreign words. The vocabulary contains over 9000 commonly used words arranged thematically.

- Vocabulary contains the most commonly used words
- Recommended as an addition to any language course
- Meets the needs of beginners and advanced learners of foreign languages
- Convenient for daily use, revision sessions, and self-testing activities
- Allows you to assess your vocabulary

Special features of the vocabulary

- Words are organized according to their meaning, not alphabetically
- Words are presented in three columns to facilitate the reviewing and self-testing processes
- Words in groups are divided into small blocks to facilitate the learning process
- The vocabulary offers a convenient and simple transcription of each foreign word

The vocabulary has 256 topics including:

Basic Concepts, Numbers, Colors, Months, Seasons, Units of Measurement, Clothing & Accessories, Food & Nutrition, Restaurant, Family Members, Relatives, Character, Feelings, Emotions, Diseases, City, Town, Sightseeing, Shopping, Money, House, Home, Office, Working in the Office, Import & Export, Marketing, Job Search, Sports, Education, Computer, Internet, Tools, Nature, Countries, Nationalities and more ...

T&P BOOKS' THEME-BASED DICTIONARIES

The Correct System for Memorizing Foreign Words

Acquiring vocabulary is one of the most important elements of learning a foreign language, because words allow us to express our thoughts, ask questions, and provide answers. An inadequate vocabulary can impede communication with a foreigner and make it difficult to understand a book or movie well.

The pace of activity in all spheres of modern life, including the learning of modern languages, has increased. Today, we need to memorize large amounts of information (grammar rules, foreign words, etc.) within a short period. However, this does not need to be difficult. All you need to do is to choose the right training materials, learn a few special techniques, and develop your individual training system.

Having a system is critical to the process of language learning. Many people fail to succeed in this regard; they cannot master a foreign language because they fail to follow a system comprised of selecting materials, organizing lessons, arranging new words to be learned, and so on. The lack of a system causes confusion and eventually, lowers self-confidence.

T&P Books' theme-based dictionaries can be included in the list of elements needed for creating an effective system for learning foreign words. These dictionaries were specially developed for learning purposes and are meant to help students effectively memorize words and expand their vocabulary.

Generally speaking, the process of learning words consists of three main elements:

- Reception (creation or acquisition) of a training material, such as a word list
- Work aimed at memorizing new words
- Work aimed at reviewing the learned words, such as self-testing

All three elements are equally important since they determine the quality of work and the final result. All three processes require certain skills and a well-thought-out approach.

New words are often encountered quite randomly when learning a foreign language and it may be difficult to include them all in a unified list. As a result, these words remain written on scraps of paper, in book margins, textbooks, and so on. In order to systematize such words, we have to create and continually update a "book of new words." A paper notebook, a netbook, or a tablet PC can be used for these purposes.

This "book of new words" will be your personal, unique list of words. However, it will only contain the words that you came across during the learning process. For example, you might have written down the words "Sunday," "Tuesday," and "Friday." However, there are additional words for days of the week, for example, "Saturday," that are missing, and your list of words would be incomplete. Using a theme dictionary, in addition to the "book of new words," is a reasonable solution to this problem.

The theme-based dictionary may serve as the basis for expanding your vocabulary.

It will be your big "book of new words" containing the most frequently used words of a foreign language already included. There are quite a few theme-based dictionaries available, and you should ensure that you make the right choice in order to get the maximum benefit from your purchase.

Therefore, we suggest using theme-based dictionaries from T&P Books Publishing as an aid to learning foreign words. Our books are specially developed for effective use in the sphere of vocabulary systematization, expansion and review.

Theme-based dictionaries are not a magical solution to learning new words. However, they can serve as your main database to aid foreign-language acquisition. Apart from theme dictionaries, you can have copybooks for writing down new words, flash cards, glossaries for various texts, as well as other resources; however, a good theme dictionary will always remain your primary collection of words.

T&P Books' theme-based dictionaries are specialty books that contain the most frequently used words in a language.

The main characteristic of such dictionaries is the division of words into themes. For example, the *City* theme contains the words "street," "crossroads," "square," "fountain," and so on. The *Talking* theme might contain words like "to talk," "to ask," "question," and "answer".

All the words in a theme are divided into smaller units, each comprising 3–5 words. Such an arrangement improves the perception of words and makes the learning process less tiresome. Each unit contains a selection of words with similar meanings or identical roots. This allows you to learn words in small groups and establish other associative links that have a positive effect on memorization.

The words on each page are placed in three columns: a word in your native language, its translation, and its transcription. Such positioning allows for the use of techniques for effective memorization. After closing the translation column, you can flip through and review foreign words, and vice versa. "This is an easy and convenient method of review – one that we recommend you do often."

Our theme-based dictionaries contain transcriptions for all the foreign words. Unfortunately, none of the existing transcriptions are able to convey the exact nuances of foreign pronunciation. That is why we recommend using the transcriptions only as a supplementary learning aid. Correct pronunciation can only be acquired with the help of sound. Therefore our collection includes audio theme-based dictionaries.

The process of learning words using T&P Books' theme-based dictionaries gives you the following advantages:

- You have correctly grouped source information, which predetermines your success at subsequent stages of word memorization
- Availability of words derived from the same root (lazy, lazily, lazybones), allowing you to memorize word units instead of separate words
- Small units of words facilitate the process of establishing associative links needed for consolidation of vocabulary
- You can estimate the number of learned words and hence your level of language knowledge
- The dictionary allows for the creation of an effective and high-quality revision process
- You can revise certain themes several times, modifying the revision methods and techniques
- Audio versions of the dictionaries help you to work out the pronunciation of words and develop your skills of auditory word perception

The T&P Books' theme-based dictionaries are offered in several variants differing in the number of words: 1.500, 3.000, 5.000, 7.000, and 9.000 words. There are also dictionaries containing 15,000 words for some language combinations. Your choice of dictionary will depend on your knowledge level and goals.

We sincerely believe that our dictionaries will become your trusty assistant in learning foreign languages and will allow you to easily acquire the necessary vocabulary.

TABLE OF CONTENTS

Medicine

HUMAN HABITAT
City

Dwelling. House. Home

PRONUNCIATION GUIDE

T&P phonetic alphabet	Egyptian Arabic example	English example
[a]	[ṭaffa] طفّى	shorter than in ask
[ā]	[exṭār] إختار	calf, palm
[e]	[setta] ستّة	elm, medal
[i]	[minā'] ميناء	shorter than in feet
[ī]	[ebrīl] إبريل	feet, meter
[o]	[oɣosṭos] أغسطس	pod, John
[ō]	[ḥalazōn] حلزون	fall, bomb
[u]	[kalkutta] كلكتا	book
[ū]	[gamūs] جاموس	fuel, tuna
[b]	[bedāya] بداية	baby, book
[d]	[sa'āda] سعادة	day, doctor
[ḍ]	[waḍʕ] وضع	[d] pharyngeal
[ʒ]	[arʒantīn] الأرجنتين	forge, pleasure
[ẓ]	[ẓahar] ظهر	[z] pharyngeal
[f]	[χafīf] خفيف	face, food
[g]	[bahga] بهجة	game, gold
[h]	[ettegāh] إتّجاه	home, have
[ḥ]	[ḥabb] حبّ	[h] pharyngeal
[y]	[dahaby] ذهبي	yes, New York
[k]	[korsy] كرسي	clock, kiss
[l]	[lammaḥ] لمّح	lace, people
[m]	[marṣad] مرصد	magic, milk
[n]	[ganūb] جنوب	sang, thing
[p]	[kaputʃino] كابتشينو	pencil, private
[q]	[wasaq] وثق	king, club
[r]	[roḥe] روح	rice, radio
[s]	[soχreya] سخرية	city, boss
[ṣ]	[me'ṣam] معصم	[s] pharyngeal
[ʃ]	['aʃā'] عشاء	machine, shark
[t]	[tanūb] تنوب	tourist, trip
[ṭ]	[χarīṭa] خريطة	[t] pharyngeal
[θ]	[mamūθ] ماموث	month, tooth
[v]	[vietnām] فيتنام	very, river
[w]	[wadda'] ودّع	vase, winter
[χ]	[baχīl] بخيل	as in Scots 'loch'
[ɣ]	[etɣadda] إتغدّى	between [g] and [h]

T&P phonetic alphabet	Egyptian Arabic example	English example
[z]	[me'za] معزة	zebra, please
['] (ayn)	[sab'a] سبعة	voiced pharyngeal fricative
['] (hamza)	[sa'al] سأل	glottal stop

ABBREVIATIONS
used in the vocabulary

Egyptian Arabic abbreviations

du	-	plural noun (double)
f	-	feminine noun
m	-	masculine noun
pl	-	plural

English abbreviations

ab.	-	about
adj	-	adjective
adv	-	adverb
anim.	-	animate
as adj	-	attributive noun used as adjective
e.g.	-	for example
etc.	-	et cetera
fam.	-	familiar
fem.	-	feminine
form.	-	formal
inanim.	-	inanimate
masc.	-	masculine
math	-	mathematics
mil.	-	military
n	-	noun
pl	-	plural
pron.	-	pronoun
sb	-	somebody
sing.	-	singular
sth	-	something
v aux	-	auxiliary verb
vi	-	intransitive verb
vi, vt	-	intransitive, transitive verb
vt	-	transitive verb

BASIC CONCEPTS

Basic concepts. Part 1

1. Pronouns

I, me	ana	أنا
you (masc.)	enta	أنت
you (fem.)	enty	أنت
he	howwa	هوّ
she	hiya	هيّ
we	eḥna	إحنا
you (to a group)	antom	أنتم
they	hamm	همّ

2. Greetings. Salutations. Farewells

Hello! (form.)	assalamu ʿalaykum!	السلام عليكم!
Good morning!	ṣabāḥ el χeyr!	صباح الخير!
Good afternoon!	neharak saʿīd!	نهارك سعيد!
Good evening!	masāʾ el χeyr!	مساء الخير!
to say hello	sallem	سلّم
Hi! (hello)	ahlan!	أهلاً!
greeting (n)	salām (m)	سلام
to greet (vt)	sallem ʿala	سلّم على
How are you?	ezzayek?	ازّيّك؟
What's new?	aχbārak eyh?	أخبارك ايه؟
Bye-Bye! Goodbye!	maʿ el salāma!	مع السلامة!
See you soon!	aʃūfak orayeb!	أشوفك قريب!
Farewell!	maʿ el salāma!	مع السلامة!
to say goodbye	waddaʿ	ودّع
So long!	bay bay!	باي باي!
Thank you!	ʃokran!	شكراً!
Thank you very much!	ʃokran geddan!	شكراً جداً!
You're welcome	el ʿafw	العفو
Don't mention it!	la ʃokr ʿala wāgeb	لا شكر على واجب
It was nothing	el ʿafw	العفو
Excuse me! (fam.)	ʿan eznak!	عن إذنك!

Excuse me! (form.)	ba'd ezn ḥadretak!	بعد إذن حضرتك!
to excuse (forgive)	'azar	عذر
to apologize (vi)	e'tazar	أعتذر
My apologies	ana 'āsef	أنا آسف
I'm sorry!	ana 'āsef!	أنا آسف!
to forgive (vt)	'afa	عفا
please (adv)	men faḍlak	من فضلك
Don't forget!	ma tensāʃ!	ما تنساش!
Certainly!	ṭab'an!	طبعاً!
Of course not!	la' ṭab'an!	لأ طبعاً!
Okay! (I agree)	ettafa'na!	إتّفقنا!
That's enough!	kefāya!	كفاية!

3. How to address

mister, sir	ya ostāz	يا أستاذ
ma'am	ya madām	يا مدام
miss	ya 'ānesa	يا آنسة
young man	ya ostāz	يا أستاذ
young man (little boy, kid)	yabny	يا ابني
miss (little girl)	ya benty	يا بنتي

4. Cardinal numbers. Part 1

0 zero	ṣefr	صفر
1 one	wāḥed	واحد
1 one (fem.)	waḥda	واحدة
2 two	etneyn	إتنين
3 three	talāta	ثلاثة
4 four	arba'a	أربعة
5 five	χamsa	خمسة
6 six	setta	ستّة
7 seven	sab'a	سبعة
8 eight	tamanya	ثمانية
9 nine	tes'a	تسعة
10 ten	'aʃara	عشرة
11 eleven	ḥedāʃar	حداشر
12 twelve	etnāʃar	إتناشر
13 thirteen	talattāʃar	تلاتّاشر
14 fourteen	arba'tāʃer	أربعتاشر
15 fifteen	χamastāʃer	خمستاشر
16 sixteen	settāʃar	ستّاشر
17 seventeen	saba'tāʃar	سبعتاشر

18 eighteen	tamantāʃar	تمنتاشر
19 nineteen	tesʿatāʃar	تسعتاشر
20 twenty	ʿeʃrīn	عشرين
21 twenty-one	wāḥed we ʿeʃrīn	واحد وعشرين
22 twenty-two	etneyn we ʿeʃrīn	إتنين وعشرين
23 twenty-three	talāta we ʿeʃrīn	ثلاثة وعشرين
30 thirty	talatīn	ثلاثين
31 thirty-one	wāḥed we talatīn	واحد وتلاتين
32 thirty-two	etneyn we talatīn	إتنين وتلاتين
33 thirty-three	talāta we talatīn	ثلاثة وثلاثين
40 forty	arbeʿīn	أربعين
41 forty-one	wāḥed we arbeʿīn	واحد وأربعين
42 forty-two	etneyn we arbeʿīn	إتنين وأربعين
43 forty-three	talāta we arbeʿīn	ثلاثة وأربعين
50 fifty	χamsīn	خمسين
51 fifty-one	wāḥed we χamsīn	واحد وخمسين
52 fifty-two	etneyn we χamsīn	إتنين وخمسين
53 fifty-three	talāta we χamsīn	ثلاثة وخمسين
60 sixty	settīn	ستّين
61 sixty-one	wāḥed we settīn	واحد وستّين
62 sixty-two	etneyn we settīn	إتنين وستّين
63 sixty-three	talāta we settīn	ثلاثة وستّين
70 seventy	sabʿīn	سبعين
71 seventy-one	wāḥed we sabʿīn	واحد وسبعين
72 seventy-two	etneyn we sabʿīn	إتنين وسبعين
73 seventy-three	talāta we sabʿīn	ثلاثة وسبعين
80 eighty	tamanīn	ثمانين
81 eighty-one	wāḥed we tamanīn	واحد وتمانين
82 eighty-two	etneyn we tamanīn	إتنين وتمانين
83 eighty-three	talāta we tamanīn	ثلاثة وثمانين
90 ninety	tesʿīn	تسعين
91 ninety-one	wāḥed we tesʿīn	واحد وتسعين
92 ninety-two	etneyn we tesʿīn	إتنين وتسعين
93 ninety-three	talāta we tesʿīn	ثلاثة وتسعين

5. Cardinal numbers. Part 2

100 one hundred	miya	ميّة
200 two hundred	meteyn	ميتين
300 three hundred	toltomiya	تلتميّة
400 four hundred	robʿomiya	ربعميّة
500 five hundred	χomsomiya	خمسميّة

600 six hundred	sotomiya	ستميّة
700 seven hundred	sob'omiya	سبعميّة
800 eight hundred	tomnome'a	ثمنمئة
900 nine hundred	tos'omiya	تسعميّة
1000 one thousand	alf	ألف
2000 two thousand	alfeyn	ألفين
3000 three thousand	talat 'ālāf	ثلاث آلاف
10000 ten thousand	'aʃaret 'ālāf	عشرة آلاف
one hundred thousand	mīt alf	ميت ألف
million	millyon (m)	مليون
billion	millyār (m)	مليار

6. Ordinal numbers

first (adj)	awwel	أوّل
second (adj)	tāny	ثاني
third (adj)	tālet	ثالث
fourth (adj)	rābe'	رابع
fifth (adj)	χāmes	خامس
sixth (adj)	sādes	سادس
seventh (adj)	sābe'	سابع
eighth (adj)	tāmen	ثامن
ninth (adj)	tāse'	تاسع
tenth (adj)	'āʃer	عاشر

7. Numbers. Fractions

fraction	kasr (m)	كسر
one half	noṣṣ	نص
one third	telt	ثلث
one quarter	rob'	ربع
one eighth	tomn	تمن
one tenth	'oʃr	عشر
two thirds	teleyn	تلتين
three quarters	talātet arbā'	ثلاثة أرباع

8. Numbers. Basic operations

subtraction	ṭarḥ (m)	طرح
to subtract (vi, vt)	ṭaraḥ	طرح
division	'esma (f)	قسمة
to divide (vt)	'asam	قسم
addition	gam' (m)	جمع

to add up (vt)	gama'	جمع
to add (vi, vt)	gama'	جمع
multiplication	ḍarb (m)	ضرب
to multiply (vt)	ḍarab	ضرب

9. Numbers. Miscellaneous

digit, figure	raqam (m)	رقم
number	'adad (m)	عدد
numeral	'adady (m)	عددي
minus sign	nā'eṣ (m)	ناقص
plus sign	zā'ed (m)	زائد
formula	mo'adla (f)	معادلة
calculation	ḥesāb (m)	حساب
to count (vi, vt)	'add	عدّ
to count up	ḥasab	حسب
to compare (vt)	qāran	قارن
How much?	kām?	كام؟
sum, total	magmū' (m)	مجموع
result	natīga (f)	نتيجة
remainder	bā'y (m)	باقي
a few (e.g., ~ years ago)	kām	كام
little (I had ~ time)	ʃewaya	شوية
the rest	el bā'y (m)	الباقي
one and a half	wāḥed w noṣṣ (m)	واحد ونصّ
dozen	desta (f)	دستة
in half (adv)	le noṣṣeyn	لنصّين
equally (evenly)	bel tasāwy	بالتساوى
half	noṣṣ (m)	نصّ
time (three ~s)	marra (f)	مرّة

10. The most important verbs. Part 1

to advise (vt)	naṣaḥ	نصح
to agree (say yes)	ettafa'	إتّفق
to answer (vi, vt)	gāwab	جاوب
to apologize (vi)	e'tazar	إعتذر
to arrive (vi)	weṣel	وصل
to ask (~ oneself)	sa'al	سأل
to ask (~ sb to do sth)	ṭalab	طلب
to be (vi)	kān	كان
to be afraid	χāf	خاف
to be hungry	'āyez 'ākol	عايز آكل

to be interested in ...	ehtamm be	إهتمّ بـ
to be needed	maṭlūb	مطلوب
to be surprised	etfāge'	إتفاجئ
to be thirsty	'āyez aʃrab	عايز أشرب
to begin (vt)	bada'	بدأ
to belong to ...	χaṣṣ	خصّ
to boast (vi)	tabāha	تباهى
to break (split into pieces)	kasar	كسر
to call (~ for help)	estaɣās	إستغاث
can (v aux)	'eder	قدر
to catch (vt)	mesek	مسك
to change (vt)	ɣayar	غيّر
to choose (select)	eχtār	إختار
to come down (the stairs)	nezel	نزل
to compare (vt)	qāran	قارن
to complain (vi, vt)	ʃaka	شكا
to confuse (mix up)	etlaχbaṭ	إتلخبط
to continue (vt)	wāṣel	واصل
to control (vt)	et-ḥakkem	إتحكّم
to cook (dinner)	ḥaḍḍar	حضّر
to cost (vt)	kallef	كلّف
to count (add up)	'add	عدّ
to count on ...	e'tamad 'ala ...	إعتمد على...
to create (vt)	'amal	عمل
to cry (weep)	baka	بكى

11. The most important verbs. Part 2

to deceive (vi, vt)	χada'	خدع
to decorate (tree, street)	zayen	زيّن
to defend (a country, etc.)	dāfa'	دافع
to demand (request firmly)	ṭāleb	طالب
to dig (vt)	ḥafar	حفر
to discuss (vt)	nā'eʃ	ناقش
to do (vt)	'amal	عمل
to doubt (have doubts)	ʃakk fe	شكّ في
to drop (let fall)	wa''a'	وقّع
to enter (room, house, etc.)	daχal	دخل
to exist (vi)	kān mawgūd	كان موجود
to expect (foresee)	tanabba'	تنبّأ
to explain (vt)	ʃaraḥ	شرح
to fall (vi)	we'e'	وقع
to find (vt)	la'a	لقى

to finish (vt)	χallaṣ	خلّص
to fly (vi)	ṭār	طار
to follow ... (come after)	tatabba'	تتبّع
to forget (vi, vt)	nesy	نسي
to forgive (vt)	'afa	عفا
to give (vt)	edda	إدّى
to give a hint	edda lamḥa	إدّى لمحة
to go (on foot)	meʃy	مشى
to go for a swim	sebeḥ	سبح
to go out (for dinner, etc.)	χarag	خرج
to guess (the answer)	χammen	خمّن
to have (vt)	malak	ملك
to have breakfast	feṭer	فطر
to have dinner	et'asʃa	إتعشّى
to have lunch	etɣadda	إتغدّى
to hear (vt)	seme'	سمع
to help (vt)	sā'ed	ساعد
to hide (vt)	χabba	خبّأ
to hope (vi, vt)	tamanna	تمنّى
to hunt (vi, vt)	eṣṭād	اصطاد
to hurry (vi)	esta'gel	إستعجل

12. The most important verbs. Part 3

to inform (vt)	'āl ly	قال لي
to insist (vi, vt)	aṣarr	أصرّ
to insult (vt)	ahān	أهان
to invite (vt)	'azam	عزم
to joke (vi)	hazzar	هزّر
to keep (vt)	ḥafaẓ	حفظ
to keep silent	seket	سكت
to kill (vt)	'atal	قتل
to know (sb)	'eref	عرف
to know (sth)	'eref	عرف
to laugh (vi)	ḍeḥek	ضحك
to liberate (city, etc.)	ḥarrar	حرّر
to like (I like ...)	'agab	عجب
to look for ... (search)	dawwar 'ala	دوّر على
to love (sb)	ḥabb	حبّ
to make a mistake	ɣeleṭ	غلط
to manage, to run	adār	أدار
to mean (signify)	'aṣad	قصد
to mention (talk about)	zakar	ذكر

to miss (school, etc.)	ɣāb	غاب
to notice (see)	lāḥaẓ	لاحظ
to object (vi, vt)	e'tarad̩	إعترض
to observe (see)	rāqab	راقب
to open (vt)	fataḥ	فتح
to order (meal, etc.)	ṭalab	طلب
to order (mil.)	amar	أمر
to own (possess)	malak	ملك
to participate (vi)	ʃārek	شارك
to pay (vi, vt)	dafa'	دفع
to permit (vt)	samaḥ	سمح
to plan (vt)	χaṭṭeṭ	خطّط
to play (children)	le'eb	لعب
to pray (vi, vt)	ṣalla	صلّى
to prefer (vt)	faḍḍal	فضّل
to promise (vt)	wa'ad	وعد
to pronounce (vt)	naṭa'	نطق
to propose (vt)	'araḍ	عرض
to punish (vt)	'āqab	عاقب

13. The most important verbs. Part 4

to read (vi, vt)	'ara	قرأ
to recommend (vt)	naṣaḥ	نصح
to refuse (vi, vt)	rafaḍ	رفض
to regret (be sorry)	nedem	ندم
to rent (sth from sb)	est'gar	إستأجر
to repeat (say again)	karrar	كرّر
to reserve, to book	ḥagaz	حجز
to run (vi)	gery	جري
to save (rescue)	anqaz	أنقذ
to say (~ thank you)	'āl	قال
to scold (vt)	wabbeχ	وبّخ
to see (vt)	ʃāf	شاف
to sell (vt)	bā'	باع
to send (vt)	arsal	أرسل
to shoot (vi)	ḍarab bel nār	ضرب بالنار
to shout (vi)	ṣarraχ	صرّخ
to show (vt)	warra	ورّى
to sign (document)	waqqa'	وقّع
to sit down (vi)	'a'ad	قعد
to smile (vi)	ebtasam	إبتسم
to speak (vi, vt)	kallem	كلّم

to steal (money, etc.)	sara'	سرق
to stop (for pause, etc.)	wa''af	وقّف
to stop (please ~ calling me)	baṭṭal	بطّل
to study (vt)	daras	درس
to swim (vi)	'ām	عام
to take (vt)	aχad	أخد
to think (vi, vt)	fakkar	فكّر
to threaten (vt)	hadded	هدّد
to touch (with hands)	lamas	لمس
to translate (vt)	targem	ترجم
to trust (vt)	wasaq	وثق
to try (attempt)	ḥāwel	حاول
to turn (e.g., ~ left)	ḥād	حاد
to underestimate (vt)	estaχaff	إستخفّ
to understand (vt)	fehem	فهِم
to unite (vt)	waḥḥed	وحّد
to wait (vt)	estanna	إستنّى
to want (wish, desire)	'āyez	عايز
to warn (vt)	ḥazzar	حذّر
to work (vi)	eʃtaɣal	إشتغل
to write (vt)	katab	كتب
to write down	katab	كتب

14. Colors

color	lone (m)	لون
shade (tint)	daraget el lōn (m)	درجة اللون
hue	ṣabɣet lōn (f)	صبغة اللون
rainbow	qose qozaḥ (m)	قوس قزح
white (adj)	abyaḍ	أبيض
black (adj)	aswad	أسود
gray (adj)	romādy	رمادي
green (adj)	aχḍar	أخضر
yellow (adj)	aṣfar	أصفر
red (adj)	aḥmar	أحمر
blue (adj)	azra'	أزرق
light blue (adj)	azra' fāteḥ	أزرق فاتح
pink (adj)	wardy	وردي
orange (adj)	bortoqāly	برتقاليّ
violet (adj)	banaffsegy	بنفسجي
brown (adj)	bonny	بنّي
golden (adj)	dahaby	ذهبي

silvery (adj)	feḍḍy	فضّي
beige (adj)	bɛ:ʒ	بيج
cream (adj)	'āgy	عاجي
turquoise (adj)	fayrūzy	فيروزي
cherry red (adj)	aḥmar karazy	أحمر كرزي
lilac (adj)	laylaky	ليّلكي
crimson (adj)	qormozy	قرمزي
light (adj)	fāteḥ	فاتح
dark (adj)	ɣāme'	غامق
bright, vivid (adj)	zāhy	زاهي
colored (pencils)	melawwen	ملوّن
color (e.g., ~ film)	melawwen	ملوّن
black-and-white (adj)	abyaḍ we aswad	أبيض وأسوَد
plain (one-colored)	sāda	سادة
multicolored (adj)	mota'added el alwān	متعددَ الألوان

15. Questions

Who?	mīn?	مين؟
What?	eyh?	ايه؟
Where? (at, in)	feyn?	فين؟
Where (to)?	feyn?	فين؟
From where?	meneyn?	منين؟
When?	emta	امتى؟
Why? (What for?)	'aʃān eyh?	عشان ايه؟
Why? (~ are you crying?)	leyh?	ليه؟
What for?	l eyh?	لـ ليه؟
How? (in what way)	ezāy?	إزاي؟
What? (What kind of ...?)	eyh?	ايه؟
Which?	ayī?	أيّ؟
To whom?	le mīn?	لمين؟
About whom?	'an mīn?	عن مين؟
About what?	'an eyh?	عن ايه؟
With whom?	ma' mīn?	مع مين؟
How many? How much?	kām?	كام؟
Whose?	betā'et mīn?	بتاعت مين؟

16. Prepositions

with (accompanied by)	ma'	مع
without	men ɣeyr	من غير
to (indicating direction)	ela	إلى
about (talking ~ ...)	'an	عن

before (in time)	'abl	قبل
in front of ...	'oddām	قدّام
under (beneath, below)	taḥt	تحت
above (over)	fo'e	فوق
on (atop)	'ala	على
from (off, out of)	men	من
of (made from)	men	من
in (e.g., ~ ten minutes)	ba'd	بعد
over (across the top of)	men 'ala	من على

17. Function words. Adverbs. Part 1

Where? (at, in)	feyn?	فين؟
here (adv)	hena	هنا
there (adv)	henāk	هناك
somewhere (to be)	fe makānen ma	في مكان ما
nowhere (not anywhere)	meʃ fi ayī makān	مش في أيّ مكان
by (near, beside)	ganb	جنب
by the window	ganb el ʃebbāk	جنب الشبّاك
Where (to)?	feyn?	فين؟
here (e.g., come ~!)	hena	هنا
there (e.g., to go ~)	henāk	هناك
from here (adv)	men hena	من هنا
from there (adv)	men henāk	من هناك
close (adv)	'arīb	قريب
far (adv)	be'īd	بعيد
near (e.g., ~ Paris)	'and	عند
nearby (adv)	'arīb	قريب
not far (adv)	meʃ be'īd	مش بعيد
left (adj)	el ʃemāl	الشمال
on the left	'alal ʃemāl	على الشمال
to the left	lel ʃemāl	للشمال
right (adj)	el yemīn	اليمين
on the right	'alal yemīn	على اليمين
to the right	lel yemīn	لليمين
in front (adv)	'oddām	قدّام
front (as adj)	amāmy	أمامي
ahead (the kids ran ~)	ela el amām	إلى الأمام
behind (adv)	wara'	وراء
from behind	men wara	من ورا

back (towards the rear)	le wara	لورا
middle	wasaṭ (m)	وسط
in the middle	fel wasaṭ	في الوسط
at the side	'ala ganb	على جنب
everywhere (adv)	fe kol makān	في كل مكان
around (in all directions)	ḥawaleyn	حوالين
from inside	men gowwah	من جوّه
somewhere (to go)	le 'ayī makān	لأي مكان
straight (directly)	'ala ṭūl	على طول
back (e.g., come ~)	rogū'	رجوع
from anywhere	men ayī makān	من أيّ مكان
from somewhere	men makānen mā	من مكان ما
firstly (adv)	awwalan	أوّلاً
secondly (adv)	sāneyan	ثانياً
thirdly (adv)	sālesan	ثالثاً
suddenly (adv)	fag'a	فجأة
at first (in the beginning)	fel bedāya	في البداية
for the first time	le 'awwel marra	لأوّل مرّة
long before ...	'abl ... be modda ṭawīla	قبل... بمدة طويلة
anew (over again)	men gedīd	من جديد
for good (adv)	lel abad	للأبد
never (adv)	abadan	أبداً
again (adv)	tāny	تاني
now (adv)	delwa'ty	دلوقتي
often (adv)	ketīr	كثير
then (adv)	wa'taha	وقتها
urgently (quickly)	'ala ṭūl	على طول
usually (adv)	'ādatan	عادةً
by the way, ...	'ala fekra ...	على فكرة...
possible (that is ~)	momken	ممكن
probably (adv)	momken	ممكن
maybe (adv)	momken	ممكن
besides ...	bel eḍāfa ela ...	بالإضافة إلى...
that's why ...	'aʃān keda	عشان كده
in spite of ...	bel raɣm men ...	بالرغم من...
thanks to ...	be faḍl ...	بفضل...
what (pron.)	elly	إللي
that (conj.)	ennu	إنّه
something	ḥāga (f)	حاجة
anything (something)	ayī ḥāga (f)	أيّ حاجة
nothing	wala ḥāga	ولا حاجة
who (pron.)	elly	إللي
someone	ḥadd	حد

somebody	ḥadd	حدّ
nobody	wala ḥadd	ولا حدّ
nowhere (a voyage to ~)	meʃ le wala makān	مش لـ ولا مكان
nobody's	wala ḥadd	ولا حدّ
somebody's	le ḥadd	لحدّ
so (I'm ~ glad)	geddan	جداً
also (as well)	kamān	كمان
too (as well)	kamān	كمان

18. Function words. Adverbs. Part 2

Why?	leyh?	ليه؟
for some reason	le sabeben ma	لسبب ما
because ...	ʻaʃān ...	... عشان
for some purpose	le hadafen mā	لهدف ما
and	w	و
or	walla	ولّا
but	bass	بسّ
for (e.g., ~ me)	ʻaʃān	عشان
too (~ many people)	ketīr geddan	كتير جدّاً
only (exclusively)	bass	بسّ
exactly (adv)	bel ḍabṭ	بالضبط
about (more or less)	naḥw	نحو
approximately (adv)	naḥw	نحو
approximate (adj)	taqrīby	تقريبي
almost (adv)	taʼrīban	تقريباً
the rest	el bāʼy (m)	الباقي
each (adj)	koll	كلّ
any (no matter which)	ayī	أيّ
many, much (a lot of)	ketīr	كتير
many people	nās ketīr	ناس كتير
all (everyone)	koll el nās	كلّ الناس
in return for ...	fi moqābel ...	... في مقابل
in exchange (adv)	fe moqābel	في مقابل
by hand (made)	bel yad	باليد
hardly (negative opinion)	bel kād	بالكاد
probably (adv)	momken	ممكن
on purpose (intentionally)	bel ʼaṣd	بالقصد
by accident (adv)	bel ṣodfa	بالصدفة
very (adv)	ʼawy	قويّ
for example (adv)	masalan	مثلاً
between	beyn	بين

among	wesṭ	وسط
so much (such a lot)	ketīr	كتير
especially (adv)	χāṣṣa	خاصّة

Basic concepts. Part 2

19. Weekdays

Monday	el etneyn (m)	الإتنين
Tuesday	el talāt (m)	التلات
Wednesday	el arbe'ā' (m)	الأربعاء
Thursday	el χamīs (m)	الخميس
Friday	el gom'a (m)	الجمعة
Saturday	el sabt (m)	السبت
Sunday	el aḥad (m)	الأحد
today (adv)	el naharda	النهارده
tomorrow (adv)	bokra	بكرة
the day after tomorrow	ba'd bokra (m)	بعد بكرة
yesterday (adv)	embāreḥ	امبارح
the day before yesterday	awwel embāreḥ	أوّل امبارح
day	yome (m)	يوم
working day	yome 'amal (m)	يوم عمل
public holiday	agāza rasmiya (f)	أجازة رسميَة
day off	yome el agāza (m)	يوم أجازة
weekend	nehāyet el osbū' (f)	نهاية الأسبوع
all day long	ṭūl el yome	طول اليوم
the next day (adv)	fel yome elly ba'dīh	في اليوم اللي بعديه
two days ago	men yomeyn	من يومين
the day before	fel yome elly 'ablo	في اليوم اللي قبله
daily (adj)	yawmy	يومي
every day (adv)	yawmiyan	يومياً
week	osbū' (m)	أسبوع
last week (adv)	el esbū' elly fāt	الأسبوع اللي فات
next week (adv)	el esbū' elly gayī	الأسبوع اللي جاي
weekly (adj)	osbū'y	أسبوعي
every week (adv)	osbū'iyan	أسبوعياً
twice a week	marreteyn fel osbū'	مرّتين في الأسبوع
every Tuesday	koll solasā'	كلّ ثلاثاء

20. Hours. Day and night

morning	ṣobḥ (m)	صبح
in the morning	fel ṣobḥ	في الصبح
noon, midday	ẓohr (m)	ظهر

in the afternoon	ba'd el ḍohr	بعد الظهر
evening	leyl (m)	ليل
in the evening	bel leyl	بالليل
night	leyl (m)	ليل
at night	bel leyl	بالليل
midnight	noṣṣ el leyl (m)	نصّ الليل
second	sanya (f)	ثانية
minute	de'ī'a (f)	دقيقة
hour	sā'a (f)	ساعة
half an hour	noṣṣ sā'a (m)	نصّ ساعة
a quarter-hour	rob' sā'a (f)	ربع ساعة
fifteen minutes	χamastāʃer de'ī'a	خمستاشر دقيقة
24 hours	arba'a we 'eʃrīn sā'a	أربعة وعشرين ساعة
sunrise	ʃorū' el ʃams (m)	شروق الشمس
dawn	fagr (m)	فجر
early morning	ṣobḥ badry (m)	صبح بدري
sunset	ɣorūb el ʃams (m)	غروب الشمس
early in the morning	el ṣobḥ badry	الصبح بدري
this morning	el naharda el ṣobḥ	النهاردة الصبح
tomorrow morning	bokra el ṣobḥ	بكرة الصبح
this afternoon	el naharda ba'd el ḍohr	النهاردة بعد الظهر
in the afternoon	ba'd el ḍohr	بعد الظهر
tomorrow afternoon	bokra ba'd el ḍohr	بكرة بعد الظهر
tonight (this evening)	el naharda bel leyl	النهاردة بالليل
tomorrow night	bokra bel leyl	بكرة بالليل
at 3 o'clock sharp	es sā'a talāta bel ḍabṭ	الساعة تلاتة بالضبط
about 4 o'clock	es sā'a arba'a ta'rīban	الساعة أربعة تقريبا
by 12 o'clock	ḥatt es sā'a etnāʃar	حتى الساعة إتناشر
in 20 minutes	fe χelāl 'eʃrīn de'ee'a	في خلال عشرين دقيقة
in an hour	fe χelāl sā'a	في خلال ساعة
on time (adv)	fe maw'edo	في موعده
a quarter of ...	ella rob'	إلّا ربع
within an hour	χelāl sā'a	خلال ساعة
every 15 minutes	koll rob' sā'a	كلّ ربع ساعة
round the clock	leyl nahār	ليل نهار

21. Months. Seasons

January	yanāyer (m)	يناير
February	febrāyer (m)	فبراير
March	māres (m)	مارس
April	ebrīl (m)	إبريل
May	māyo (m)	مايو

June	yonyo (m)	يونيو
July	yolyo (m)	يوليو
August	oɣosṭos (m)	أغسطس
September	sebtamber (m)	سبتمبر
October	oktober (m)	أكتوبر
November	november (m)	نوفمبر
December	desember (m)	ديسمبر
spring	rabee' (m)	ربيع
in spring	fel rabee'	في الربيع
spring (as adj)	rabee'y	ربيعي
summer	ṣeyf (m)	صيف
in summer	fel ṣeyf	في الصيف
summer (as adj)	ṣeyfy	صيفي
fall	χarīf (m)	خريف
in fall	fel χarīf	في الخريف
fall (as adj)	χarīfy	خريفي
winter	ʃetā' (m)	شتاء
in winter	fel ʃetā'	في الشتاء
winter (as adj)	ʃetwy	شتوي
month	ʃahr (m)	شهر
this month	fel ʃahr da	في الشهر ده
next month	el ʃahr el gayī	الشهر الجايّ
last month	el ʃahr elly fāt	الشهر اللي فات
a month ago	men ʃahr	من شهر
in a month (a month later)	ba'd ʃahr	بعد شهر
in 2 months (2 months later)	ba'd ʃahreyn	بعد شهرين
the whole month	el ʃahr kollo	الشهر كلّه
all month long	ṭawāl el ʃahr	طوال الشهر
monthly (~ magazine)	ʃahry	شهري
monthly (adv)	ʃahry	شهري
every month	koll ʃahr	كلّ شهر
twice a month	marreteyn fel ʃahr	مرّتين في الشهر
year	sana (f)	سنة
this year	el sana di	السنة دي
next year	el sana el gaya	السنة الجايّة
last year	el sana elly fātet	السنة اللي فاتت
a year ago	men sana	من سنة
in a year	ba'd sana	بعد سنة
in two years	ba'd sanateyn	بعد سنتين
the whole year	el sana kollaha	السنة كلّها
all year long	ṭūl el sana	طول السنة
every year	koll sana	كلّ سنة

annual (adj)	sanawy	سنوي
annually (adv)	koll sana	كلّ سنة
4 times a year	arbaʿ marrāt fel sana	أربع مرات في السنة
date (e.g., today's ~)	tarīχ (m)	تاريخ
date (e.g., ~ of birth)	tarīχ (m)	تاريخ
calendar	natīga (f)	نتيجة
half a year	noṣṣ sana	نصّ سنة
six months	settet aʃ-hor (f)	ستّة أشهر
season (summer, etc.)	faṣl (m)	فصل
century	qarn (m)	قرن

22. Time. Miscellaneous

time	wa'ʾt (m)	وقت
moment	laḥza (f)	لحظة
instant (n)	laḥza (f)	لحظة
instant (adj)	laḥza	لحظة
lapse (of time)	fatra (f)	فترة
life	ḥayah (f)	حياة
eternity	abadiya (f)	أبديّة
epoch	ʿahd (m)	عهد
era	ʿaṣr (m)	عصر
cycle	dawra (f)	دورة
period	fatra (f)	فترة
term (short-~)	fatra (f)	فترة
the future	el mostaqbal (m)	المستقبل
future (as adj)	elly gayī	اللي جاي
next time	el marra el gaya	المرّة الجايّة
the past	el māḍy (m)	الماضي
past (recent)	elly fāt	اللي فات
last time	el marra elly fātet	المرّة اللي فاتت
later (adv)	baʿdeyn	بعدين
after (prep.)	baʿd	بعد
nowadays (adv)	el ayām di	الأيام دي
now (adv)	delwaʾty	دلوقتي
immediately (adv)	ḥālan	حالاً
soon (adv)	ʾarīb	قريب
in advance (beforehand)	moʾaddaman	مقدّماً
a long time ago	men zamān	من زمان
recently (adv)	men ʾorayeb	من قريّب
destiny	maṣīr (m)	مصير
memories (childhood ~)	zekra (f)	زكرى
archives	arʃīf (m)	أرشيف
during ...	esnāʾ...	إثناء...

long, a long time (adv)	modda ṭawīla	مدّة طويلة
not long (adv)	le fatra 'aṣīra	لفترة قصيرة
early (in the morning)	badry	بدري
late (not early)	met'akχer	متأخّر
forever (for good)	lel abad	للأبد
to start (begin)	bada'	بدأ
to postpone (vt)	aggel	أجّل
at the same time	fe nafs el waqt	في نفس الوقت
permanently (adv)	be ʃakl dā'em	بشكل دائم
constant (noise, pain)	mostamerr	مستمرّ
temporary (adj)	mo'akkatan	مؤقتاً
sometimes (adv)	sa'āt	ساعات
rarely (adv)	nāderan	نادراً
often (adv)	ketīr	كثير

23. Opposites

rich (adj)	ɣany	غني
poor (adj)	fa'īr	فقير
ill, sick (adj)	marīḍ	مريض
well (not sick)	salīm	سليم
big (adj)	kebīr	كبير
small (adj)	ṣaɣīr	صغير
quickly (adv)	bosor'a	بسرعة
slowly (adv)	bo boṭ'	ببطء
fast (adj)	saree'	سريع
slow (adj)	baṭī'	بطيء
glad (adj)	farḥān	فرحان
sad (adj)	ḥazīn	حزين
together (adv)	ma' ba'ḍ	مع بعض
separately (adv)	le waḥdo	لوحده
aloud (to read)	beṣote 'āly	بصوت عالي
silently (to oneself)	beṣamt	بصمت
tall (adj)	'āly	عالي
low (adj)	wāṭy	واطي
deep (adj)	'amīq	عميق
shallow (adj)	ḍaḥl	ضحل
yes	aywa	أيوه

no	la'	لأ
distant (in space)	be'īd	بعيد
nearby (adj)	'arīb	قريب
far (adv)	be'īd	بعيد
nearby (adv)	'arīb	قريب
long (adj)	ṭawīl	طويل
short (adj)	'aṣīr	قصير
good (kindhearted)	ṭayeb	طيّب
evil (adj)	ʃerrīr	شرير
married (adj)	metgawwez	متجوّز
single (adj)	a'zab	أعزب
to forbid (vt)	mana'	منع
to permit (vt)	samaḥ	سمح
end	nehāya (f)	نهاية
beginning	bedāya (f)	بداية
left (adj)	el ʃemāl	الشمال
right (adj)	el yemīn	اليمين
first (adj)	awwel	أوّل
last (adj)	'āχer	آخر
crime	garīma (f)	جريمة
punishment	'eqāb (m)	عقاب
to order (vt)	amar	أمر
to obey (vi, vt)	ṭā'	طاع
straight (adj)	mostaqīm	مستقيم
curved (adj)	monḥany	منحني
paradise	el ganna (f)	الجنّة
hell	el gaḥīm (f)	الجحيم
to be born	etwalad	إتولّد
to die (vi)	māt	مات
strong (adj)	'awy	قوّي
weak (adj)	ḍa'īf	ضعيف
old (adj)	'agūz	عجوز
young (adj)	ʃāb	شاب
old (adj)	'adīm	قديم
new (adj)	gedīd	جديد
hard (adj)	ṣalb	صلب

soft (adj)	ṭary	طري
warm (tepid)	dāfy	دافي
cold (adj)	bāred	بارد
fat (adj)	teχīn	تخين
thin (adj)	rofaya'	رفيّع
narrow (adj)	ḍaye'	ضيّق
wide (adj)	wāse'	واسع
good (adj)	kewayes	كويّس
bad (adj)	weḥeʃ	وحش
brave (adj)	ʃogā'	شجاع
cowardly (adj)	gabān	جبان

24. Lines and shapes

square	morabba' (m)	مربّع
square (as adj)	morabba'	مربّع
circle	dayra (f)	دايرة
round (adj)	medawwar	مدوّر
triangle	mosallas (m)	مثلّث
triangular (adj)	mosallasy el ʃakl	مثلّثي الشكل
oval	bayḍawy (m)	بيضوّي
oval (as adj)	bayḍawy	بيضوّي
rectangle	mostaṭīl (m)	مستطيل
rectangular (adj)	mostaṭīly	مستطيلي
pyramid	haram (m)	هرم
rhombus	mo'ayen (m)	معيّن
trapezoid	ʃebh el monḥaref (m)	شبه المنحرف
cube	moka'ab (m)	مكعّب
prism	manʃūr (m)	منشور
circumference	moḥīṭ monḥany moɣlaq (m)	محيط منحنى مغلق
sphere	kora (f)	كرة
ball (solid sphere)	kora (f)	كرة
diameter	qaṭr (m)	قطر
radius	noṣṣ qaṭr (m)	نصّ قطر
perimeter (circle's ~)	moḥīṭ (m)	محيط
center	wasaṭ (m)	وسط
horizontal (adj)	ofoqy	أفقي
vertical (adj)	'amūdy	عمودي
parallel (n)	motawāz (m)	متواز
parallel (as adj)	motawāzy	متوازي
line	χaṭṭ (m)	خطّ
stroke	ḥaraka (m)	حركة

straight line	χaṭṭ mostaqīm (m)	خطّ مستقيم
curve (curved line)	χaṭṭ monḥany (m)	خطّ منحني
thin (line, etc.)	rofaya'	رفيّع
contour (outline)	kontūr (m)	كنتور
intersection	taqāṭo' (m)	تقاطع
right angle	zawya mostaqīma (f)	زاوية مستقيمة
segment	'eṭ'a (f)	قطعة
sector	qaṭā' (m)	قطاع
side (of triangle)	gāneb (m)	جانب
angle	zawya (f)	زاوية

25. Units of measurement

weight	wazn (m)	وزن
length	ṭūl (m)	طول
width	'arḍ (m)	عرض
height	ertefā' (m)	إرتفاع
depth	'omq (m)	عمق
volume	ḥagm (m)	حجم
area	mesāḥa (f)	مساحة
gram	gram (m)	جرام
milligram	milligrām (m)	ملّيغرام
kilogram	kilogrām (m)	كيلوغرام
ton	ṭenn (m)	طنّ
pound	reṭl (m)	رطل
ounce	onṣa (f)	أونصة
meter	metr (m)	متر
millimeter	millimetr (m)	ملّيمتر
centimeter	santimetr (m)	سنتيمتر
kilometer	kilometr (m)	كيلومتر
mile	mīl (m)	ميل
inch	boṣa (f)	بوصة
foot	'adam (m)	قدم
yard	yarda (f)	ياردة
square meter	metr morabba' (m)	متر مربّع
hectare	hektār (m)	هكتار
liter	litre (m)	لتر
degree	daraga (f)	درجة
volt	volt (m)	فولت
ampere	ambere (m)	أمبير
horsepower	ḥoṣān (m)	حصان
quantity	kemiya (f)	كميّة
a little bit of ...	ʃewayet ...	شويّة...

half	noṣṣ (m)	نصّ
dozen	desta (f)	دستة
piece (item)	waḥda (f)	وحدة
size	ḥagm (m)	حجم
scale (map ~)	me'yās (m)	مقياس
minimal (adj)	el adna	الأدنى
the smallest (adj)	el aṣɣar	الأصغر
medium (adj)	motawasseṭ	متوّسط
maximal (adj)	el aqṣa	الأقصى
the largest (adj)	el akbar	الأكبر

26. Containers

canning jar (glass ~)	barṭamān (m)	برطمان
can	kanz (m)	كانز
bucket	gardal (m)	جردل
barrel	barmīl (m)	برميل
wash basin (e.g., plastic ~)	ḥoḍe lel ɣasīl (m)	حوض للغسيل
tank (100L water ~)	χazzān (m)	خزّان
hip flask	zamzamiya (f)	زمزميّة
jerrycan	ʒerken (m)	جركن
tank (e.g., tank car)	χazzān (m)	خزّان
mug	mugg (m)	ماجّ
cup (of coffee, etc.)	fengān (m)	فنجان
saucer	ṭaba' fengān (m)	طبق فنجان
glass (tumbler)	kobbāya (f)	كوبّاية
wine glass	kāsa (f)	كاسة
stock pot (soup pot)	ḥalla (f)	حلّة
bottle (~ of wine)	ezāza (f)	إزازة
neck (of the bottle, etc.)	'onq (m)	عنق
carafe (decanter)	dawra' zogāgy (m)	دوّرق زجاجي
pitcher	ebrī' (m)	إبريق
vessel (container)	we'ā' (m)	وعاء
pot (crock, stoneware ~)	aṣīṣ (m)	أصيص
vase	vāza (f)	فازة
bottle (perfume ~)	ezāza (f)	إزازة
vial, small bottle	ezāza (f)	إزازة
tube (of toothpaste)	anbūba (f)	أنبوبة
sack (bag)	kīs (m)	كيس
bag (paper ~, plastic ~)	kīs (m)	كيس
pack (of cigarettes, etc.)	'elba (f)	علبة
box (e.g., shoebox)	'elba (f)	علبة

crate	ṣandū' (m)	صندوق
basket	salla (f)	سلّة

27. Materials

material	madda (f)	مادّة
wood (n)	χaʃab (m)	خشب
wood-, wooden (adj)	χaʃaby	خشبي
glass (n)	ezāz (m)	إزاز
glass (as adj)	ezāz	إزاز
stone (n)	ḥagar (m)	حجر
stone (as adj)	ḥagary	حجري
plastic (n)	blastik (m)	بلاستيك
plastic (as adj)	men el blastik	من البلاستيك
rubber (n)	maṭṭāṭ (m)	مطّاط
rubber (as adj)	maṭṭāṭy	مطّاطي
cloth, fabric (n)	'omāʃ (m)	قماش
fabric (as adj)	men el 'omāʃ	من القماش
paper (n)	wara' (m)	ورق
paper (as adj)	wara'y	ورقي
cardboard (n)	kartōn (m)	كرتون
cardboard (as adj)	kartony	كرتوني
polyethylene	bolyetylen (m)	بولي ايثيلين
cellophane	sellofān (m)	سيلوفان
plywood	ablakāʃ (m)	أبلكاش
porcelain (n)	borsalīn (m)	بورسلين
porcelain (as adj)	men el borsalīn	من البورسلين
clay (n)	ṭīn (m)	طين
clay (as adj)	fokχāry	فخّاري
ceramic (n)	seramīk (m)	سيراميك
ceramic (as adj)	men el seramik	من السيراميك

28. Metals

metal (n)	ma'dan (m)	معدن
metal (as adj)	ma'dany	معدني
alloy (n)	sebīka (f)	سبيكة
gold (n)	dahab (m)	ذهب
gold, golden (adj)	dahaby	ذهبي

silver (n)	faḍḍa (f)	فضّة
silver (as adj)	feḍḍy	فضّي
iron (n)	ḥadīd (m)	حديد
iron-, made of iron (adj)	ḥadīdy	حديدي
steel (n)	fulāz (m)	فولاذ
steel (as adj)	folāzy	فولاذي
copper (n)	neḥās (m)	نحاس
copper (as adj)	neḥāsy	نحاسي
aluminum (n)	aluminyum (m)	الومينيوم
aluminum (as adj)	aluminyum	الومينيوم
bronze (n)	bronze (m)	برونز
bronze (as adj)	bronzy	برونزي
brass	neḥās aṣfar (m)	نحاس أصفر
nickel	nikel (m)	نيكل
platinum	blatīn (m)	بلاتين
mercury	ze'baq (m)	زئبق
tin	'aṣdīr (m)	قصدير
lead	roṣāṣ (m)	رصاص
zinc	zink (m)	زنك

HUMAN BEING

Human being. The body

29. Humans. Basic concepts

human being	ensān (m)	إنسان
man (adult male)	rāgel (m)	راجل
woman	set (f)	ست
child	ṭefl (m)	طفل
girl	bent (f)	بنت
boy	walad (m)	ولد
teenager	morāheq (m)	مراهق
old man	ʿagūz (m)	عجوز
old woman	ʿagūza (f)	عجوزة

30. Human anatomy

organism (body)	ʿoḍw (m)	عضو
heart	ʾalb (m)	قلب
blood	damm (m)	دم
artery	ʃeryān (m)	شريان
vein	ʿerʾ (m)	عرق
brain	mokχ (m)	مخّ
nerve	ʿaṣab (m)	عصب
nerves	aʿṣāb (pl)	أعصاب
vertebra	faqra (f)	فقرة
spine (backbone)	ʿamūd faqry (m)	عمود فقري
stomach (organ)	meʿda (f)	معدة
intestines, bowels	amʿāʾ (pl)	أمعاء
intestine (e.g., large ~)	maʿy (m)	معى
liver	kebd (f)	كبد
kidney	kelya (f)	كلية
bone	ʿaḍm (m)	عظم
skeleton	haykal ʿazmy (m)	هيكل عظمي
rib	ḍelʿ (m)	ضلع
skull	gomgoma (f)	جمجمة
muscle	ʿaḍala (f)	عضلة
biceps	biseps (f)	بايسبس

triceps	triseps (f)	ترايسبس
tendon	watar (m)	وتر
joint	mefṣal (m)	مفصل
lungs	re'ateyn (du)	رئتين
genitals	a'ḍā' tanasoliya (pl)	أعضاء تناسلية
skin	boʃra (m)	بشرة

31. Head

head	ra's (m)	رأس
face	weʃ (m)	وش
nose	manaχīr (m)	مناخير
mouth	bo' (m)	بوء
eye	'eyn (f)	عين
eyes	'oyūn (pl)	عيون
pupil	ḥad'a (f)	حدقة
eyebrow	ḥāgeb (m)	حاجب
eyelash	remʃ (m)	رمش
eyelid	gefn (m)	جفن
tongue	lesān (m)	لسان
tooth	senna (f)	سنّة
lips	ʃafāyef (pl)	شفايف
cheekbones	'aḍmet el χadd (f)	عضمة الخدّ
gum	lassa (f)	لثّة
palate	ḥanak (m)	حنك
nostrils	manaχer (pl)	مناخر
chin	da''n (m)	دقن
jaw	fakk (m)	فكّ
cheek	χadd (m)	خدّ
forehead	gabha (f)	جبهة
temple	ṣedɣ (m)	صدغ
ear	wedn (f)	ودن
back of the head	'afa (m)	قفا
neck	ra'aba (f)	رقبة
throat	zore (m)	زور
hair	ʃa'r (m)	شعر
hairstyle	tasrīḥa (f)	تسريحة
haircut	tasrīḥa (f)	تسريحة
wig	barūka (f)	باروكة
mustache	ʃanab (pl)	شنب
beard	leḥya (f)	لحية
to have (a beard, etc.)	'ando	عنده
braid	ḍefīra (f)	ضفيرة
sideburns	sawālef (pl)	سوالف

red-haired (adj)	aḥmar el ʃaʿr	أحمر الشعر
gray (hair)	ʃaʿr abyaḍ	شعر أبيض
bald (adj)	aṣlaʿ	أصلع
bald patch	ṣalaʿ (m)	صلع
ponytail	deyl ḥoṣān (m)	ديل حصان
bangs	ʾoṣṣa (f)	قصّة

32. Human body

hand	yad (m)	يد
arm	derāʿ (f)	دراع
finger	ṣobāʿ (m)	صباع
toe	ṣobāʿ el ʾadam (m)	صباع القدم
thumb	ebhām (m)	إبهام
little finger	xonṣor (m)	خنصر
nail	ḍefr (m)	ضفر
fist	qabḍa (f)	قبضة
palm	kaff (f)	كفّ
wrist	meʿṣam (m)	معصم
forearm	sāʿed (m)	ساعد
elbow	kūʿ (m)	كوع
shoulder	ketf (f)	كتف
leg	regl (f)	رجل
foot	qadam (f)	قدم
knee	rokba (f)	ركبة
calf (part of leg)	semmāna (f)	سمّانة
hip	faxd (f)	فخد
heel	kaʿb (m)	كعب
body	gesm (m)	جسم
stomach	baṭn (m)	بطن
chest	ṣedr (m)	صدر
breast	sady (m)	ثدي
flank	ganb (m)	جنب
back	ḍahr (m)	ضهر
lower back	asfal el ḍahr (m)	أسفل الضهر
waist	wesṭ (f)	وسط
navel (belly button)	sorra (f)	سرّة
buttocks	ardāf (pl)	أرداف
bottom	debr (m)	دبر
beauty mark	ʃāma (f)	شامة
birthmark (café au lait spot)	waḥma	وحمة
tattoo	waʃm (m)	وشم
scar	nadba (f)	ندبة

Clothing & Accessories

33. Outerwear. Coats

clothes	malābes (pl)	ملابس
outerwear	malābes fo'aniya (pl)	ملابس فوقانيّة
winter clothing	malābes ʃetwiya (pl)	ملابس شتويّة
coat (overcoat)	balṭo (m)	بالطو
fur coat	balṭo farww (m)	بالطو فروّ
fur jacket	ʒaket farww (m)	جاكيت فروّ
down coat	balṭo maḥʃy rīʃ (m)	بالطو محشي ريش
jacket (e.g., leather ~)	ʒæket (m)	جاكيت
raincoat (trenchcoat, etc.)	ʒæket lel maṭar (m)	جاكيت للمطر
waterproof (adj)	wāqy men el maya	واقي من الميّة

34. Men's & women's clothing

shirt (button shirt)	'amīṣ (m)	قميص
pants	banṭalone (f)	بنطلون
jeans	ʒeans (m)	جينز
suit jacket	ʒæket (f)	جاكت
suit	badla (f)	بدلة
dress (frock)	fostān (m)	فستان
skirt	ʒība (f)	جيبة
blouse	bloza (f)	بلوزة
knitted jacket (cardigan, etc.)	kardigan (m)	كارديجن
jacket (of woman's suit)	ʒæket (m)	جاكيت
T-shirt	ti ʃirt (m)	تي شيرت
shorts (short trousers)	ʃort (m)	شورت
tracksuit	treneng (m)	ترينج
bathrobe	robe el ḥammām (m)	روب حمّام
pajamas	beʒāma (f)	بيجاما
sweater	blover (f)	بلوفر
pullover	blover (m)	بلوفر
vest	vest (m)	فيست
tailcoat	badlet sahra ṭawīla (f)	بدلة سهرة طويلة
tuxedo	badla (f)	بدلة

uniform	zayī muwaḥḥad (m)	زيّ موحّد
workwear	lebs el ʃoɣl (m)	لبس الشغل
overalls	overall (m)	اوفر اول
coat (e.g., doctor's smock)	balṭo (m)	بالطو

35. Clothing. Underwear

underwear	malābes dāχeliya (pl)	ملابس داخلية
boxers, briefs	sirwāl dāχly rigāly (m)	سروال داخلي رجالي
panties	sirwāl dāχly nisā'y (m)	سروال داخلي نسائي
undershirt (A-shirt)	fanella (f)	فانلّا
socks	ʃarāb (m)	شراب
nightgown	'amīṣ nome (m)	قميص نوم
bra	setyāna (f)	ستيانة
knee highs (knee-high socks)	ʃarabāt ṭawīla (pl)	شرابات طويلة
pantyhose	klone (m)	كلون
stockings (thigh highs)	gawāreb (pl)	جوارب
bathing suit	mayo (m)	مايّوه

36. Headwear

hat	ṭa'iya (f)	طاقيّة
fedora	borneyṭa (f)	برنيطة
baseball cap	base bāl kāb (m)	بيس بول كاب
flatcap	ṭa'iya mosaṭṭaḥa (f)	طاقيّة مسطحة
beret	bereyh (m)	بيريه
hood	ɣaṭa' (f)	غطاء
panama hat	qobba'et banama (f)	قبّعة بناما
knit cap (knitted hat)	ays kāb (m)	آيس كاب
headscarf	eʃarb (m)	إيشارب
women's hat	borneyṭa (f)	برنيطة
hard hat	χawza (f)	خوذة
garrison cap	kāb (m)	كاب
helmet	χawza (f)	خوذة
derby	qobba'a (f)	قبّعة
top hat	qobba'a rasmiya (f)	قبّعة رسمية

37. Footwear

footwear	gezam (pl)	جزم
shoes (men's shoes)	gazma (f)	جزمة

shoes (women's shoes)	gazma (f)	جزمة
boots (e.g., cowboy ~)	būt (m)	بوت
slippers	ʃebʃeb (m)	شبشب
tennis shoes (e.g., Nike ~)	kotʃy tennis (m)	كوتشي تنس
sneakers (e.g., Converse ~)	kotʃy (m)	كوتشي
sandals	ṣandal (pl)	صندل
cobbler (shoe repairer)	eskāfy (m)	إسكافي
heel	ka'b (m)	كعب
pair (of shoes)	goze (m)	جوز
shoestring	ʃerī'ṭ (m)	شريط
to lace (vt)	rabaṭ	ربط
shoehorn	labbāsa el gazma (f)	لبّاسة الجزمة
shoe polish	warnīʃ el gazma (m)	ورنيش الجزمة

38. Textile. Fabrics

cotton (n)	'oṭn (m)	قطن
cotton (as adj)	'oṭny	قطني
flax (n)	kettān (m)	كتّان
flax (as adj)	men el kettān	من الكتّان
silk (n)	ḥarīr (m)	حرير
silk (as adj)	ḥarīry	حريري
wool (n)	ṣūf (m)	صوف
wool (as adj)	ṣūfiya	صوفية
velvet	moχmal (m)	مخمل
suede	geld maz'abar (m)	جلد مزأبر
corduroy	'oṭṭn 'aṭīfa (f)	قطن قطيفة
nylon (n)	nylon (m)	نايلون
nylon (as adj)	men el naylon	من النيلون
polyester (n)	bolyester (m)	بوليستر
polyester (as adj)	men el bolyastar	من البوليستر
leather (n)	geld (m)	جلد
leather (as adj)	men el geld	من الجلد
fur (n)	farww (m)	فروّ
fur (e.g., ~ coat)	men el farww	من الفروّ

39. Personal accessories

gloves	gwanty (m)	جوانتي
mittens	gwanty men ɣeyr aṣābe' (m)	جوانتي من غير أصابع

scarf (muffler)	skarf (m)	سكارف
glasses (eyeglasses)	naḍḍāra (f)	نظّارة
frame (eyeglass ~)	eṭār (m)	إطار
umbrella	ʃamsiya (f)	شمسيّة
walking stick	ʿaṣāya (f)	عصاية
hairbrush	forʃet ʃaʿr (f)	فرشة شعر
fan	marwaḥa (f)	مروّحة
tie (necktie)	karavetta (f)	كرافتة
bow tie	bebyona (m)	بيبيونة
suspenders	ḥammala (f)	حمّالة
handkerchief	mandīl (m)	منديل
comb	meʃṭ (m)	مشط
barrette	dabbūs (m)	دبّوس
hairpin	bensa (m)	بنسة
buckle	bokla (f)	بكلة
belt	ḥezām (m)	حزام
shoulder strap	ḥammalet el ketf (f)	حمّالة الكتف
bag (handbag)	ʃanṭa (f)	شنطة
purse	ʃanṭet yad (f)	شنطة يد
backpack	ʃanṭet ḍahr (f)	شنطة ظهر

40. Clothing. Miscellaneous

fashion	mūḍa (f)	موضة
in vogue (adj)	fel moḍa	في الموضة
fashion designer	moṣammem azyāʾ (m)	مصمّم أزياء
collar	yāʾa (f)	ياقة
pocket	geyb (m)	جيب
pocket (as adj)	geyb	جيب
sleeve	komm (m)	كمّ
hanging loop	ʿelāqa (f)	علّاقة
fly (on trousers)	lesān (m)	لسان
zipper (fastener)	sosta (f)	سوستة
fastener	maʃbak (m)	مشبك
button	zerr (m)	زرّ
buttonhole	ʿarwa (f)	عروة
to come off (ab. button)	weʾeʿ	وقع
to sew (vi, vt)	χayaṭ	خيّط
to embroider (vi, vt)	ṭarraz	طرّز
embroidery	taṭrīz (m)	تطريز
sewing needle	ebra (f)	إبرة
thread	χeyṭ (m)	خيط
seam	derz (m)	درز

to get dirty (vi)	ettwassaχ	إتّوَسّخ
stain (mark, spot)	bo''a (f)	بقعة
to crease, crumple (vi)	takarmaʃ	تكرمش
to tear, to rip (vt)	'aṭa'	قطع
clothes moth	'etta (f)	عثّة

41. Personal care. Cosmetics

toothpaste	ma'gūn asnān (m)	معجون أسنان
toothbrush	forʃet senān (f)	فرشة أسنان
to brush one's teeth	naḍḍaf el asnān	نظّف الأسنان
razor	mūs (m)	موس
shaving cream	krīm ḥelā'a (m)	كريم حلاقة
to shave (vi)	ḥala'	حلق
soap	ṣabūn (m)	صابون
shampoo	ʃambū (m)	شامبو
scissors	ma'aṣ (m)	مقص
nail file	mabrad (m)	مبرد
nail clippers	mel'aṭ (m)	ملقط
tweezers	mel'aṭ (m)	ملقط
cosmetics	mawād tagmīl (pl)	مواد تجميل
face mask	mask (m)	ماسك
manicure	monekīr (m)	مونيكير
to have a manicure	'amal monikīr	عمل مونيكير
pedicure	badikīr (m)	باديكير
make-up bag	ʃanṭet mekyāʒ (f)	شنطة مكياج
face powder	bodret weʃ (f)	بودرة وش
powder compact	'elbet bodra (f)	علبة بودرة
blusher	aḥmar χodūd (m)	أحمر خدود
perfume (bottled)	barfān (m)	بارفان
toilet water (lotion)	kolonya (f)	كولونيا
lotion	loʃion (m)	لوشن
cologne	kolonya (f)	كولونيا
eyeshadow	eyeʃadow (m)	ايّ شادو
eyeliner	koḥl (m)	كحل
mascara	maskara (f)	ماسكارا
lipstick	rūʒ (m)	روج
nail polish, enamel	monekīr (m)	مونيكير
hair spray	mosabbet el ʃa'r (m)	مثبّت الشعر
deodorant	mozīl 'ara' (m)	مزيل عرق
cream	krīm (m)	كريم
face cream	krīm lel weʃ (m)	كريم للوش

hand cream	krīm eyd (m)	كريم أيد
anti-wrinkle cream	krīm moḍād lel taga'īd (m)	كريم مضاد للتجاعيد
day cream	krīm en nahār (m)	كريم النهار
night cream	krīm el leyl (m)	كريم الليل
day (as adj)	nahāry	نهاري
night (as adj)	layly	لَيلي
tampon	tambon (m)	تانبون
toilet paper (toilet roll)	wara' twalet (m)	ورق تواليت
hair dryer	seʃwār (m)	سشوار

42. Jewelry

jewelry	mogawharāt (pl)	مجوّهرات
precious (e.g., ~ stone)	ɣāly	غالي
hallmark stamp	damɣa (f)	دمغة
ring	χātem (m)	خاتم
wedding ring	deblet el faraḥ (m)	دبلة الفرح
bracelet	eswera (m)	إسوَرة
earrings	ḥala' (m)	حلق
necklace (~ of pearls)	'o'd (m)	عقد
crown	tāg (m)	تاج
bead necklace	'o'd χaraz (m)	عقد خرز
diamond	almāz (m)	ألماز
emerald	zomorrod (m)	زمرّد
ruby	ya'ūt aḥmar (m)	ياقوت أحمر
sapphire	ya'ūt azra' (m)	ياقوت أزرق
pearl	lo'lo' (m)	لؤلؤ
amber	kahramān (m)	كهرمان

43. Watches. Clocks

watch (wristwatch)	sā'a (f)	ساعة
dial	wag-h el sā'a (m)	وجه الساعة
hand (of clock, watch)	'a'rab el sā'a (m)	عقرب الساعة
metal watch band	ʃerī'ṭ sā'a ma'daniya (m)	شريط ساعة معدنية
watch strap	ʃerī'ṭ el sā'a (m)	شريط الساعة
battery	baṭṭariya (f)	بطّاريّة
to be dead (battery)	χelṣet	خلصت
to change a battery	ɣayar el baṭṭariya	غيّر البطّاريّة
to run fast	saba'	سبق
to run slow	ta'akχar	تأخّر
wall clock	sā'et ḥeyṭa (f)	ساعة حيطة
hourglass	sā'a ramliya (f)	ساعة رمليّة

sundial	sā'a ʃamsiya (f)	ساعة شمسيَة
alarm clock	monabbeh (m)	منبّه
watchmaker	sa'āty (m)	ساعاتي
to repair (vt)	ṣallaḥ	صلّح

Food. Nutricion

44. Food

meat	laḥma (f)	لحمة
chicken	ferāχ (m)	فراخ
Rock Cornish hen (poussin)	farrūg (m)	فروج
duck	baṭṭa (f)	بطّة
goose	wezza (f)	وزّة
game	ṣeyd (m)	صيد
turkey	dīk rūmy (m)	ديك رومي
pork	laḥm el χanazīr (m)	لحم الخنزير
veal	laḥm el ʿegl (m)	لحم العجل
lamb	laḥm ḍāny (m)	لحم ضاني
beef	laḥm baqary (m)	لحم بقري
rabbit	laḥm arāneb (m)	لحم أرانب
sausage (bologna, pepperoni, etc.)	sogo'' (m)	سجق
vienna sausage (frankfurter)	sogo'' (m)	سجق
bacon	bakon (m)	بيكون
ham	hām(m)	هام
gammon	faχd χanzīr (m)	فخد خنزير
pâté	maʿgūn laḥm (m)	معجون لحم
liver	kebda (f)	كبدة
hamburger (ground beef)	hamburger (m)	هامبورجر
tongue	lesān (m)	لسان
egg	beyḍa (f)	بيضة
eggs	beyḍ (m)	بيض
egg white	bayāḍ el beyḍ (m)	بياض البيض
egg yolk	ṣafār el beyḍ (m)	صفار البيض
fish	samak (m)	سمك
seafood	sīfūd (pl)	سي فود
caviar	kaviar (m)	كافيار
crab	kaboria (m)	كابوريا
shrimp	gammbary (m)	جمبري
oyster	maḥār (m)	محار
spiny lobster	estakoza (m)	استاكوزا
octopus	aχṭabūṭ (m)	أخطبوط

squid	kalmāry (m)	كالماري
sturgeon	samak el ḥaff (m)	سمك الحفش
salmon	salamon (m)	سلمون
halibut	samak el halbūt (m)	سمك الهلبوت
cod	samak el qadd (m)	سمك القد
mackerel	makerel (m)	ماكريل
tuna	tuna (f)	تونة
eel	ḥankalīs (m)	حنكليس
trout	salamon mera''aṭ (m)	سلمون مرقّط
sardine	sardīn (m)	سردين
pike	samak el karāky (m)	سمك الكراكي
herring	renga (f)	رنجة
bread	ʿeyʃ (m)	عيش
cheese	gebna (f)	جبنة
sugar	sokkar (m)	سكّر
salt	melḥ (m)	ملح
rice	rozz (m)	رزّ
pasta (macaroni)	makaruna (f)	مكرونة
noodles	nūdles (f)	نودلز
butter	zebda (f)	زبدة
vegetable oil	zeyt (m)	زيت
sunflower oil	zeyt ʿabbād el ʃams (m)	زيت عبّاد الشمس
margarine	margarīn (m)	مارجرين
olives	zaytūn (m)	زيتون
olive oil	zeyt el zaytūn (m)	زيت الزيتون
milk	laban (m)	لبن
condensed milk	ḥalīb mokassaf (m)	حليب مكثّف
yogurt	zabādy (m)	زبادي
sour cream	kreyma ḥamḍa (f)	كريمة حامضة
cream (of milk)	krīma (f)	كريمة
mayonnaise	mayonnɛ:z (m)	مايونيز
buttercream	krīmet zebda (f)	كريمة زبدة
cereal grains (wheat, etc.)	ḥobūb ʾamḥ (pl)	حبوب قمح
flour	deʾī (m)	دقيق
canned food	moʿallabāt (pl)	معلّبات
cornflakes	korn fleks (m)	كورن فليكس
honey	ʿasal (m)	عسل
jam	mrabba (m)	مربّى
chewing gum	lebān (m)	لبان

45. Drinks

water	meyāh (f)	مياه
drinking water	mayet ʃorb (m)	ميّة شرب
mineral water	maya ma'daniya (f)	ميّة معدنية
still (adj)	rakeda	راكدة
carbonated (adj)	kanz	كانز
sparkling (adj)	kanz	كانز
ice	talg (m)	ثلج
with ice	bel talg	بالتلج
non-alcoholic (adj)	men ɣeyr koḥūl	من غير كحول
soft drink	maʃrūb ɣāzy (m)	مشروب غازي
refreshing drink	ḥāga sa''a (f)	حاجة ساقعة
lemonade	limonāta (f)	ليموناتة
liquors	maʃrūbāt koḥūliya (pl)	مشروبات كحولية
wine	χamra (f)	خمرة
white wine	nebīz abyaḍ (m)	نبيذ أبيض
red wine	nebī aḥmar (m)	نبيذ أحمر
liqueur	liqure (m)	ليكيور
champagne	ʃambania (f)	شمبانيا
vermouth	vermote (m)	فيرموت
whiskey	wiski (m)	ويسكي
vodka	vodka (f)	فودكا
gin	ʒin (m)	جين
cognac	konyāk (m)	كونياك
rum	rum (m)	رم
coffee	'ahwa (f)	قهوة
black coffee	'ahwa sāda (f)	قهوة سادة
coffee with milk	'ahwa bel ḥalīb (f)	قهوة بالحليب
cappuccino	kaputʃino (m)	كابتشينو
instant coffee	neskafe (m)	نيسكافيه
milk	laban (m)	لبن
cocktail	koktayl (m)	كوكتيل
milkshake	milk ʃejk (m)	ميلك شيك
juice	'aṣīr (m)	عصير
tomato juice	'aṣīr ṭamāṭem (m)	عصير طماطم
orange juice	'aṣīr bortoqāl (m)	عصير برتقال
freshly squeezed juice	'aṣīr freʃ (m)	عصير فريش
beer	bīra (f)	بيرة
light beer	bīra χafīfa (f)	بيرة خفيفة
dark beer	bīra ɣam'a (f)	بيرة غامقة
tea	ʃāy (m)	شاي

black tea	ʃāy aḥmar (m)	شاي أحمر
green tea	ʃāy aχḍar (m)	شاي أخضر

46. Vegetables

vegetables	χoḍār (pl)	خضار
greens	χoḍrawāt waraqiya (pl)	خضروات ورقية
tomato	ṭamāṭem (f)	طماطم
cucumber	χeyār (m)	خيار
carrot	gazar (m)	جزر
potato	baṭāṭes (f)	بطاطس
onion	baṣal (m)	بصل
garlic	tūm (m)	ثوم
cabbage	koronb (m)	كرنب
cauliflower	'arnabīṭ (m)	قرنبيط
Brussels sprouts	koronb broksel (m)	كرنب بروكسل
broccoli	brokkoli (m)	بركولي
beetroot	bangar (m)	بنجر
eggplant	bātengān (m)	باذنجان
zucchini	kōsa (f)	كوسة
pumpkin	qarʿ ʿasaly (m)	قرع عسلي
turnip	left (m)	لفت
parsley	ba'dūnes (m)	بقدونس
dill	ʃabat (m)	شبت
lettuce	χass (m)	خسّ
celery	karfas (m)	كرفس
asparagus	helione (m)	هليون
spinach	sabāneχ (m)	سبانخ
pea	besella (f)	بسلّة
beans	fūl (m)	فول
corn (maize)	dora (f)	ذرة
kidney bean	faṣolya (f)	فاصوليا
bell pepper	felfel (m)	فلفل
radish	fegl (m)	فجل
artichoke	χarʃūf (m)	خرشوف

47. Fruits. Nuts

fruit	faχa (f)	فاكهة
apple	toffāḥa (f)	تفّاحة
pear	komettra (f)	كمّثرى
lemon	lymūn (m)	ليمون

orange	bortoqāl (m)	برتقال
strawberry (garden ~)	farawla (f)	فراولة
mandarin	yosfy (m)	يوسفي
plum	bar'ū' (m)	برقوق
peach	χawχa (f)	خوخة
apricot	meʃmeʃ (f)	مشمش
raspberry	tūt el 'alī' el aḥmar (m)	توت العليق الأحمر
pineapple	ananās (m)	أناناس
banana	moze (m)	موز
watermelon	baṭṭīχ (m)	بطّيخ
grape	'enab (m)	عنب
cherry	karaz (m)	كرز
melon	ʃammām (f)	شمّام
grapefruit	grabe frūt (m)	جريب فروت
avocado	avokado (f)	افوكاتو
papaya	babāya (m)	ببايا
mango	manga (m)	مانجة
pomegranate	rommān (m)	رمان
redcurrant	keʃmeʃ aḥmar (m)	كشمش أحمر
blackcurrant	keʃmeʃ aswad (m)	كشمش أسود
gooseberry	'enab el sa'lab (m)	عنب الثعلب
bilberry	'enab al aḥrāg (m)	عنب الأحراج
blackberry	tūt aswad (m)	توت أسود
raisin	zebīb (m)	زبيب
fig	tīn (m)	تين
date	tamr (m)	تمر
peanut	fūl sudāny (m)	فول سوداني
almond	loze (m)	لوز
walnut	'eyn gamal (f)	عين الجمل
hazelnut	bondo' (m)	بندق
coconut	goze el hend (m)	جوز هند
pistachios	fosto' (m)	فستق

48. Bread. Candy

bakers' confectionery (pastry)	ḥalawīāt (pl)	حلويّات
bread	'eyʃ (m)	عيش
cookies	baskawīt (m)	بسكويت
chocolate (n)	ʃokolāta (f)	شكولاتة
chocolate (as adj)	bel ʃokolāṭa	بالشكولاتة
candy (wrapped)	bonbony (m)	بونبوني
cake (e.g., cupcake)	keyka (f)	كيكة

cake (e.g., birthday ~)	torta (f)	تورتة
pie (e.g., apple ~)	feṭīra (f)	فطيرة
filling (for cake, pie)	ḥaʃwa (f)	حشوة
jam (whole fruit jam)	mrabba (m)	مربّى
marmalade	marmalād (f)	مرملاد
waffles	waffles (pl)	وافلز
ice-cream	'ays krīm (m)	آيس كريم
pudding	būding (m)	بودنج

49. Cooked dishes

course, dish	wagba (f)	وجبة
cuisine	maṭbaχ (m)	مطبخ
recipe	waṣfa (f)	وصفة
portion	naṣīb (m)	نصيب
salad	solṭa (f)	سلطة
soup	ʃorba (f)	شوربة
clear soup (broth)	mara'a (m)	مرقة
sandwich (bread)	sandawitʃ (m)	ساندويتش
fried eggs	beyḍ ma'ly (m)	بيض مقلي
hamburger (beefburger)	hamburger (m)	هامبورجر
beefsteak	steak laḥm (m)	ستيك لحم
side dish	ṭaba' gāneby (m)	طبق جانبي
spaghetti	spaɣetti (m)	سباجيتي
mashed potatoes	baṭāṭes mahrūsa (f)	بطاطس مهروسة
pizza	bītza (f)	بيتزا
porridge (oatmeal, etc.)	'aṣīda (f)	عصيدة
omelet	omlette (m)	اومليت
boiled (e.g., ~ beef)	maslū'	مسلوق
smoked (adj)	modakχen	مدخّن
fried (adj)	ma'ly	مقلي
dried (adj)	mogaffaf	مجفّف
frozen (adj)	mogammad	مجمّد
pickled (adj)	meχallel	مخلّل
sweet (sugary)	mesakkar	مسكّر
salty (adj)	māleḥ	مالح
cold (adj)	bāred	بارد
hot (adj)	soχn	سخن
bitter (adj)	morr	مرّ
tasty (adj)	ḥelw	حلو
to cook in boiling water	sala'	سلق
to cook (dinner)	ḥaḍḍar	حضّر

to fry (vt)	'ala	قلي
to heat up (food)	sakχan	سخّن
to salt (vt)	ras∫ malḥ	رشّ ملح
to pepper (vt)	ras∫ felfel	رشّ فلفل
to grate (vt)	bara∫	برش
peel (n)	'e∫ra (f)	قشرة
to peel (vt)	'as∫ar	قشّر

50. Spices

salt	melḥ (m)	ملح
salty (adj)	māleḥ	مالح
to salt (vt)	ras∫ malḥ	رشّ ملح
black pepper	felfel aswad (m)	فلفل أسود
red pepper (milled ~)	felfel aḥmar (m)	فلفل أحمر
mustard	mosṭarda (m)	مسطردة
horseradish	fegl ḥār (m)	فجل حار
condiment	bahār (m)	بهار
spice	bahār (m)	بهار
sauce	ṣalṣa (f)	صلصة
vinegar	χall (m)	خلّ
anise	yansūn (m)	ينسون
basil	rīḥān (m)	ريحان
cloves	'oronfol (m)	قرنفل
ginger	zangabīl (m)	زنجبيل
coriander	kozbora (f)	كزبرة
cinnamon	'erfa (f)	قرفة
sesame	semsem (m)	سمسم
bay leaf	wara' el ɣār (m)	ورق الغار
paprika	babrika (f)	بابريكا
caraway	karawya (f)	كراوية
saffron	za'farān (m)	زعفران

51. Meals

food	akl (m)	أكل
to eat (vi, vt)	akal	أكل
breakfast	foṭūr (m)	فطور
to have breakfast	feṭer	فطر
lunch	ɣada' (m)	غداء
to have lunch	etɣadda	إتغدّى
dinner	'a∫ā' (m)	عشاء

to have dinner	et'asʃa	إتعشّى
appetite	ʃahiya (f)	شهيّة
Enjoy your meal!	bel hana wel ʃefa!	!بالهنا والشفا
to open (~ a bottle)	fataḥ	فتح
to spill (liquid)	dala'	دلق
to spill out (vi)	dala'	دلق
to boil (vi)	ɣely	غلى
to boil (vt)	ɣely	غلى
boiled (~ water)	maɣly	مغلي
to chill, cool down (vt)	barrad	برّد
to chill (vi)	barrad	برّد
taste, flavor	ṭa'm (m)	طعم
aftertaste	ṭa'm ma ba'd el mazāq (m)	طعم ما بعد المذاق
to slim down (lose weight)	χass	خسّ
diet	reʒīm (m)	رجيم
vitamin	vitamīn (m)	فيتامين
calorie	so'ra ḥarāriya (f)	سعرة حراريّة
vegetarian (n)	nabāty (m)	نباتي
vegetarian (adj)	nabāty	نباتي
fats (nutrient)	dohūn (pl)	دهون
proteins	brotenāt (pl)	بروتينات
carbohydrates	naʃawīāt (pl)	نشويّات
slice (of lemon, ham)	ʃarīḥa (f)	شريحة
piece (of cake, pie)	'eṭ'a (f)	قطعة
crumb (of bread, cake, etc.)	fattāta (f)	فتاتة

52. Table setting

spoon	ma'la'a (f)	معلقة
knife	sekkīna (f)	سكّينة
fork	ʃawka (f)	شوكة
cup (e.g., coffee ~)	fengān (m)	فنجان
plate (dinner ~)	ṭaba' (m)	طبق
saucer	ṭaba' fengān (m)	طبق فنجان
napkin (on table)	mandīl wara' (m)	منديل ورق
toothpick	χallet senān (f)	خلة سنان

53. Restaurant

restaurant	maṭ'am (m)	مطعم
coffee house	'ahwa (f), kaféih (m)	قهوة ,كافيه

pub, bar	bār (m)	بار
tearoom	ṣalone ʃāy (m)	صالون شاي
waiter	garsone (m)	جرسون
waitress	garsona (f)	جرسونة
bartender	bārman (m)	بارمان
menu	qā'emet el ṭa'ām (f)	قائمة طعام
wine list	qā'emet el χomūr (f)	قائمة خمور
to book a table	ḥagaz sofra	حجز سفرة
course, dish	wagba (f)	وجبة
to order (meal)	ṭalab	طلب
to make an order	ṭalab	طلب
aperitif	ʃarāb (m)	شراب
appetizer	moqabbelāt (pl)	مقبّلات
dessert	ḥalawīāt (pl)	حلويّات
check	ḥesāb (m)	حساب
to pay the check	dafa' el ḥesāb	دفع الحساب
to give change	edda el bā'y	ادّي الباقي
tip	ba'ʃīʃ (m)	بقشيش

Family, relatives and friends

54. Personal information. Forms

name (first name)	esm (m)	اسم
surname (last name)	esm el 'a'ela (m)	اسم العائلة
date of birth	tarīχ el melād (m)	تاريخ الميلاد
place of birth	makān el melād (m)	مكان الميلاد
nationality	gensiya (f)	جنسيّة
place of residence	maqarr el eqāma (m)	مقرّ الإقامة
country	balad (m)	بلد
profession (occupation)	mehna (f)	مهنة
gender, sex	ginss (m)	جنس
height	ṭūl (m)	طول
weight	wazn (m)	وزن

55. Family members. Relatives

mother	walda (f)	والدة
father	wāled (m)	والد
son	walad (m)	ولد
daughter	bent (f)	بنت
younger daughter	el bent el saɣīra (f)	البنت الصغيرة
younger son	el ebn el saɣīr (m)	الابن الصغير
eldest daughter	el bent el kebīra (f)	البنت الكبيرة
eldest son	el ebn el kabīr (m)	الابن الكبير
brother	aχ (m)	أخ
elder brother	el aχ el kibīr (m)	الأخ الكبير
younger brother	el aχ el ṣoɣeyyir (m)	الأخ الصغير
sister	oχt (f)	أخت
elder sister	el uχt el kibīra (f)	الأخت الكبيرة
younger sister	el uχt el ṣoɣeyyira (f)	الأخت الصغيرة
cousin (masc.)	ibn 'amm (m), ibn χāl (m)	إبن عمّ, إبن خال
cousin (fem.)	bint 'amm (f), bint χāl (f)	بنت عمّ, بنت خال
mom, mommy	mama (f)	ماما
dad, daddy	baba (m)	بابا
parents	waldeyn (du)	والدين
child	ṭefl (m)	طفل
children	aṭfāl (pl)	أطفال

grandmother	gedda (f)	جدّة
grandfather	gadd (m)	جدّ
grandson	ḥafīd (m)	حفيد
granddaughter	ḥafīda (f)	حفيدة
grandchildren	aḥfād (pl)	أحفاد
uncle	ʿamm (m), χāl (m)	عمّ, خال
aunt	ʿamma (f), χāla (f)	عمة, خالة
nephew	ibn el aχ (m), ibn el uχt (m)	إبن الأخ, إبن الأخت
niece	bint el aχ (f), bint el uχt (f)	بنت الأخ, بنت الأخت
mother-in-law (wife's mother)	ḥamah (f)	حماة
father-in-law (husband's father)	ḥama (m)	حما
son-in-law (daughter's husband)	goze el bent (m)	جوز البنت
stepmother	merāt el abb (f)	مرات الأب
stepfather	goze el omm (m)	جوز الأم
infant	ṭefl raḍeeʿ (m)	طفل رضيع
baby (infant)	mawlūd (m)	موَلود
little boy, kid	walad ṣaɣīr (m)	ولد صغير
wife	goza (f)	جوزة
husband	goze (m)	جوز
spouse (husband)	goze (m)	جوز
spouse (wife)	goza (f)	جوزة
married (masc.)	metgawwez	متجوّز
married (fem.)	metgawweza	متجوّزة
single (unmarried)	aʿzab	أعزب
bachelor	aʿzab (m)	أعزب
divorced (masc.)	moṭallaq (m)	مطلّق
widow	armala (f)	أرملة
widower	armal (m)	أرمل
relative	ʾarīb (m)	قريب
close relative	nesīb ʾarīb (m)	نسيب قريب
distant relative	nesīb beʿīd (m)	نسيب بعيد
relatives	aqāreb (pl)	أقارب
orphan (boy or girl)	yatīm (m)	يتيم
guardian (of a minor)	walyī amr (m)	وليّ أمر
to adopt (a boy)	tabanna	تبنّى
to adopt (a girl)	tabanna	تبنّى

56. Friends. Coworkers

friend (masc.)	ṣadīq (m)	صديق
friend (fem.)	ṣadīqa (f)	صديقة

friendship	ṣadāqa (f)	صداقة
to be friends	ṣādaq	صادق
buddy (masc.)	ṣāḥeb (m)	صاحب
buddy (fem.)	ṣaḥba (f)	صاحبة
partner	rafī' (m)	رفيق
chief (boss)	ra'īs (m)	رئيس
superior (n)	el arfa' maqāman (m)	الأرفع مقاماً
owner, proprietor	ṣāḥib (m)	صاحب
subordinate (n)	tābe' (m)	تابع
colleague	zamīl (m)	زميل
acquaintance (person)	ma'refa (m)	معرفة
fellow traveler	rafī' safar (m)	رفيق سفر
classmate	zamīl fel ṣaff (m)	زميل في الصفّ
neighbor (masc.)	gār (m)	جار
neighbor (fem.)	gāra (f)	جارة
neighbors	gerān (pl)	جيران

57. Man. Woman

woman	set (f)	ست
girl (young woman)	bent (f)	بنت
bride	'arūsa (f)	عروسة
beautiful (adj)	gamīla	جميلة
tall (adj)	ṭawīla	طويلة
slender (adj)	raʃīqa	رشيقة
short (adj)	'aṣīra	قصيرة
blonde (n)	ʃa'ra (f)	شقراء
brunette (n)	zāt al ʃa'r el dāken (f)	ذات الشعر الداكن
ladies' (adj)	sayedāt	سيّدات
virgin (girl)	'azrā' (f)	عذراء
pregnant (adj)	ḥāmel	حامل
man (adult male)	rāgel (m)	راجل
blond (n)	aʃ'ar (m)	أشقر
brunet (n)	zu el ʃa'r el dāken (m)	ذو الشعر الداكن
tall (adj)	ṭawīl	طويل
short (adj)	'aṣīr	قصير
rude (rough)	waqeḥ	وقح
stocky (adj)	malyān	مليان
robust (adj)	matīn	متين
strong (adj)	'awy	قوّي
strength	'owwa (f)	قوّة

stout, fat (adj)	teχīn	تخين
swarthy (adj)	asmar	أسمر
slender (well-built)	raʃīq	رشيق
elegant (adj)	anīq	أنيق

58. Age

age	ʿomr (m)	عمر
youth (young age)	ʃabāb (m)	شباب
young (adj)	ʃāb	شاب
younger (adj)	aṣɣar	أصغر
older (adj)	akbar	أكبر
young man	ʃāb (m)	شاب
teenager	morāheq (m)	مراهق
guy, fellow	ʃāb (m)	شاب
old man	ʿagūz (m)	عجوز
old woman	ʿagūza (f)	عجوزة
adult (adj)	rāʃed (m)	راشد
middle-aged (adj)	fe montaṣaf el ʿomr	في منتصف العمر
elderly (adj)	ʿagūz	عجوز
old (adj)	ʿagūz	عجوز
retirement	maʿāʃ (m)	معاش
to retire (from job)	oḥīl ʿala el maʿāʃ	أحيل على المعاش
retiree	motaqāʿed (m)	متقاعد

59. Children

child	ṭefl (m)	طفل
children	aṭfāl (pl)	أطفال
twins	tawʾam (du)	توأم
cradle	mahd (m)	مهد
rattle	χoʃχeyʃa (f)	خشخيشة
diaper	bambarz, ḥaffāḍ (m)	بامبرز, حفاض
pacifier	bazzāza (f)	بزّازة
baby carriage	ʿarabet aṭfāl (f)	عربة أطفال
kindergarten	rawḍet aṭfāl (f)	روضة أطفال
babysitter	dāda (f)	دادة
childhood	ṭofūla (f)	طفولة
doll	ʿarūsa (f)	عروسة
toy	leʿba (f)	لعبة

construction set (toy)	moka''abāt (pl)	مكعّبات
well-bred (adj)	mo'addab	مؤدّب
ill-bred (adj)	'alīl el adab	قليل الأدب
spoiled (adj)	metdalla'	متدلّع
to be naughty	ʃefy	شقي
mischievous (adj)	la'ūb	لعوب
mischievousness	ez'āg (m)	إزعاج
mischievous child	ṭefl la'ūb (m)	طفل لعوب
obedient (adj)	moṭee'	مطيع
disobedient (adj)	'āq	عاقّ
docile (adj)	'ā'el	عاقل
clever (smart)	zaky	ذكي
child prodigy	ṭefl mo'geza (m)	طفل معجزة

60. Married couples. Family life

to kiss (vt)	bās	باس
to kiss (vi)	bās	باس
family (n)	'eyla (f)	عيلة
family (as adj)	'ā'ely	عائلي
couple	gozeyn (du)	جوزين
marriage (state)	gawāz (m)	جواز
hearth (home)	beyt (m)	بيت
dynasty	solāla ḥākema (f)	سلالة حاكمة
date	maw'ed (m)	موعد
kiss	bosa (f)	بوسة
love (for sb)	ḥobb (m)	حبّ
to love (sb)	ḥabb	حبّ
beloved	ḥabīb	حبيب
tenderness	ḥanān (m)	حنان
tender (affectionate)	ḥanūn	حنون
faithfulness	el eχlāṣ (m)	الإخلاص
faithful (adj)	moχleṣ	مخلص
care (attention)	'enāya (f)	عناية
caring (~ father)	mohtamm	مهتمّ
newlyweds	'arūseyn (du)	عروسين
honeymoon	ʃahr el 'asal (m)	شهر العسل
to get married (ab. woman)	tagawwaz	تجوّز
to get married (ab. man)	tagawwaz	تجوّز
wedding	faraḥ (m)	فرح
golden wedding	el zekra el χamsīn lel gawāz (f)	الذكرى الخمسين للجواز

anniversary	zekra sanawiya (f)	ذكرى سنوية
lover (masc.)	ḥabīb (m)	حبيب
mistress (lover)	ḥabība (f)	حبيبة
adultery	χeyāna zawgiya (f)	خيانة زوّجية
to cheat on ... (commit adultery)	χān	خان
jealous (adj)	ɣayūr	غيّور
to be jealous	ɣār	غار
divorce	ṭalā' (m)	طلاق
to divorce (vi)	ṭalla'	طلّق
to quarrel (vi)	etχāne'	إتخانق
to be reconciled (after an argument)	taṣālaḥ	تصالح
together (adv)	ma' ba'ḍ	مع بعض
sex	ginss (m)	جنس
happiness	sa'āda (f)	سعادة
happy (adj)	sa'īd	سعيد
misfortune (accident)	moṣība (m)	مصيبة
unhappy (adj)	ta'īs	تعيس

Character. Feelings. Emotions

61. Feelings. Emotions

feeling (emotion)	ʃoʻūr (m)	شعور
feelings	maʃāʻer (pl)	مشاعر
to feel (vt)	ʃaʻar	شعر
hunger	gūʻ (m)	جوع
to be hungry	ʻāyez ʼākol	عايز آكل
thirst	ʻaṭaʃ (m)	عطش
to be thirsty	ʻāyez aʃrab	عايز أشرب
sleepiness	neʻās (m)	نعاس
to feel sleepy	neʻes	نعس
tiredness	taʻab (m)	تعب
tired (adj)	taʻbān	تعبان
to get tired	teʻeb	تعب
mood (humor)	mazāg (m)	مزاج
boredom	malal (m)	ملل
to be bored	zeheʼ	زهق
seclusion	ʻozla (f)	عزلة
to seclude oneself	ʻazal	عزل
to worry (make anxious)	aʼlaʼ	أقلق
to be worried	ʼeleʼ	قلق
worrying (n)	ʼalaʼ (m)	قلق
anxiety	ʼalaʼ (m)	قلق
preoccupied (adj)	maʃɣūl el bāl	مشغول البال
to be nervous	etwattar	إتوّتر
to panic (vi)	etχaḍḍ	إتخضّ
hope	amal (m)	أمل
to hope (vi, vt)	tamanna	تمنّى
certainty	yaqīn (m)	يقين
certain, sure (adj)	motaʼakked	متأكّد
uncertainty	ʻadam el taʼakkod (m)	عدم التأكّد
uncertain (adj)	meʃ motaʼakked	مش متأكّد
drunk (adj)	sakrān	سكران
sober (adj)	ṣāḥy	صاحي
weak (adj)	ḍaʻīf	ضعيف
happy (adj)	saʻīd	سعيد
to scare (vt)	χawwef	خوّف

fury (madness)	ɣaḍab ʃedīd (m)	غضب شديد
rage (fury)	ɣaḍab (m)	غضب
depression	ekte'āb (m)	إكتئاب
discomfort (unease)	'adam erteyāḥ (m)	عدم إرتياح
comfort	rāḥa (f)	راحة
to regret (be sorry)	nedem	ندم
regret	nadam (m)	ندم
bad luck	sū' ḥaẓẓ (m)	سوء حظ
sadness	ḥozn (f)	حزن
shame (remorse)	χagal (m)	خجل
gladness	farah (m)	فرح
enthusiasm, zeal	ḥamās (m)	حماس
enthusiast	motaḥammes (m)	متحمّس
to show enthusiasm	taḥammas	تحمّس

62. Character. Personality

character	ʃaχṣiya (f)	شخصية
character flaw	'eyb (m)	عيب
mind, reason	'a'l (m)	عقل
conscience	ḍamīr (m)	ضمير
habit (custom)	'āda (f)	عادة
ability (talent)	qodra (f)	قدرة
can (e.g., ~ swim)	'eref	عرف
patient (adj)	ṣabūr	صبور
impatient (adj)	'alīl el ṣabr	قليل الصبر
curious (inquisitive)	foḍūly	فضولي
curiosity	foḍūl (m)	فضول
modesty	tawāḍo' (m)	تواضع
modest (adj)	motawāḍe'	متواضع
immodest (adj)	meʃ motawāḍe'	مش متواضع
laziness	kasal (m)	كسل
lazy (adj)	kaslān	كسلان
lazy person (masc.)	kaslān (m)	كسلان
cunning (n)	makr (m)	مكر
cunning (as adj)	makkār	مكّار
distrust	'adam el seqa (m)	عدم الثقة
distrustful (adj)	ʃakkāk	شكّاك
generosity	karam (m)	كرم
generous (adj)	karīm	كريم
talented (adj)	mawhūb	موهوب
talent	mawheba (f)	موهبة

courageous (adj)	ʃogāʿ	شجاع
courage	ʃagāʿa (f)	شجاعة
honest (adj)	amīn	أمين
honesty	amāna (f)	أمانة
careful (cautious)	ḥazer	حذر
brave (courageous)	ʃogāʿ	شجاع
serious (adj)	gād	جاد
strict (severe, stern)	ṣārem	صارم
decisive (adj)	ḥāsem	حاسم
indecisive (adj)	motaradded	متردّد
shy, timid (adj)	χagūl	خجول
shyness, timidity	χagal (m)	خجل
confidence (trust)	seqa (f)	ثقة
to believe (trust)	wasaq	وثق
trusting (credulous)	saree' el taṣdīq	سريع التصديق
sincerely (adv)	beṣarāḥa	بصراحة
sincere (adj)	moχleṣ	مخلص
sincerity	eχlāṣ (m)	إخلاص
open (person)	ṣarīḥ	صريح
calm (adj)	hady	هادئ
frank (sincere)	ṣarīḥ	صريح
naïve (adj)	sāzeg	ساذج
absent-minded (adj)	ʃāred el fekr	شارد الفكر
funny (odd)	moḍḥek	مضحك
greed	boχl (m)	بخل
greedy (adj)	ṭammāʿ	طماع
stingy (adj)	baχīl	بخيل
evil (adj)	ʃerrīr	شرير
stubborn (adj)	ʿanīd	عنيد
unpleasant (adj)	karīh	كريه
selfish person (masc.)	anāny (m)	أناني
selfish (adj)	anāny	أناني
coward	gabān (m)	جبان
cowardly (adj)	gabān	جبان

63. Sleep. Dreams

to sleep (vi)	nām	نام
sleep, sleeping	nome (m)	نوم
dream	ḥelm (m)	حلم
to dream (in sleep)	ḥelem	حلم
sleepy (adj)	naʿsān	نعسان
bed	serīr (m)	سرير

mattress	martaba (f)	مرتبة
blanket (comforter)	baṭṭaniya (f)	بطّانيّة
pillow	maχadda (f)	مخدّة
sheet	melāya (f)	ملاية
insomnia	araq (m)	أرق
sleepless (adj)	bodūn nome	بدون نوم
sleeping pill	monawwem (m)	منوّم
to take a sleeping pill	aχad monawwem	اخد منوّم
to feel sleepy	neʿes	نعس
to yawn (vi)	ettāweb	إتّاوب
to go to bed	rāḥ lel serīr	راح للسرير
to make up the bed	waḍḍab el serīr	وضّب السرير
to fall asleep	nām	نام
nightmare	kabūs (m)	كابوس
snore, snoring	ʃeχīr (m)	شخير
to snore (vi)	ʃakχar	شخّر
alarm clock	monabbeh (m)	منبّه
to wake (vt)	ṣaḥḥa	صحّى
to wake up	ṣeḥy	صحي
to get up (vi)	ʾām	قام
to wash up (wash face)	ɣasal	غسل

64. Humour. Laughter. Gladness

humor (wit, fun)	hezār (m)	هزار
sense of humor	ḥess fokāhy (m)	حسّ فكاهي
to enjoy oneself	estamtaʿ	إستمتع
cheerful (merry)	farḥān	فرحان
merriment (gaiety)	bahga (f)	بهجة
smile	ebtesāma (f)	إبتسامة
to smile (vi)	ebtasam	إبتسم
to start laughing	badaʾ yeḍḥak	بدأ يضحك
to laugh (vi)	ḍeḥek	ضحك
laugh, laughter	ḍeḥka (f)	ضحكة
anecdote	ḥekāya (f)	حكاية
funny (anecdote, etc.)	moḍḥek	مضحك
funny (odd)	moḍḥek	مضحك
to joke (vi)	hazzar	هزّر
joke (verbal)	nokta (f)	نكتة
joy (emotion)	saʿāda (f)	سعادة
to rejoice (vi)	mereḥ	مرح
joyful (adj)	saʿīd	سعيد

65. Discussion, conversation. Part 1

communication	tawāṣol (m)	تواصل
to communicate	tawāṣal	تواصل
conversation	moḥadsa (f)	محادثة
dialog	ḥewār (m)	حوار
discussion (discourse)	mona'ʃa (f)	مناقشة
dispute (debate)	χelāf (m)	خلاف
to dispute	χālef	خالف
interlocutor	muḥāwer (m)	محاوِر
topic (theme)	mawḍūʿ (m)	موضوع
point of view	weg-het naẓar (f)	وجهة نظر
opinion (point of view)	ra'yī (m)	رأي
speech (talk)	χeṭāb (m)	خطاب
discussion (of report, etc.)	mona'ʃa (f)	مناقشة
to discuss (vt)	nā'eʃ	ناقش
talk (conversation)	ḥadīs (m)	حديث
to talk (to chat)	dardeʃ	دردش
meeting	leqā' (m)	لقاء
to meet (vi, vt)	'ābel	قابل
proverb	masal (m)	مثل
saying	maqūla (f)	مقولة
riddle (poser)	loɣz (m)	لغز
to pose a riddle	toʃakkel loɣz	تشكّل لغز
password	kelmet el morūr (f)	كلمة مرور
secret	serr (m)	سرّ
oath (vow)	qasam (m)	قسم
to swear (an oath)	aqsam	أقسم
promise	waʿd (m)	وعد
to promise (vt)	waʿad	وعد
advice (counsel)	naṣīḥa (f)	نصيحة
to advise (vt)	naṣaḥ	نصح
to follow one's advice	tatabbaʿ naṣīḥa	تتبّع نصيحة
to listen to ... (obey)	aṭāʿ	أطاع
news	aχbār (m)	أخبار
sensation (news)	ḍagga (f)	ضجّة
information (data)	maʿlumāt (pl)	معلومات
conclusion (decision)	estentāg (f)	إستنتاج
voice	ṣote (m)	صوت
compliment	madḥ (m)	مدح
kind (nice)	laṭīf	لطيف
word	kelma (f)	كلمة
phrase	ʿebāra (f)	عبارة

answer	gawāb (m)	جواب
truth	ḥaʔīʔa (f)	حقيقة
lie	kezb (m)	كذب
thought	fekra (f)	فكرة
idea (inspiration)	fekra (f)	فكرة
fantasy	χayāl (m)	خيال

66. Discussion, conversation. Part 2

respected (adj)	moḥtaram	محترم
to respect (vt)	eḥtaram	إحترم
respect	eḥterām (m)	إحترام
Dear ... (letter)	ʿazīzy ...	عزيزي...
to introduce (sb to sb)	ʿarraf	عرّف
to make acquaintance	taʿarraf	تعرّف
intention	niya (f)	نيّة
to intend (have in mind)	nawa	نوى
wish	omniya (f)	أمنية
to wish (~ good luck)	tamanna	تمنّى
surprise (astonishment)	mofagʾa (f)	مفاجأة
to surprise (amaze)	fāgaʾ	فاجئ
to be surprised	etfāgeʾ	إتفاجئ
to give (vt)	edda	أدّى
to take (get hold of)	aχad	أخد
to give back	radd	ردّ
to return (give back)	raggaʿ	رجّع
to apologize (vi)	eʿtazar	إعتذر
apology	eʿtezār (m)	إعتذار
to forgive (vt)	ʿafa	عفا
to talk (speak)	etkallem	إتكلّم
to listen (vi)	semeʿ	سمع
to hear out	semeʿ	سمع
to understand (vt)	fehem	فهم
to show (to display)	ʿaraḍ	عرض
to look at ...	baṣṣ	بصّ
to call (yell for sb)	nāda	نادى
to distract (disturb)	ʃaɣal	شغل
to disturb (vt)	azʿag	أزعج
to pass (to hand sth)	sallem	سلّم
demand (request)	ṭalab (m)	طلب
to request (ask)	ṭalab	طلب
demand (firm request)	maṭlab (m)	مطلب

to demand (request firmly)	ṭāleb	طالب
to tease (call names)	ɣāẓ	غاظ
to mock (make fun of)	saχar	سخر
mockery, derision	soχreya (f)	سخرية
nickname	esm el ʃohra (m)	اسم الشهرة
insinuation	talmīḥ (m)	تلميح
to insinuate (imply)	lammaḥ	لمّح
to mean (vt)	'aṣad	قصد
description	waṣf (m)	وصف
to describe (vt)	waṣaf	وصف
praise (compliments)	madḥ (m)	مدح
to praise (vt)	madaḥ	مدح
disappointment	χeybet amal (f)	خيبة أمل
to disappoint (vt)	χayab	خيّب
to be disappointed	χābet 'āmalo	خابت آماله
supposition	efterāḍ (m)	إفتراض
to suppose (assume)	eftaraḍ	إفترض
warning (caution)	taḥzīr (m)	تحذير
to warn (vt)	ḥazzar	حذّر

67. Discussion, conversation. Part 3

to talk into (convince)	aqnaʿ	أقنع
to calm down (vt)	ṭam'an	طمأن
silence (~ is golden)	sokūt (m)	سكوت
to be silent (not speaking)	seket	سكت
to whisper (vi, vt)	hamas	همس
whisper	hamsa (f)	همسة
frankly, sincerely (adv)	beṣarāḥa	بصراحة
in my opinion ...	fi ra'yi ...	... في رأيي
detail (of the story)	tafṣīl (m)	تفصيل
detailed (adj)	mofaṣṣal	مفصّل
in detail (adv)	bel tafṣīl	بالتفصيل
hint, clue	talmīḥ (m)	تلميح
to give a hint	edda lamḥa	أدى لمحة
look (glance)	naẓra (f)	نظرة
to have a look	alqa nazra	ألقى نظرة
fixed (look)	sābet	ثابت
to blink (vi)	ramaʃ	رمش
to wink (vi)	ɣamaz	غمز
to nod (in assent)	haz rāso	هزّ رأسه

sigh	tanhīda (f)	تنهيدة
to sigh (vi)	tanahhad	تنهّد
to shudder (vi)	erta'aʃ	ارتعش
gesture	eʃāret yad (f)	إشارة يد
to touch (one's arm, etc.)	lamas	لمس
to seize (e.g., ~ by the arm)	mesek	مسك
to tap (on the shoulder)	ḥazz	حزّ
Look out!	χally bālak!	!خللي بالك
Really?	fe'lan	فعلاً؟
Are you sure?	enta mota'akked?	أنت متأكّد؟
Good luck!	bel tawfī'!	!بالتوفيق
I see!	wāḍeḥ!	!واضح
What a pity!	ya χesāra!	!يا خسارة

68. Agreement. Refusal

consent	mowafʼa (f)	موافقة
to consent (vi)	wāfe'	وافق
approval	'obūl (m)	قبول
to approve (vt)	'abal	قبل
refusal	rafḍ (m)	رفض
to refuse (vi, vt)	rafaḍ	رفض
Great!	'azīm!	!عظيم
All right!	tamām!	!تمام
Okay! (I agree)	ettafa'na!	!إتّفقنا
forbidden (adj)	mamnū'	ممنوع
it's forbidden	mamnū'	ممنوع
it's impossible	mostaḥīl	مستحيل
incorrect (adj)	ɣeleṭ	غلط
to reject (~ a demand)	rafaḍ	رفض
to support (cause, idea)	ayed	أيّد
to accept (~ an apology)	'abal	قبل
to confirm (vt)	akkad	أكّد
confirmation	ta'kīd (m)	تأكيد
permission	samāḥ (m)	سماح
to permit (vt)	samaḥ	سمح
decision	qarār (m)	قرار
to say nothing (hold one's tongue)	ṣamt	صمت
condition (term)	ʃarṭ (m)	شرط
excuse (pretext)	'ozr (m)	عذر
praise (compliments)	madḥ (m)	مدح
to praise (vt)	madaḥ	مدح

69. Success. Good luck. Failure

success	nagāḥ (m)	نجاح
successfully (adv)	be nagāḥ	بنجاح
successful (adj)	nāgeḥ	ناجح
luck (good luck)	ḥazz (m)	حظّ
Good luck!	bel tawfī'!	بالتوفيق!
lucky (e.g., ~ day)	maḥẓūẓ	محظوظ
lucky (fortunate)	maḥẓūẓ	محظوظ
failure	faʃal (m)	فشل
misfortune	sū' el ḥazz (m)	سوء الحظّ
bad luck	sū' el ḥazz (m)	سوء الحظّ
unsuccessful (adj)	ɣayr nāgeḥ	غير ناجح
catastrophe	karsa (f)	كارثة
pride	faχr (m)	فخر
proud (adj)	faχūr	فخور
to be proud	eftaχar	إفتخر
winner	fā'ez (m)	فائز
to win (vi)	fāz	فاز
to lose (not win)	χeser	خسر
try	moḥawla (f)	محاولة
to try (vi)	ḥāwel	حاول
chance (opportunity)	forṣa (f)	فرصة

70. Quarrels. Negative emotions

shout (scream)	ṣarχa (f)	صرخة
to shout (vi)	ṣarraχ	صرّخ
to start to cry out	ṣarraχ	صرّخ
quarrel	χenā'a (f)	خناقة
to quarrel (vi)	etχāne'	إتخانق
fight (squabble)	χenā'a (f)	خناقة
to make a scene	taʃāgar	تشاجر
conflict	χelāf (m)	خلاف
misunderstanding	sū' tafāhom (m)	سوء تفاهم
insult	ehāna (f)	إهانة
to insult (vt)	ahān	أهان
insulted (adj)	mohān	مهان
resentment	esteyā' (m)	إستياء
to offend (vt)	ahān	أهان
to take offense	estā'	إستاء
indignation	saχṭ (m)	سخط
to be indignant	estā'	إستاء

complaint	ʃakwa (f)	شكوَى
to complain (vi, vt)	ʃaka	شكا
apology	e'tezār (m)	إعتذار
to apologize (vi)	e'tazar	إعتذر
to beg pardon	e'tazar	إعتذر
criticism	naqd (m)	نقد
to criticize (vt)	naqad	نقد
accusation	ettehām (m)	إتّهام
to accuse (vt)	ettaham	إتّهم
revenge	enteqām (m)	إنتقام
to avenge (get revenge)	entaqam	إنتقم
to pay back	radd	ردّ
disdain	ezderā' (m)	إزدراء
to despise (vt)	eḥtaqar	إحتقر
hatred, hate	korh (f)	كره
to hate (vt)	kereh	كره
nervous (adj)	'aṣaby	عصبي
to be nervous	etwattar	إتوّتر
angry (mad)	ɣaḍbān	غضبان
to make angry	narfez	نرفز
humiliation	ezlāl (m)	إذلال
to humiliate (vt)	zallel	ذلّل
to humiliate oneself	tazallal	تذلّل
shock	ṣadma (f)	صدمة
to shock (vt)	ṣadam	صدم
trouble (e.g., serious ~)	moʃkela (f)	مشكلة
unpleasant (adj)	karīh	كريه
fear (dread)	χofe (m)	خوف
terrible (storm, heat)	ʃedīd	شديد
scary (e.g., ~ story)	moχīf	مخيف
horror	ro'b (m)	رعب
awful (crime, news)	baʃe'	بشع
to begin to tremble	erta'aʃ	إرتعش
to cry (weep)	baka	بكى
to start crying	bada' yebky	بدأ يبكي
tear	dama'a (f)	دمعة
fault	ɣalṭa (f)	غلطة
guilt (feeling)	zanb (m)	ذنب
dishonor (disgrace)	'ār (m)	عار
protest	eḥtegāg (m)	إحتجاج
stress	tawattor (m)	توتّر

to disturb (vt)	azʿag	أزعج
to be furious	ɣeḍeb	غضب
mad, angry (adj)	ɣaḍbān	غضبان
to end (~ a relationship)	anha	أنهى
to swear (at sb)	ʃatam	شتم
to scare (become afraid)	χāf	خاف
to hit (strike with hand)	ḍarab	ضرب
to fight (street fight, etc.)	χāneʾ	خانق
to settle (a conflict)	sawwa	سوّى
discontented (adj)	meʃ rāḍy	مش راضي
furious (adj)	ɣaḍbān	غضبان
It's not good!	keda meʃ kwayes!	!كده مش كويّس
It's bad!	keda weḥeʃ!	كده وحش!

Medicine

71. Diseases

sickness	maraḍ (m)	مرض
to be sick	mereḍ	مرض
health	ṣeḥḥa (f)	صحّة
runny nose (coryza)	raʃ-ḥ fel anf (m)	رشح في الأنف
tonsillitis	eltehāb el lawzateyn (m)	إلتهاب اللوزتين
cold (illness)	zokām (m)	زكام
to catch a cold	gālo bard	جاله برد
bronchitis	eltehāb ʃoʿaby (m)	إلتهاب شعبيّ
pneumonia	eltehāb raʾawy (m)	إلتهاب رئوي
flu, influenza	influenza (f)	إنفلونزا
nearsighted (adj)	ʾaṣīr el naẓar	قصير النظر
farsighted (adj)	beʿīd el naẓar	بعيد النظر
strabismus (crossed eyes)	ḥawal (m)	حوَل
cross-eyed (adj)	aḥwal	أحوَل
cataract	katarakt (f)	كاتاراكت
glaucoma	glawkoma (f)	جلوكوما
stroke	sakta (f)	سكتة
heart attack	azma ʾalbiya (f)	أزمة قلبية
myocardial infarction	nawba ʾalbiya (f)	نوبة قلبية
paralysis	ʃalal (m)	شلل
to paralyze (vt)	ʃall	شلّ
allergy	ḥasasiya (f)	حساسيّة
asthma	rabw (m)	ربو
diabetes	dāʾ el sokkary (m)	داء السكّري
toothache	alam asnān (m)	ألم الأسنان
caries	naχr el asnān (m)	نخر الأسنان
diarrhea	es-hāl (m)	إسهال
constipation	emsāk (m)	إمساك
stomach upset	edṭrāb el meʿda (m)	إضطراب المعدة
food poisoning	tasammom (m)	تسمّم
to get food poisoning	etsammem	إتسمّم
arthritis	eltehāb el mafāṣel (m)	إلتهاب المفاصل
rickets	kosāḥ el aṭfāl (m)	كساح الأطفال
rheumatism	rheumatism (m)	روماتزم

atherosclerosis	taṣṣallob el ʃarayīn (m)	تصلّب الشرايين
gastritis	eltehāb el me'da (m)	إلتهاب المعدة
appendicitis	eltehāb el zayda el dūdiya (m)	إلتهاب الزائدة الدودية
cholecystitis	eltehāb el marāra (m)	إلتهاب المرارة
ulcer	qorḥa (f)	قرحة
measles	maraḍ el ḥaṣba (m)	مرض الحصبة
rubella (German measles)	el ḥaṣba el almaniya (f)	الحصبة الألمانية
jaundice	yaraqān (m)	يرقان
hepatitis	eltehāb el kabed el vayrūsy (m)	إلتهاب الكبد الفيروسي
schizophrenia	fuṣām (m)	فصام
rabies (hydrophobia)	dā' el kalb (m)	داء الكلب
neurosis	eḍṭrāb 'aṣaby (m)	إضطراب عصبي
concussion	ertegāg el moχ (m)	إرتجاج المخ
cancer	saraṭān (m)	سرطان
sclerosis	taṣṣallob (m)	تصلّب
multiple sclerosis	taṣṣallob mota'added (m)	تصلّب متعدّد
alcoholism	edmān el χamr (m)	إدمان الخمر
alcoholic (n)	modmen el χamr (m)	مدمن الخمر
syphilis	syfilis el zehry (m)	سفلس الزهري
AIDS	el eydz (m)	الايدز
tumor	waram (m)	ورم
malignant (adj)	χabīs	خبيث
benign (adj)	ḥamīd (m)	حميد
fever	ḥomma (f)	حمّى
malaria	malaria (f)	ملاريا
gangrene	ɣanɣarīna (f)	غنغرينا
seasickness	dawār el baḥr (m)	دوار البحر
epilepsy	maraḍ el ṣara' (m)	مرض الصرع
epidemic	wabā' (m)	وباء
typhus	tyfus (m)	تيفوس
tuberculosis	maraḍ el soll (m)	مرض السلّ
cholera	kōlīra (f)	كوليرا
plague (bubonic ~)	ṭa'ūn (m)	طاعون

72. Symptoms. Treatments. Part 1

symptom	'araḍ (m)	عرض
temperature	ḥarāra (f)	حرارة
high temperature (fever)	ḥomma (f)	حمّى
pulse	nabḍ (m)	نبض
dizziness (vertigo)	dawχa (f)	دوخة

hot (adj)	soχn	سخن
shivering	ra'ʃa (f)	رعشة
pale (e.g., ~ face)	aṣfar	أصفر
cough	koḥḥa (f)	كحّة
to cough (vi)	kaḥḥ	كحّ
to sneeze (vi)	'aṭas	عطس
faint	dawχa (f)	دوخة
to faint (vi)	oɣma 'aleyh	أغمي عليه
bruise (hématome)	kadma (f)	كدمة
bump (lump)	tawarrom (m)	تورّم
to bang (bump)	etχabaṭ	إتخبط
contusion (bruise)	raḍḍa (f)	رضّة
to get a bruise	etkadam	إتكدم
to limp (vi)	'arag	عرج
dislocation	χal' (m)	خلع
to dislocate (vt)	χala'	خلع
fracture	kasr (m)	كسر
to have a fracture	enkasar	إنكسر
cut (e.g., paper ~)	garḥ (m)	جرح
to cut oneself	garaḥ nafsoh	جرح نفسه
bleeding	nazīf (m)	نزيف
burn (injury)	ḥar' (m)	حرق
to get burned	et-ḥara'	إتحرق
to prick (vt)	waχaz	وخز
to prick oneself	waχaz nafso	وخز نفسه
to injure (vt)	aṣāb	أصاب
injury	eṣāba (f)	إصابة
wound	garḥ (m)	جرح
trauma	ṣadma (f)	صدمة
to be delirious	haza	هذى
to stutter (vi)	tala'sam	تلعثم
sunstroke	ḍarabet ʃams (f)	ضربة شمس

73. Symptoms. Treatments. Part 2

pain, ache	alam (m)	ألم
splinter (in foot, etc.)	ʃazya (f)	شظية
sweat (perspiration)	'er' (m)	عرق
to sweat (perspire)	'ere'	عرق
vomiting	targee' (m)	ترجيع
convulsions	taʃonnogāt (pl)	تشنّجات
pregnant (adj)	ḥāmel	حامل

to be born	etwalad	اتوّلد
delivery, labor	welāda (f)	ولادة
to deliver (~ a baby)	walad	ولد
abortion	eg-hāḍ (m)	إجهاض
breathing, respiration	tanaffos (m)	تنفّس
in-breath (inhalation)	estenʃāq (m)	إستنشاق
out-breath (exhalation)	zafīr (m)	زفير
to exhale (breathe out)	zafar	زفر
to inhale (vi)	estanʃaq	إستنشق
disabled person	mo'āq (m)	معاق
cripple	moq'ad (m)	مقعد
drug addict	modmen moχaddarāt (m)	مدمن مخدّرات
deaf (adj)	aṭraʃ	أطرش
mute (adj)	aχras	أخرس
deaf mute (adj)	aṭraʃ aχras	أطرش أخرس
mad, insane (adj)	magnūn (m)	مجنون
madman (demented person)	magnūn (m)	مجنون
madwoman	magnūna (f)	مجنونة
to go insane	etgannen	اتجنّن
gene	ʒīn (m)	جين
immunity	manā'a (f)	مناعة
hereditary (adj)	werāsy	وراثي
congenital (adj)	χolqy men el welāda	خلقي من الولادة
virus	virūs (m)	فيروس
microbe	mikrūb (m)	ميكروب
bacterium	garsūma (f)	جرثومة
infection	'adwa (f)	عدوى

74. Symptoms. Treatments. Part 3

hospital	mostaʃfa (m)	مستشفى
patient	marīḍ (m)	مريض
diagnosis	taʃχīṣ (m)	تشخيص
cure	ʃefā' (m)	شفاء
medical treatment	'elāg ṭebby (m)	علاج طبي
to get treatment	et'āleg	اتعالج
to treat (~ a patient)	'ālag	عالج
to nurse (look after)	marraḍ	مرّض
care (nursing ~)	'enāya (f)	عناية
operation, surgery	'amaliya grāḥiya (f)	عمليّة جراحية
to bandage (head, limb)	ḍammad	ضمّد

bandaging	taḏmīd (m)	تضميد
vaccination	talqīḥ (m)	تلقيح
to vaccinate (vt)	laqqaḥ	لقّح
injection, shot	ḥo'na (f)	حقنة
to give an injection	ḥa'an ebra	حقن إبرة
attack	nawba (f)	نوبة
amputation	batr (m)	بتر
to amputate (vt)	batr	بتر
coma	ɣaybūba (f)	غيبوبة
to be in a coma	kān fi ḥālet ɣaybūba	كان في حالة غيبوبة
intensive care	el 'enāya el morakkaza (f)	العناية المركّزة
to recover (~ from flu)	ʃefy	شفي
condition (patient's ~)	ḥāla (f)	حالة
consciousness	wa'y (m)	وعي
memory (faculty)	zākera (f)	ذاكرة
to pull out (tooth)	χala'	خلع
filling	ḥaʃww (m)	حشو
to fill (a tooth)	ḥaʃa	حشا
hypnosis	el tanwīm el meɣnaṭīsy (m)	التنويم المغناطيسى
to hypnotize (vt)	nawwem	نوّم

75. Doctors

doctor	doktore (m)	دكتور
nurse	momarreḍa (f)	ممرّضة
personal doctor	doktore ʃaχṣy (m)	دكتور شخصي
dentist	doktore asnān (m)	دكتور أسنان
eye doctor	doktore el 'oyūn (m)	دكتور العيون
internist	ṭabīb baṭna (m)	طبيب باطنة
surgeon	garrāḥ (m)	جرّاح
psychiatrist	doktore nafsāny (m)	دكتور نفساني
pediatrician	doktore aṭfāl (m)	دكتور أطفال
psychologist	aχeṣā'y 'elm el nafs (m)	أخصائي علم النفس
gynecologist	doktore nesa (m)	دكتور نسا
cardiologist	doktore 'alb (m)	دكتور قلب

76. Medicine. Drugs. Accessories

medicine, drug	dawā' (m)	دواء
remedy	'elāg (m)	علاج
to prescribe (vt)	waṣaf	وصف
prescription	waṣfa (f)	وصفة

tablet, pill	'orṣ (m)	قرص
ointment	marham (m)	مرهم
ampule	ambūla (f)	أمبولة
mixture	dawā' ʃorb (m)	دواء شراب
syrup	ʃarāb (m)	شراب
pill	ḥabba (f)	حبّة
powder	zorūr (m)	ذرور
gauze bandage	ḍammāda ʃāʃ (f)	ضمادة شاش
cotton wool	'oṭn (m)	قطن
iodine	yūd (m)	يود
Band-Aid	blaster (m)	بلاستر
eyedropper	'aṭṭāra (f)	قطّارة
thermometer	termometr (m)	ترمومتر
syringe	serennga (f)	سرنّجة
wheelchair	korsy motaḥarrek (m)	كرسي متحرك
crutches	'okkāz (m)	عكّاز
painkiller	mosakken (m)	مسكّن
laxative	molayen (m)	مليّن
spirits (ethanol)	etanol (m)	إيثانول
medicinal herbs	a'ʃāb ṭebbiya (pl)	أعشاب طبّية
herbal (~ tea)	'oʃby	عشبي

77. Smoking. Tobacco products

tobacco	tabɣ (m)	تبغ
cigarette	segāra (f)	سيجارة
cigar	segār (m)	سيجار
pipe	ɣelyone (m)	غليون
pack (of cigarettes)	'elba (f)	علبة
matches	kebrīt (m)	كبريت
matchbox	'elbet kebrīt (f)	علبة كبريت
lighter	wallā'a (f)	ولّاعة
ashtray	ṭa'ṭū'a (f)	طقطوقة
cigarette case	'elbet sagāyer (f)	علبة سجائر
cigarette holder	ḥamelet segāra (f)	حاملة سيجارة
filter (cigarette tip)	filter (m)	فلتر
to smoke (vi, vt)	dakχen	دخّن
to light a cigarette	walla' segāra	ولّع سيجارة
smoking	tadχīn (m)	تدخين
smoker	modakχen (m)	مدخّن
stub, butt (of cigarette)	'aqab segāra (m)	عقب سيجارة
smoke, fumes	dokχān (m)	دخّان
ash	ramād (m)	رماد

HUMAN HABITAT

City

78. City. Life in the city

city, town	madīna (f)	مدينة
capital city	'āṣema (f)	عاصمة
village	qarya (f)	قرية
city map	χarīṭet el madinah (f)	خريطة المدينة
downtown	wesṭ el balad (m)	وسط البلد
suburb	ḍāḥeya (f)	ضاحية
suburban (adj)	el ḍawāḥy	الضواحي
outskirts	aṭrāf el madīna (pl)	أطراف المدينة
environs (suburbs)	ḍawāḥy el madīna (pl)	ضواحي المدينة
city block	ḥayī (m)	حي
residential block (area)	ḥayī sakany (m)	حي سكني
traffic	ḥaraket el morūr (f)	حركة المرور
traffic lights	eʃārāt el morūr (pl)	إشارات المرور
public transportation	wasā'el el na'l (pl)	وسائل النقل
intersection	taqāṭo' (m)	تقاطع
crosswalk	ma'bar (m)	معبر
pedestrian underpass	nafa' moʃāh (m)	نفق مشاه
to cross (~ the street)	'abar	عبر
pedestrian	māʃy (m)	ماشي
sidewalk	raṣīf (m)	رصيف
bridge	kobry (m)	كبري
embankment (river walk)	korneyʃ (m)	كورنيش
fountain	nafūra (f)	نافورة
allée (garden walkway)	mamʃa (m)	ممشى
park	ḥadīqa (f)	حديقة
boulevard	bolvār (m)	بولفار
square	medān (m)	ميدان
avenue (wide street)	ʃāre' (m)	شارع
street	ʃāre' (m)	شارع
side street	zo'ā' (m)	زقاق
dead end	ṭarī' masdūd (m)	طريق مسدود
house	beyt (m)	بيت
building	mabna (m)	مبنى

skyscraper	nāṭeḥet sahāb (f)	ناطحة سحاب
facade	waɣa (f)	واجهة
roof	sa'f (m)	سقف
window	ʃebbāk (m)	شبّاك
arch	qose (m)	قوس
column	ʿamūd (m)	عمود
corner	zawya (f)	زاوية
store window	vatrīna (f)	فترينة
signboard (store sign, etc.)	yafṭa, lāfeta (f)	لافتة, يافطة
poster	boster (m)	بوستر
advertising poster	boster eʿlān (m)	بوستر إعلان
billboard	lawḥet eʿlanāt (f)	لوحة إعلانات
garbage, trash	zebāla (f)	زبالة
trashcan (public ~)	ṣandū' zebāla (m)	صندوق زبالة
to litter (vi)	rama zebāla	رمى زبالة
garbage dump	mazbala (f)	مزبلة
phone booth	koʃk telefōn (m)	كشك تليفون
lamppost	ʿamūd nūr (m)	عمود نور
bench (park ~)	korsy (m)	كرسي
police officer	ʃorṭy (m)	شرطي
police	ʃorṭa (f)	شرطة
beggar	ʃaḥḥāt (m)	شحّات
homeless (n)	motaʃarred (m)	متشرّد

79. Urban institutions

store	maḥal (m)	محل
drugstore, pharmacy	ṣaydaliya (f)	صيدليّة
eyeglass store	maḥal naḍḍārāt (m)	محل نضّارات
shopping mall	mole (m)	مول
supermarket	subermarket (m)	سوبرماركت
bakery	maχbaz (m)	مخبز
baker	χabbāz (m)	خبّاز
pastry shop	ḥalawāny (m)	حلواني
grocery store	ba''āla (f)	بقّالة
butcher shop	gezāra (f)	جزارة
produce store	dokkān χoḍār (m)	دكّان خضار
market	sū' (f)	سوق
coffee house	'ahwa (f), kaféih (m)	قهوة, كافيه
restaurant	maṭʿam (m)	مطعم
pub, bar	bār (m)	بار
pizzeria	maḥal pizza (m)	محل بيتزا
hair salon	ṣalone ḥelā'a (m)	صالون حلاقة

post office	maktab el barīd (m)	مكتب البريد
dry cleaners	dray klīn (m)	دراي كلين
photo studio	estudio taṣwīr (m)	إستوديو تصوير
shoe store	maḥal gezam (m)	محل جزم
bookstore	maḥal kotob (m)	محل كتب
sporting goods store	maḥal mostalzamāt reyaḍiya (m)	محل مستلزمات رياضية
clothes repair shop	maḥal χeyāṭet malābes (m)	محل خياطة ملابس
formal wear rental	ta'gīr malābes rasmiya (m)	تأجير ملابس رسمية
video rental store	maḥal ta'gīr video (m)	محل تأجير فيديو
circus	serk (m)	سيرك
zoo	ḥadīqet el ḥayawān (f)	حديقة حيوان
movie theater	sinema (f)	سينما
museum	mat-ḥaf (m)	متحف
library	maktaba (f)	مكتبة
theater	masraḥ (m)	مسرح
opera (opera house)	obra (f)	أوبرا
nightclub	malha leyly (m)	ملهى ليَلي
casino	kazino (m)	كازينو
mosque	masged (m)	مسجد
synagogue	kenīs (m)	كنيس
cathedral	katedra'iya (f)	كاتدرائية
temple	ma'bad (m)	معبد
church	kenīsa (f)	كنيسة
college	kolliya (m)	كليّة
university	gam'a (f)	جامعة
school	madrasa (f)	مدرسة
prefecture	moqaṭ'a (f)	مقاطعة
city hall	baladiya (f)	بلديّة
hotel	fondo' (m)	فندق
bank	bank (m)	بنك
embassy	safāra (f)	سفارة
travel agency	ʃerket seyāḥa (f)	شركة سياحة
information office	maktab el este'lāmāt (m)	مكتب الإستعلامات
currency exchange	ṣarrāfa (f)	صرّافة
subway	metro (m)	مترو
hospital	mostaʃfa (m)	مستشفى
gas station	maḥaṭṭet banzīn (f)	محطّة بنزين
parking lot	maw'ef el 'arabeyāt (m)	موقف العربيات

80. Signs

signboard (store sign, etc.)	yafṭa, lāfeta (f)	لافتة, يافطة
notice (door sign, etc.)	bayān (m)	بيان
poster	boster (m)	بوستر
direction sign	'alāmet (f)	علامة إتجاه
arrow (sign)	'alāmet eʃāra (f)	علامة إشارة
caution	taḥzīr (m)	تحذير
warning sign	lāfetat taḥzīr (f)	لافتة تحذير
to warn (vt)	ḥazzar	حذّر
rest day (weekly ~)	yome 'oṭla (m)	يوم عطلة
timetable (schedule)	gadwal (m)	جدوَل
opening hours	aw'āt el 'amal (pl)	أوقات العمل
WELCOME!	ahlan w sahlan!	!أهلاَ وسهلا
ENTRANCE	doχūl	دخول
EXIT	χorūg	خروج
PUSH	edfa'	إدفع
PULL	es-ḥab	إسحب
OPEN	maftūḥ	مفتوح
CLOSED	moɣlaq	مغلق
WOMEN	lel sayedāt	للسيدات
MEN	lel regāl	للرجال
DISCOUNTS	χoṣomāt	خصومات
SALE	taχfeḍāt	تخفيضات
NEW!	gedīd!	جديد!
FREE	maggānan	مجّاناً
ATTENTION!	entebāh!	!إنتباه
NO VACANCIES	koll el amāken maḥgūza	كلّ الأماكن محجوزة
RESERVED	maḥgūz	محجوز
ADMINISTRATION	edāra	إدارة
STAFF ONLY	lel 'amelīn faqaṭ	للعاملين فقط
BEWARE OF THE DOG!	eḥzar wogūd kalb	إحذر وجود الكلب
NO SMOKING	mamnū' el tadχīn	ممنوع التدخين
DO NOT TOUCH!	'adam el lams	عدم اللمس
DANGEROUS	χaṭīr	خطير
DANGER	χaṭar	خطر
HIGH VOLTAGE	tayār 'āly	تيّار عالي
NO SWIMMING!	el sebāḥa mamnū'a	السباحة ممنوعة
OUT OF ORDER	mo'aṭṭal	معطّل
FLAMMABLE	saree' el eʃte'āl	سريع الإشتعال
FORBIDDEN	mamnū'	ممنوع

NO TRESPASSING!	mamnū' el morūr	ممنوع المرور
WET PAINT	eḥzar ṭelā' ɣayr gāf	احذر طلاء غير جاف

81. Urban transportation

bus	buṣ (m)	باص
streetcar	trām (m)	ترام
trolley bus	trolly buṣ (m)	ترولي باص
route (of bus, etc.)	χaṭṭ (m)	خطّ
number (e.g., bus ~)	raqam (m)	رقم
to go by ...	rāḥ be ...	راح بـ ...
to get on (~ the bus)	rekeb	ركب
to get off ...	nezel men	نزل من
stop (e.g., bus ~)	maw'af (m)	موقف
next stop	el maḥaṭṭa el gaya (f)	المحطة الجايّة
terminus	'āχer maw'af (m)	آخر موقف
schedule	gadwal (m)	جدول
to wait (vt)	estanna	إستنّى
ticket	tazkara (f)	تذكرة
fare	ogra (f)	أجرة
cashier (ticket seller)	kaʃier (m)	كاشيير
ticket inspection	taftīʃ el tazāker (m)	تفتيش التذاكر
ticket inspector	mofatteʃ tazāker (m)	مفتّش تذاكر
to be late (for ...)	met'akχer	متأخّر
to miss (~ the train, etc.)	ta'akχar	تأخّر
to be in a hurry	mesta'gel	مستعجل
taxi, cab	taksi (m)	تاكسي
taxi driver	sawwā' taksi (m)	سوّاق تاكسي
by taxi	bel taksi	بالتاكسي
taxi stand	maw'ef taksi (m)	موقف تاكسي
to call a taxi	kallem taksi	كلّم تاكسي
to take a taxi	aχad taksi	أخد تاكسي
traffic	ḥaraket el morūr (f)	حركة المرور
traffic jam	zaḥmet el morūr (f)	زحمة المرور
rush hour	sā'et el zorwa (f)	ساعة الذروة
to park (vi)	rakan	ركن
to park (vt)	rakan	ركن
parking lot	maw'ef el 'arabeyāt (m)	موقف العربيات
subway	metro (m)	مترو
station	maḥaṭṭa (f)	محطّة
to take the subway	aχad el metro	أخد المترو
train	qeṭār, 'aṭṭr (m)	قطار
train station	maḥaṭṭet qeṭār (f)	محطّة قطار

82. Sightseeing

monument	temsāl (m)	تمثال
fortress	ʾalʿa (f)	قلعة
palace	ʾaṣr (m)	قصر
castle	ʾalʿa (f)	قلعة
tower	borg (m)	برج
mausoleum	ḍarīḥ (m)	ضريح
architecture	handasa meʿmāriya (f)	هندسة معمارية
medieval (adj)	men el qorūn el wosṭa	من القرون الوسطى
ancient (adj)	ʿatīq	عتيق
national (adj)	waṭany	وطني
famous (monument, etc.)	maʃ-hūr	مشهور
tourist	sāʾeḥ (m)	سائح
guide (person)	morʃed (m)	مرشد
excursion, sightseeing tour	gawla (f)	جولة
to show (vt)	warra	ورّى
to tell (vt)	ʾāl	قال
to find (vt)	laʾa	لقى
to get lost (lose one's way)	ḍāʿ	ضاع
map (e.g., subway ~)	χarīṭa (f)	خريطة
map (e.g., city ~)	χarīṭa (f)	خريطة
souvenir, gift	tezkār (m)	تذكار
gift shop	maḥal hadāya (m)	محل هدايا
to take pictures	ṣawwar	صوّر
to have one's picture taken	etṣawwar	إتصوّر

83. Shopping

to buy (purchase)	eʃtara	إشترى
purchase	ḥāga (f)	حاجة
to go shopping	eʃtara	إشترى
shopping	ʃobbing (m)	شوبينج
to be open (ab. store)	maftūḥ	مفتوح
to be closed	moɣlaq	مغلق
footwear, shoes	gezam (pl)	جزم
clothes, clothing	malābes (pl)	ملابس
cosmetics	mawād tagmīl (pl)	مواد تجميل
food products	akl (m)	أكل
gift, present	hediya (f)	هديّة
salesman	bayāʿ (m)	بيّاع
saleswoman	bayāʿa (f)	بيّاعة

check out, cash desk	ṣandū' el daf' (m)	صندوق الدفع
mirror	merāya (f)	مراية
counter (store ~)	manḍada (f)	منضدة
fitting room	ɣorfet el 'eyās (f)	غرفة القياس
to try on	garrab	جرّب
to fit (ab. dress, etc.)	nāseb	ناسب
to like (I like ...)	'agab	عجب
price	se'r (m)	سعر
price tag	tiket el se'r (m)	تيكت السعر
to cost (vt)	kallef	كلّف
How much?	bekām?	بكام؟
discount	χaṣm (m)	خصم
inexpensive (adj)	meʃ ɣāly	مش غالي
cheap (adj)	reχīṣ	رخيص
expensive (adj)	ɣāly	غالي
It's expensive	da ɣāly	ده غالي
rental (n)	este'gār (m)	إستئجار
to rent (~ a tuxedo)	est'gar	إستأجر
credit (trade credit)	e'temān (m)	إئتمان
on credit (adv)	bel ta'seeṭ	بالتقسيط

84. Money

money	folūs (pl)	فلوس
currency exchange	taḥwīl 'omla (m)	تحويل عملة
exchange rate	se'r el ṣarf (m)	سعر الصرف
ATM	makinet ṣarrāf 'āly (f)	ماكينة صرّاف آلي
coin	'erʃ (m)	قرش
dollar	dolār (m)	دولار
euro	yoro (m)	يورو
lira	lira (f)	ليرة
Deutschmark	el mark el almāny (m)	المارك الألماني
franc	frank (m)	فرنك
pound sterling	geneyh esterlīny (m)	جنيه استرليني
yen	yen (m)	ين
debt	deyn (m)	دين
debtor	modīn (m)	مدين
to lend (money)	sallef	سلّف
to borrow (vi, vt)	estalaf	إستلف
bank	bank (m)	بنك
account	ḥesāb (m)	حساب
to deposit (vt)	awda'	أودع

to deposit into the account	awdaʿ fel ḥesāb	أوّدع في الحساب
to withdraw (vt)	saḥab men el ḥesāb	سحب من الحساب
credit card	kredit kard (f)	كريدت كارد
cash	kæʃ (m)	كاش
check	ʃīk (m)	شيك
to write a check	katab ʃīk	كتب شيك
checkbook	daftar ʃikāt (m)	دفتر شيكات
wallet	maḥfaẓa (f)	محفظة
change purse	maḥfazet fakka (f)	محفظة فكّة
safe	χazzāna (f)	خزّانة
heir	wāres (m)	وارث
inheritance	werāsa (f)	وراثة
fortune (wealth)	sarwa (f)	ثروّة
lease	ʿa'd el egār (m)	عقد الإيجار
rent (money)	ogret el sakan (f)	أجرة السكن
to rent (sth from sb)	est'gar	إستأجر
price	seʿr (m)	سعر
cost	taman (m)	ثمن
sum	mablaɣ (m)	مبلغ
to spend (vt)	ṣaraf	صرف
expenses	maṣarīf (pl)	مصاريف
to economize (vi, vt)	waffar	وفّر
economical	mowaffer	موّفر
to pay (vi, vt)	dafaʿ	دفع
payment	dafʿ (m)	دفع
change (give the ~)	el bā'y (m)	الباقي
tax	ḍarība (f)	ضريبة
fine	ɣarāma (f)	غرامة
to fine (vt)	faraḍ ɣarāma	فرض غرامة

85. Post. Postal service

post office	maktab el barīd (m)	مكتب البريد
mail (letters, etc.)	el barīd (m)	البريد
mailman	sāʿy el barīd (m)	ساعي البريد
opening hours	aw'āt el ʿamal (pl)	أوقات العمل
letter	resāla (f)	رسالة
registered letter	resāla mosaggala (f)	رسالة مسجّلة
postcard	kart barīdy (m)	كرت بريدي
telegram	barqiya (f)	برقيّة
package (parcel)	ṭard (m)	طرد

money transfer	ḥewāla māliya (f)	حوالة مالية
to receive (vt)	estalam	إستلم
to send (vt)	arsal	أرسل
sending	ersāl (m)	إرسال
address	ʿenwān (m)	عنوان
ZIP code	raqam el barīd (m)	رقم البريد
sender	morsel (m)	مرسل
receiver	morsel elayh (m)	مرسل إليه
name (first name)	esm (m)	اسم
surname (last name)	esm el ʿaʾela (m)	اسم العائلة
postage rate	taʿrīfa (f)	تعريفة
standard (adj)	ʿādy	عادي
economical (adj)	mowaffer	موَفر
weight	wazn (m)	وزن
to weigh (~ letters)	wazan	وزن
envelope	ẓarf (m)	ظرف
postage stamp	ṭābeʿ (m)	طابع
to stamp an envelope	alṣaq ṭābeʿ	ألصق طابع

Dwelling. House. Home

86. House. Dwelling

house	beyt (m)	بيت
at home (adv)	fel beyt	في البيت
yard	sāḥa (f)	ساحة
fence (iron ~)	sūr (m)	سور
brick (n)	ṭūb (m)	طوب
brick (as adj)	men el ṭūb	من الطوب
stone (n)	ḥagar (m)	حجر
stone (as adj)	ḥagary	حجري
concrete (n)	χarasāna (f)	خرسانة
concrete (as adj)	χarasāny	خرساني
new (new-built)	gedīd	جديد
old (adj)	'adīm	قديم
decrepit (house)	'āayel lel soqūṭ	آيل للسقوط
modern (adj)	mo'āṣer	معاصر
multistory (adj)	mota'added el ṭawābeq	متعدّد الطوابق
tall (~ building)	'āly	عالي
floor, story	dore (m)	دور
single-story (adj)	zu ṭābeq wāḥed	ذو طابق واحد
1st floor	el dore el awwal (m)	الدور الأوّل
top floor	ṭābe' 'olwy (m)	طابق علوي
roof	sa'f (m)	سقف
chimney	madχana (f)	مدخنة
roof tiles	qarmīd (m)	قرميد
tiled (adj)	men el qarmīd	من القرميد
attic (storage place)	'elya (f)	علية
window	ʃebbāk (m)	شبّاك
glass	ezāz (m)	إزاز
window ledge	ḥāfet el ʃebbāk (f)	حافة الشبّاك
shutters	ʃīʃ (m)	شيش
wall	ḥeyṭa (f)	حيطة
balcony	balakona (f)	بلكونة
downspout	masūret el taṣrīf (f)	ماسورة التصريف
upstairs (to be ~)	fo'e	فوق
to go upstairs	ṭele'	طلع
to come down (the stairs)	nezel	نزل
to move (to new premises)	na'al	نقل

87. House. Entrance. Lift

entrance	madχal (m)	مدخل
stairs (stairway)	sellem (m)	سلّم
steps	daragāt (pl)	درجات
banister	drabzīn (m)	درابزين
lobby (hotel ~)	ṣāla (f)	صالة
mailbox	ṣandū' el barīd (m)	صندوق البريد
garbage can	ṣandū' el zebāla (m)	صندوق الزبالة
trash chute	manfaz el zebāla (m)	منفذ الزبالة
elevator	asanseyr (m)	اسانسير
freight elevator	asanseyr el ʃaḥn (m)	اسانسير الشحن
elevator cage	kabīna (f)	كابينة
to take the elevator	rekeb el asanseyr	ركب الاسانسير
apartment	ʃa''a (f)	شقّة
residents (~ of a building)	sokkān (pl)	سكّان
neighbor (masc.)	gār (m)	جار
neighbor (fem.)	gāra (f)	جارة
neighbors	gerān (pl)	جيران

88. House. Electricity

electricity	kahraba' (m)	كهرباء
light bulb	lammba (f)	لمبة
switch	meftāḥ (m)	مفتاح
fuse (plug fuse)	fuse (m)	فيوز
cable, wire (electric ~)	selk (m)	سلك
wiring	aslāk (pl)	أسلاك
electricity meter	'addād (m)	عدّاد
readings	qerā'a (f)	قراءة

89. House. Doors. Locks

door	bāb (m)	باب
gate (vehicle ~)	bawwāba (f)	بوّابة
handle, doorknob	okret el bāb (f)	اوكرة الباب
to unlock (unbolt)	fataḥ	فتح
to open (vt)	fataḥ	فتح
to close (vt)	'afal	قفل
key	meftāḥ (m)	مفتاح
bunch (of keys)	rabṭa (f)	ربطة
to creak (door, etc.)	ṣarr	صر

creak	ṣarīr (m)	صرير
hinge (door ~)	mafaṣṣla (f)	مفصّلة
doormat	seggādet bāb (f)	سجّادة باب
door lock	'efl el bāb (m)	قفل الباب
keyhole	χorm el meftāḥ (m)	خرم المفتاح
crossbar (sliding bar)	terbās (m)	ترباس
door latch	terbās (m)	ترباس
padlock	'efl (m)	قفل
to ring (~ the door bell)	rann	رنّ
ringing (sound)	ranīn (m)	رنين
doorbell	garas (m)	جرس
doorbell button	zerr (m)	زرّ
knock (at the door)	ṭar', da'' (m)	طرق, دقّ
to knock (vi)	χabbaṭ	خبّط
code	kōd (m)	كود
combination lock	kōd (m)	كود
intercom	garas el bāb (m)	جرس الباب
number (on the door)	raqam (m)	رقم
doorplate	lawḥa (f)	لوحة
peephole	el 'eyn el seḥriya (m)	العين السحرية

90. Country house

village	qarya (f)	قرية
vegetable garden	bostān χoḍār (m)	بستان خضار
fence	sūr (m)	سور
picket fence	sūr (m)	سور
wicket gate	bawwāba far'iya (f)	بوّابة فرعيّة
granary	ʃouna (f)	شونة
root cellar	serdāb (m)	سرداب
shed (garden ~)	sa'īfa (f)	سقيفة
well (water)	bīr (m)	بير
stove (wood-fired ~)	forn (m)	فرن
to stoke the stove	awqad el botogāz	أوقد البوتاجاز
firewood	ḥaṭab (m)	حطب
log (firewood)	'eṭ'et ḥaṭab (f)	قطعة حطب
veranda	varannda (f)	فاراندة
deck (terrace)	ʃorfa (f)	شرفة
stoop (front steps)	sellem (m)	سلّم
swing (hanging seat)	morgeyḥa (f)	مرجيحة

91. Villa. Mansion

country house	villa rīfiya (f)	فيلا ريفيّة
villa (seaside ~)	villa (f)	فيلا
wing (~ of a building)	genāḥ (m)	جناح
garden	geneyna (f)	جنينة
park	ḥadīqa (f)	حديقة
tropical greenhouse	dafī'a (f)	دفيئة
to look after (garden, etc.)	ehtamm	إهتمّ
swimming pool	ḥammām sebāḥa (m)	حمّام سباحة
gym (home gym)	gīm (m)	جيم
tennis court	mal'ab tennis (m)	ملعب تنس
home theater (room)	sinema manzeliya (f)	سينما منزليّة
garage	garāʒ (m)	جراج
private property	melkiya χāṣa (f)	ملكيّة خاصّة
private land	arḍ χāṣa (m)	أرض خاصّة
warning (caution)	taḥzīr (m)	تحذير
warning sign	lāfetat taḥzīr (f)	لافتة تحذير
security	ḥerāsa (f)	حراسة
security guard	ḥāres amn (m)	حارس أمن
burglar alarm	gehāz enzār (m)	جهاز إنذار

92. Castle. Palace

castle	'al'a (f)	قلعة
palace	'aṣr (m)	قصر
fortress	'al'a (f)	قلعة
wall (round castle)	sūr (m)	سور
tower	borg (m)	برج
keep, donjon	borbg ra'īsy (m)	برج رئيسي
portcullis	bāb motaḥarrek (m)	باب متحرّك
underground passage	serdāb (m)	سرداب
moat	χondoq mā'y (m)	خندق مائي
chain	selsela (f)	سلسلة
arrow loop	mozɣal (m)	مزغل
magnificent (adj)	rā'e'	رائع
majestic (adj)	mohīb	مهيب
impregnable (adj)	manee'	منيع
medieval (adj)	men el qorūn el wosṭa	من القرون الوسطى

93. Apartment

apartment	ʃa''a (f)	شقّة
room	oḍa (f)	أوضة
bedroom	oḍet el nome (f)	أوضة النوم
dining room	oḍet el sofra (f)	أوضة السفرة
living room	oḍet el esteqbāl (f)	أوضة الإستقبال
study (home office)	maktab (m)	مكتب
entry room	madχal (m)	مدخل
bathroom (room with a bath or shower)	ḥammām (m)	حمّام
half bath	ḥammām (m)	حمّام
ceiling	sa'f (m)	سقف
floor	arḍiya (f)	أرضية
corner	zawya (f)	زاوية

94. Apartment. Cleaning

to clean (vi, vt)	naḍḍaf	نظّف
to put away (to stow)	ʃāl	شال
dust	γobār (m)	غبار
dusty (adj)	meγabbar	مغبّر
to dust (vt)	masaḥ el γobār	مسح الغبار
vacuum cleaner	maknasa kahraba'iya (f)	مكنسة كهربائيّة
to vacuum (vt)	naḍḍaf be maknasa kahrabā'iya	نظّف بمكنسة كهربائيّة
to sweep (vi, vt)	kanas	كنس
sweepings	qomāma (f)	قمامة
order	nezām (m)	نظام
disorder, mess	fawḍa (m)	فوّضى
mop	ʃarʃūba (f)	شرشوبة
dust cloth	mamsaḥa (f)	ممسحة
short broom	ma'sʃa (f)	مقشّة
dustpan	lammāma (f)	لمّامة

95. Furniture. Interior

furniture	asās (m)	أثاث
table	maktab (m)	مكتب
chair	korsy (m)	كرسي
bed	serīr (m)	سرير
couch, sofa	kanaba (f)	كنبة
armchair	korsy (m)	كرسي

bookcase	χazzānet kotob (f)	خزّانة كتب
shelf	raff (m)	رفّ
wardrobe	dolāb (m)	دولاب
coat rack (wall-mounted ~)	ʃammā'a (f)	شمّاعة
coat stand	ʃammā'a (f)	شمّاعة
bureau, dresser	dolāb adrāg (m)	دولاب أدراج
coffee table	ṭarabeyzet el 'ahwa (f)	طرابيزة القهوة
mirror	merāya (f)	مراية
carpet	seggāda (f)	سجّادة
rug, small carpet	seggāda (f)	سجّادة
fireplace	daffāya (f)	دفّاية
candle	ʃam'a (f)	شمعة
candlestick	ʃam'adān (m)	شمعدان
drapes	satā'er (pl)	ستائر
wallpaper	wara' ḥā'eṭ (m)	ورق حائط
blinds (jalousie)	satā'er ofoqiya (pl)	ستائر أفقيّة
table lamp	abāʒūr (f)	اباجورة
wall lamp (sconce)	lammbet ḥā'eṭ (f)	لمّبة حائط
floor lamp	meṣbāḥ arḍy (m)	مصباح أرضي
chandelier	nagafa (f)	نجفة
leg (of chair, table)	regl (f)	رجل
armrest	masnad (m)	مسند
back (backrest)	masnad (m)	مسند
drawer	dorg (m)	درج

96. Bedding

bedclothes	bayāḍāt el serīr (pl)	بياضات السرير
pillow	maχadda (f)	مخدّة
pillowcase	kīs el maχadda (m)	كيس المخدّة
duvet, comforter	leḥāf (m)	لحاف
sheet	melāya (f)	ملاية
bedspread	ɣaṭā' el serīr (m)	غطاء السرير

97. Kitchen

kitchen	maṭbaχ (m)	مطبخ
gas	ɣāz (m)	غاز
gas stove (range)	botoɣāz (m)	بوتوغاز
electric stove	forn kaharabā'y (m)	فرن كهربائي
oven	forn (m)	فرن

microwave oven	mikroweyv (m)	ميكروويف
refrigerator	tallāga (f)	ثلاجة
freezer	freyzer (m)	فريزر
dishwasher	ɣassālet aṭbā' (f)	غسّالة أطباق
meat grinder	farrāmet laḥm (f)	فرّامة لحم
juicer	'aṣṣāra (f)	عصّارة
toaster	maḥmaṣet χobz (f)	محمصة خبز
mixer	χallāṭ (m)	خلّاط
coffee machine	makinet ṣon' el 'ahwa (f)	ماكينة صنع القهوة
coffee pot	ɣallāya kahraba'iya (f)	غلّاية القهوة
coffee grinder	maṭ-ḥanet 'ahwa (f)	مطحنة قهوة
kettle	ɣallāya (f)	غلّاية
teapot	barrād el ʃāy (m)	برّاد الشاي
lid	ɣaṭā' (m)	غطاء
tea strainer	maṣfāh el ʃāy (f)	مصفاة الشاي
spoon	ma'la'a (f)	معلقة
teaspoon	ma'la'et ʃāy (f)	معلقة شاي
soup spoon	ma'la'a kebīra (f)	ملعقة كبيرة
fork	ʃawka (f)	شوكة
knife	sekkīna (f)	سكّينة
tableware (dishes)	awāny (pl)	أواني
plate (dinner ~)	ṭaba' (m)	طبق
saucer	ṭaba' fengān (m)	طبق فنجان
shot glass	kāsa (f)	كاسة
glass (tumbler)	kobbāya (f)	كوبّاية
cup	fengān (m)	فنجان
sugar bowl	sokkariya (f)	سكّريّة
salt shaker	mamlaḥa (f)	مملحة
pepper shaker	mobhera (f)	مبهرة
butter dish	ṭaba' zebda (m)	طبق زبدة
stock pot (soup pot)	ḥalla (f)	حلّة
frying pan (skillet)	ṭāsa (f)	طاسة
ladle	maɣrafa (f)	مغرفة
colander	maṣfāh (f)	مصفاه
tray (serving ~)	ṣeniya (f)	صينيّة
bottle	ezāza (f)	إزازة
jar (glass)	barṭamān (m)	برطمان
can	kanz (m)	كانز
bottle opener	fattāḥa (f)	فتّاحة
can opener	fattāḥa (f)	فتّاحة
corkscrew	barrīma (f)	بريّمة
filter	filter (m)	فلتر

to filter (vt)	ṣaffa	صفّى
trash, garbage (food waste, etc.)	zebāla (f)	زبالة
trash can (kitchen ~)	ṣandū' el zebāla (m)	صندوق الزبالة

98. Bathroom

bathroom	ḥammām (m)	حمّام
water	meyāh (f)	مياه
faucet	ḥanafiya (f)	حنفيّة
hot water	maya soχna (f)	مايّة سخنة
cold water	maya barda (f)	مايّة باردة
toothpaste	ma'gūn asnān (m)	معجون أسنان
to brush one's teeth	naḍḍaf el asnān	نظّف الأسنان
toothbrush	forʃet senān (f)	فرشة أسنان
to shave (vi)	ḥala'	حلق
shaving foam	raɣwa lel ḥelā'a (f)	رغوة للحلاقة
razor	mūs (m)	موس
to wash (one's hands, etc.)	ɣasal	غسل
to take a bath	estaḥamma	إستحمّى
shower	doʃ (m)	دوش
to take a shower	aχad doʃ	أخد دوش
bathtub	banyo (m)	بانيو
toilet (toilet bowl)	twalet (m)	تواليت
sink (washbasin)	ḥoḍe (m)	حوض
soap	ṣabūn (m)	صابون
soap dish	ṣabbāna (f)	صبّانة
sponge	līfa (f)	ليفة
shampoo	ʃambū (m)	شامبو
towel	fūṭa (f)	فوطة
bathrobe	robe el ḥammām (m)	روب حمّام
laundry (process)	ɣasīl (m)	غسيل
washing machine	ɣassāla (f)	غسّالة
to do the laundry	ɣasal el malābes	غسل الملابس
laundry detergent	mas-ḥū' ɣasīl (m)	مسحوق غسيل

99. Household appliances

TV set	televizion (m)	تليفزيون
tape recorder	gehāz tasgīl (m)	جهاز تسجيل
VCR (video recorder)	'āla tasgīl video (f)	آلة تسجيل فيديو

radio	gehāz radio (m)	جهاز راديو
player (CD, MP3, etc.)	blayer (m)	بليير
video projector	gehāz 'arḍ (m)	جهاز عرض
home movie theater	sinema manzeliya (f)	سينما منزليّة
DVD player	dividī blayer (m)	دي في دي بليير
amplifier	mokabbaer el ṣote (m)	مكبّر الصوت
video game console	'ātāry (m)	أتاري
video camera	kamera video (f)	كاميرا فيديو
camera (photo)	kamera (f)	كاميرا
digital camera	kamera diʒital (f)	كاميرا ديجيتال
vacuum cleaner	maknasa kahraba'iya (f)	مكنسة كهربائيّة
iron (e.g., steam ~)	makwa (f)	مكواة
ironing board	lawḥet kayī (f)	لوحة كيّ
telephone	telefon (m)	تليفون
cell phone	mobile (m)	موبايل
typewriter	'āla katba (f)	آلة كاتبة
sewing machine	makanet el χeyāṭa (f)	مكنة الخياطة
microphone	mikrofon (m)	ميكروفون
headphones	samma'āt ra'siya (pl)	سمّاعات رأسية
remote control (TV)	remowt kontrol (m)	ريموت كنترول
CD, compact disc	sidī (m)	سي دي
cassette, tape	kasett (m)	كاسيت
vinyl record	esṭewāna mūsīqa (f)	أسطوانة موسيقى

100. Repairs. Renovation

renovations	tagdīdāt (m)	تجديدات
to renovate (vt)	gadded	جدّد
to repair, to fix (vt)	ṣallaḥ	صلّح
to put in order	nazzam	نظّم
to redo (do again)	'ād	عاد
paint	dehān (m)	دهان
to paint (~ a wall)	dahhen	دهّن
house painter	dahhān (m)	دهّان
paintbrush	forʃet dehān (f)	فرشاة الدهان
whitewash	maḥlūl mobayeḍ (m)	محلول مبيّض
to whitewash (vt)	beyḍ	بيّض
wallpaper	wara' ḥā'eṭ (m)	ورق حائط
to wallpaper (vt)	laṣaq wara' el ḥā'eṭ	لصق ورق الحائط
varnish	warnīʃ (m)	ورنيش
to varnish (vt)	ṭala bel warnīʃ	طلى بالورنيش

101. Plumbing

water	meyāh (f)	مياه
hot water	maya soχna (f)	مايّة سخنة
cold water	maya barda (f)	مايّة باردة
faucet	ḥanafiya (f)	حنفيّة
drop (of water)	'aṭra (f)	قطرة
to drip (vi)	'aṭṭar	قطّر
to leak (ab. pipe)	sarrab	سرّب
leak (pipe ~)	tasarrob (m)	تسرب
puddle	berka (f)	بركة
pipe	masūra (f)	ماسورة
valve (e.g., ball ~)	ṣamām (m)	صمام
to be clogged up	kān masdūd	كان مسدود
tools	adawāt (pl)	أدوات
adjustable wrench	el meftāḥ el englīzy (m)	المفتاح الإنجليزي
to unscrew (lid, filter, etc.)	fataḥ	فتح
to screw (tighten)	aḥkam el ʃadd	أحكم الشدّ
to unclog (vt)	sallek	سلّك
plumber	samkary (m)	سمكري
basement	badrome (m)	بدروم
sewerage (system)	ʃabaket el magāry (f)	شبكة المجاري

102. Fire. Conflagration

fire (accident)	ḥarī' (m)	حريق
flame	lahab (m)	لهب
spark	ʃarāra (f)	شرارة
smoke (from fire)	dokχān (m)	دخّان
torch (flaming stick)	ʃo'la (f)	شعلة
campfire	nār moχayem (m)	نار مخيّم
gas, gasoline	banzīn (m)	بنزين
kerosene (type of fuel)	kerosīn (m)	كيروسين
flammable (adj)	qābel lel eḥterāq	قابل للإحتراق
explosive (adj)	māda motafaggera	مادة متفجّرة
NO SMOKING	mamnū' el tadχīn	ممنوع التدخين
safety	amn (m)	أمن
danger	χaṭar (m)	خطر
dangerous (adj)	χaṭīr	خطير
to catch fire	eʃta'al	إشتعل
explosion	enfegār (m)	إنفجار
to set fire	aʃ'al el nār	أشعل النار

arsonist	moʃel ḥarīq ʿan ʿamd (m)	مشعل حريق عن عمد
arson	eḥrāq el momtalakāt (m)	إحراق الممتلكات
to blaze (vi)	awhag	أوهج
to burn (be on fire)	et-ḥaraʾ	إتحرق
to burn down	et-ḥaraʾ	إتحرق
to call the fire department	kallim ʾism el ḥarīʾ	كلّم قسم الحريق
firefighter, fireman	rāgel el maṭāfy (m)	راجل المطافي
fire truck	sayāret el maṭāfy (f)	سيّارة المطافي
fire department	ʾesm el maṭāfy (f)	قسم المطافي
fire truck ladder	sellem el maṭāfy (m)	سلّم المطافي
fire hose	χarṭūm el mayya (m)	خرطوم الميّة
fire extinguisher	ṭaffayet ḥarīʾ (f)	طفّاية حريق
helmet	χawza (f)	خوذة
siren	sarīna (f)	سرينة
to cry (for help)	ṣarraχ	صرّخ
to call for help	estaɣās	إستغاث
rescuer	monqez (m)	منقذ
to rescue (vt)	anqaz	أنقذ
to arrive (vi)	weṣel	وصل
to extinguish (vt)	ṭaffa	طفّى
water	meyāh (f)	مياه
sand	raml (m)	رمل
ruins (destruction)	ḥeṭām (pl)	حطام
to collapse (building, etc.)	enhār	إنهار
to fall down (vi)	enhār	إنهار
to cave in (ceiling, floor)	enhār	إنهار
piece of debris	ʾeṭʿet ḥeṭām (f)	قطعة حطام
ash	ramād (m)	رماد
to suffocate (die)	eθχanaʾ	إتخنق
to be killed (perish)	māt	مات

HUMAN ACTIVITIES

Job. Business. Part 1

103. Office. Working in the office

office (company ~)	maktab (m)	مكتب
office (of director, etc.)	maktab (m)	مكتب
reception desk	esteʾbāl (m)	إستقبال
secretary	sekerteyr (m)	سكرتير
director	modīr (m)	مدير
manager	modīr (m)	مدير
accountant	muḥāseb (m)	محاسب
employee	mowazzaf (m)	موظّف
furniture	asās (m)	أثاث
desk	maktab (m)	مكتب
desk chair	korsy (m)	كرسي
drawer unit	weḥdet adrāg (f)	وحدة أدراج
coat stand	ʃammāʿa (f)	شمّاعة
computer	kombuter (m)	كمبيوتر
printer	ṭābeʿa (f)	طابعة
fax machine	faks (m)	فاكس
photocopier	ʾālet nasχ (f)	آلة نسخ
paper	waraʾ (m)	ورق
office supplies	adawāt maktabiya (pl)	أدوات مكتبية
mouse pad	maws bād (m)	ماوس باد
sheet (of paper)	waraʾa (f)	ورقة
binder	malaff (m)	ملفّ
catalog	fehras (m)	فهرس
phone directory	dalīl el telefone (m)	دليل التليفون
documentation	wasāʾeq (pl)	وثائق
brochure (e.g., 12 pages ~)	naʃra (f)	نشرة
leaflet (promotional ~)	manʃūr (m)	منشور
sample	namūzag (m)	نموذج
training meeting	egtemāʿ tadrīb (m)	إجتماع تدريب
meeting (of managers)	egtemāʿ (m)	إجتماع
lunch time	fatret el ɣadaʾ (f)	فترة الغذاء
to make a copy	ṣawwar	صوّر

to make multiple copies	ṣawwar	صوّر
to receive a fax	estalam faks	إستلم فاكس
to send a fax	ba'at faks	بعت فاكس
to call (by phone)	ettaṣal	إتّصل
to answer (vt)	gāwab	جاوب
to put through	waṣṣal	وصّل
to arrange, to set up	ḥadded	حدّد
to demonstrate (vt)	'araḍ	عرض
to be absent	ɣāb	غاب
absence	ɣeyāb (m)	غياب

104. Business processes. Part 1

occupation	ʃoɣl (m)	شغل
firm	ʃerka (f)	شركة
company	ʃerka (f)	شركة
corporation	mo'assasa tegariya (f)	مؤسسة تجارية
enterprise	ʃerka (f)	شركة
agency	wekāla (f)	وكالة
agreement (contract)	ettefaqiya (f)	إتّفاقية
contract	'a'd (m)	عقد
deal	ṣafqa (f)	صفقة
order (to place an ~)	ṭalab (m)	طلب
terms (of the contract)	ʃorūṭ (pl)	شروط
wholesale (adv)	bel gomla	بالجملة
wholesale (adj)	el gomla	الجملة
wholesale (n)	bey' bel gomla (m)	بيع بالجملة
retail (adj)	yebee' bel tagze'a	يبيع بالتجزئة
retail (n)	maḥal yebee' bel tagze'a (m)	محل يبيع بالتجزئة
competitor	monāfes (m)	منافس
competition	monafsa (f)	منافسة
to compete (vi)	nāfes	نافس
partner (associate)	ʃerīk (m)	شريك
partnership	ʃarāka (f)	شراكة
crisis	azma (f)	أزمة
bankruptcy	eflās (m)	إفلاس
to go bankrupt	falles	فلّس
difficulty	ṣo'ūba (f)	صعوبة
problem	moʃkela (f)	مشكلة
catastrophe	karsa (f)	كارثة
economy	eqtiṣād (m)	إقتصاد
economic (~ growth)	eqteṣādy	إقتصادي

economic recession	rokūd eqteṣādy (m)	ركود إقتصادي
goal (aim)	hadaf (m)	هدف
task	mohemma (f)	مهمّة
to trade (vi)	tāger	تاجر
network (distribution ~)	ʃabaka (f)	شبكة
inventory (stock)	el maχzūn (m)	المخزون
range (assortment)	taʃkīla (f)	تشكيلة
leader (leading company)	qā'ed (m)	قائد
large (~ company)	kebīr	كبير
monopoly	eḥtekār (m)	إحتكار
theory	naẓariya (f)	نظريّة
practice	momarsa (f)	ممارسة
experience (in my ~)	χebra (f)	خبرة
trend (tendency)	ettegāh (m)	إتّجاه
development	tanmeya (f)	تنمية

105. Business processes. Part 2

profit (foregone ~)	rebḥ (m)	ربح
profitable (~ deal)	morbeḥ	مربح
delegation (group)	wafd (m)	وفد
salary	morattab (m)	مرتّب
to correct (an error)	ṣaḥḥaḥ	صحّح
business trip	reḥlet ʿamal (f)	رحلة عمل
commission	lagna (f)	لجنة
to control (vt)	et-ḥakkem	إتحكّم
conference	mo'tamar (m)	مؤتمر
license	roχṣa (f)	رخصة
reliable (~ partner)	mawsūq	موثوق
initiative (undertaking)	mobadra (f)	مبادرة
norm (standard)	meʿyār (m)	معيار
circumstance	ẓarf (m)	ظرف
duty (of employee)	wāgeb (m)	واجب
organization (company)	monaẓẓama (f)	منظّمة
organization (process)	tanẓīm (m)	تنظيم
organized (adj)	monaẓẓam	منظّم
cancellation	elɣā' (m)	إلغاء
to cancel (call off)	alɣa	ألغى
report (official ~)	ta'rīr (m)	تقرير
patent	bara'et el eχterāʿ (f)	براءة الإختراع
to patent (obtain patent)	saggel barā'et eχterāʿ	سجّل براءة الإختراع
to plan (vt)	χaṭṭeṭ	خطّط

bonus (money)	ʿalāwa (f)	علاوة
professional (adj)	mehany	مهني
procedure	egrā' (m)	إجراء
to examine (contract, etc.)	baḥs fi	بحث في
calculation	ḥesāb (m)	حساب
reputation	somʿa (f)	سمعة
risk	moχaṭra (f)	مخاطرة
to manage, to run	adār	أدار
information	maʿlumāt (pl)	معلومات
property	melkiya (f)	ملكيّة
union	etteḥād (m)	إتّحاد
life insurance	ta'mīn ʿalal ḥayah (m)	تأمين على الحياة
to insure (vt)	ammen	أمّن
insurance	ta'mīn (m)	تأمين
auction (~ sale)	mazād (m)	مزاد
to notify (inform)	ballaɣ	بلّغ
management (process)	edāra (f)	إدارة
service (~ industry)	χadma (f)	خدمة
forum	nadwa (f)	ندوة
to function (vi)	adda waẓīfa	أدّى وظيفة
stage (phase)	marḥala (f)	مرحلة
legal (~ services)	qanūniya	قانونية
lawyer (legal advisor)	muḥāmy (m)	محامي

106. Production. Works

plant	maṣnaʿ (m)	مصنع
factory	maṣnaʿ (m)	مصنع
workshop	warʃa (f)	ورشة
works, production site	maṣnaʿ (m)	مصنع
industry (manufacturing)	ṣenāʿa (f)	صناعة
industrial (adj)	ṣenāʿy	صناعي
heavy industry	ṣenāʿa teʾīla (f)	صناعة ثقيلة
light industry	ṣenāʿa χafīfa (f)	صناعة خفيفة
products	montagāt (pl)	منتجات
to produce (vt)	antag	أنتج
raw materials	mawād χām (pl)	مواد خام
foreman (construction ~)	ra'īs el ʿommāl (m)	رئيس العمّال
workers team (crew)	farīʾ el ʿommāl (m)	فريق العمّال
worker	ʿāmel (m)	عامل
working day	yome ʿamal (m)	يوم عمل
pause (rest break)	rāḥa (f)	راحة

meeting	egtemā‘ (m)	إجتماع
to discuss (vt)	nā’eʃ	ناقش
plan	χeṭṭa (f)	خطّة
to fulfill the plan	naffez el χeṭṭa	نفّذ الخطّة
rate of output	mo‘addal el entāg (m)	معدّل الإنتاج
quality	gawda (f)	جودة
control (checking)	taftīʃ (m)	تفتيش
quality control	ḍabṭ el gawda (m)	ضبط الجودة
workplace safety	salāmet makān el ‘amal (f)	سلامة مكان العمل
discipline	enḍebāṭ (m)	إنضباط
violation (of safety rules, etc.)	moχalfa (f)	مخالفة
to violate (rules)	χālef	خالف
strike	eḍrāb (m)	إضراب
striker	moḍrab (m)	مضرب
to be on strike	aḍrab	أضرب
labor union	etteḥād el ‘omāl (m)	إتّحاد العمال
to invent (machine, etc.)	eχtara‘	إخترع
invention	eχterā‘ (m)	إختراع
research	baḥs (m)	بحث
to improve (make better)	ḥassen	حسّن
technology	teknoloʒia (f)	تكنولوجيا
technical drawing	rasm teqany (m)	رسم تقني
load, cargo	ʃaḥn (m)	شحن
loader (person)	ʃayāl (m)	شيّال
to load (vehicle, etc.)	ʃaḥn	شحن
loading (process)	taḥmīl (m)	تحميل
to unload (vi, vt)	farraɣ	فرّغ
unloading	tafrīɣ (m)	تفريغ
transportation	wasā’el el na’l (pl)	وسائل النقل
transportation company	ʃerket na’l (f)	شركة نقل
to transport (vt)	na’al	نقل
freight car	‘arabet ʃaḥn (f)	عربة شحن
tank (e.g., oil ~)	χazzān (m)	خزّان
truck	ʃāḥena (f)	شاحنة
machine tool	makana (f)	مكنة
mechanism	’āliya (f)	آليّة
industrial waste	moχallafāt ṣena‘iya (pl)	مخلفات صناعية
packing (process)	ta‘be’a (f)	تعبئة
to pack (vt)	‘abba	عبّأ

107. Contract. Agreement

contract	'a'd (m)	عقد
agreement	ettefā' (m)	إتّفاق
addendum	molḥa' (m)	ملحق
to sign a contract	waqqa' 'ala 'a'd	وقّع على عقد
signature	tawqee' (m)	توقيع
to sign (vt)	waqqa'	وقّع
seal (stamp)	χetm (m)	ختم
subject of contract	mawḍū' el 'a'd (m)	موضوع العقد
clause	band (m)	بند
parties (in contract)	aṭrāf (pl)	أطراف
legal address	'enwān qanūny (m)	عنوان قانوني
to violate the contract	χālef el 'a'd	خالف العقد
commitment (obligation)	eltezām (m)	إلتزام
responsibility	mas'oliya (f)	مسؤوليّة
force majeure	'owwa qāhera (m)	قوّة قاهرة
dispute	χelāf (m)	خلاف
penalties	'oqobāt (pl)	عقوبات

108. Import & Export

import	esterād (m)	إستيراد
importer	mostawred (m)	مستورّد
to import (vt)	estawrad	إستورّد
import (as adj.)	wāred	وارد
export (exportation)	taṣdīr (m)	تصدير
exporter	moṣadder (m)	مصدّر
to export (vi, vt)	ṣaddar	صدّر
export (as adj.)	sādir	صادر
goods (merchandise)	baḍā'e' (pl)	بضائع
consignment, lot	ʃoḥna (f)	شحنة
weight	wazn (m)	وزن
volume	ḥagm (m)	حجم
cubic meter	metr moka''ab (m)	متر مكعّب
manufacturer	el ʃerka el moṣanne'a (f)	الشركة المصنّعة
transportation company	ʃerket na'l (f)	شركة نقل
container	ḥāweya (f)	حاوية
border	ḥadd (m)	حدّ
customs	gamārek (pl)	جمارك
customs duty	rasm gomroky (m)	رسم جمركي

customs officer	mowazzaf el gamārek (m)	موظّف الجمارك
smuggling	tahrīb (m)	تهريب
contraband (smuggled goods)	beḍā'a moharraba (pl)	بضاعة مهربة

109. Finances

stock (share)	sahm (m)	سهم
bond (certificate)	sanad (m)	سند
promissory note	kembyāla (f)	كمبيالة
stock exchange	borṣa (f)	بورصة
stock price	se'r el sahm (m)	سعر السهم
to go down (become cheaper)	reχeṣ	رخص
to go up (become more expensive)	ʃely	غلي
share	naṣīb (m)	نصيب
controlling interest	el magmū'a el mosayṭara (f)	المجموعة المسيطرة
investment	estesmār (pl)	إستثمار
to invest (vt)	estasmar	إستثمر
percent	bel me'a - bel miya	بالمئة
interest (on investment)	fayda (f)	فائدة
profit	rebḥ (m)	ربح
profitable (adj)	morbeḥ	مربح
tax	ḍarība (f)	ضريبة
currency (foreign ~)	'omla (f)	عملَة
national (adj)	waṭany	وطني
exchange (currency ~)	taḥwīl (m)	تحويل
accountant	muḥāseb (m)	محاسب
accounting	maḥasba (f)	محاسبة
bankruptcy	eflās (m)	إفلاس
collapse, crash	enheyār (m)	إنهيار
ruin	eflās (m)	إفلاس
to be ruined (financially)	falles	فلّس
inflation	taḍakχom māly (m)	تضخّم مالي
devaluation	taχfīḍ qīmet 'omla (m)	تخفيض قيمة عملة
capital	ra's māl (m)	رأس مال
income	daχl (m)	دخل
turnover	dawret ra's el māl (f)	دورة رأس المال
resources	mawāred (pl)	موارد
monetary resources	el mawāred el naqdiya (pl)	الموارد النقديّة

overhead	nafa'āt 'āmma (pl)	نفقات عامّة
to reduce (expenses)	χaffaḍ	خفّض

110. Marketing

marketing	taswī' (m)	تسويق
market	sū' (f)	سوق
market segment	qaṭā' el sū' (m)	قطاع السوق
product	montag (m)	منتج
goods (merchandise)	baḍā'e' (pl)	بضائع
brand	mārka (f)	ماركة
trademark	marka tegāriya (f)	ماركة تجاريّة
logotype	ʃe'ār (m)	شعار
logo	ʃe'ār (m)	شعار
demand	ṭalab (m)	طلب
supply	mU'İddāt (pl)	معدّات
need	ḥāga (f)	حاجة
consumer	mostahlek (m)	مستهلك
analysis	taḥlīl (m)	تحليل
to analyze (vt)	ḥallel	حلّل
positioning	waḍ' (m)	وضع
to position (vt)	waḍa'	وضع
price	se'r (m)	سعر
pricing policy	seyāset el as'ār (f)	سياسة الأسعار
price formation	taʃkīl el as'ār (m)	تشكيل الأسعار

111. Advertising

advertising	e'lān (m)	إعلان
to advertise (vt)	a'lan	أعلن
budget	mezaniya (f)	ميزانية
ad, advertisement	e'lān (m)	إعلان
TV advertising	e'lān fel televizīōn (m)	إعلان في التليفزيون
radio advertising	e'lān fel radio (m)	إعلان في الراديو
outdoor advertising	e'lān zahery (m)	إعلان ظاهري
mass media	wasā'el el e'lām (pl)	وسائل الإعلام
periodical (n)	magalla dawriya (f)	مجلّة دوريّة
image (public appearance)	imyʒ (m)	إيميج
slogan	ʃe'ār (m)	شعار
motto (maxim)	ʃe'ār (m)	شعار
campaign	ḥamla (f)	حملة

advertising campaign	ḥamla e'laniya (f)	حملة إعلانيّة
target group	magmū'a mostahdafa (f)	مجموعة مستهدفة
business card	kart el 'amal (m)	كارت العمل
leaflet (promotional ~)	manʃūr (m)	منشور
brochure (e.g., 12 pages ~)	naʃra (f)	نشرة
pamphlet	kotayeb (m)	كتيّب
newsletter	naʃra eχbariya (f)	نشرة إخبارية
signboard (store sign, etc.)	yafṭa, lāfeta (f)	لافتة, يافطة
poster	boster (m)	بوستر
billboard	lawḥet e'lanāt (f)	لوحة إعلانات

112. Banking

bank	bank (m)	بنك
branch (of bank, etc.)	far' (m)	فرع
bank clerk, consultant	mowazzaf bank (m)	موظّف بنك
manager (director)	modīr (m)	مدير
bank account	ḥesāb bank (m)	حساب بنك
account number	raqam el ḥesāb (m)	رقم الحساب
checking account	ḥesāb gāry (m)	حساب جاري
savings account	ḥesāb tawfīr (m)	حساب توّفير
to open an account	fataḥ ḥesāb	فتح حساب
to close the account	'afal ḥesāb	قفل حساب
to deposit into the account	awda' fel ḥesāb	أودع في الحساب
to withdraw (vt)	saḥab men el ḥesāb	سحب من الحساب
deposit	wadee'a (f)	وديعة
to make a deposit	awda'	أودع
wire transfer	ḥewāla maṣrefiya (f)	حوالة مصرفيّة
to wire, to transfer	ḥawwel	حوّل
sum	mablaɣ (m)	مبلغ
How much?	kām?	كام؟
signature	tawqee' (m)	توقيع
to sign (vt)	waqqa'	وقّع
credit card	kredit kard (f)	كريدت كارد
code (PIN code)	kōd (m)	كود
credit card number	raqam el kredit kard (m)	رقم الكريدت كارد
ATM	makinet ṣarrāf 'āly (f)	ماكينة صرّاف آلي
check	ʃīk (m)	شيك
to write a check	katab ʃīk	كتب شيك

checkbook	daftar ʃikāt (m)	دفتر شيكات
loan (bank ~)	qarḍ (m)	قرض
to apply for a loan	'addem ṭalab 'ala qarḍ	قدّم طلب على قرض
to get a loan	ḥaṣal 'ala qarḍ	حصل على قرض
to give a loan	edda qarḍ	ادّى قرض
guarantee	ḍamān (m)	ضمان

113. Telephone. Phone conversation

telephone	telefon (m)	تليفون
cell phone	mobile (m)	موبايل
answering machine	gehāz radd 'alal mokalmāt (m)	جهاز ردّ على المكالمات
to call (by phone)	ettaṣal	إتّصل
phone call	mokalma telefoniya (f)	مكالمة تليفونية
to dial a number	ettaṣal be raqam	إتّصل برقم
Hello!	alo!	ألو!
to ask (vt)	sa'al	سأل
to answer (vi, vt)	radd	ردّ
to hear (vt)	seme'	سمع
well (adv)	kewayes	كويّس
not well (adv)	meʃ kowayīs	مش كويّس
noises (interference)	taʃwīʃ (m)	تشويش
receiver	sammā'a (f)	سمّاعة
to pick up (~ the phone)	rafa' el sammā'a	رفع السمّاعة
to hang up (~ the phone)	'afal el sammā'a	قفل السمّاعة
busy (engaged)	maʃɣūl	مشغول
to ring (ab. phone)	rann	رنّ
telephone book	dalīl el telefone (m)	دليل التليفون
local (adj)	maḥalliyya	ة محليّة
local call	mokalma maḥalliya (f)	مكالمة محليّة
long distance (~ call)	bi'īd	بعيد
long-distance call	mokalma bi'īda (f)	مكالمة بعيدة المدى
international (adj)	dowly	دوّلي
international call	mokalma dowliya (f)	مكالمة دوليّة

114. Cell phone

cell phone	mobile (m)	موبايل
display	'arḍ (m)	عرض
button	zerr (m)	زرّ
SIM card	sim kard (m)	سيم كارد

battery	baṭṭariya (f)	بطّاريّة
to be dead (battery)	χelṣet	خلصت
charger	ʃāḥen (m)	شاحن
menu	qā'ema (f)	قائمة
settings	awḍā' (pl)	أوضاع
tune (melody)	naɣama (f)	نغمة
to select (vt)	eχtār	إختار
calculator	'āla ḥasba (f)	آلة حاسبة
voice mail	barīd ṣawty (m)	بريد صوتي
alarm clock	monabbeh (m)	منبّه
contacts	gehāt el etteṣāl (pl)	جهات الإتّصال
SMS (text message)	resāla 'aṣīra ɛsɛmɛs (f)	sms رسالة قصيرة
subscriber	moʃtarek (m)	مشترك

115. Stationery

ballpoint pen	'alam gāf (m)	قلم جاف
fountain pen	'alam rīʃa (m)	قلم ريشة
pencil	'alam roṣāṣ (m)	قلم رصاص
highlighter	markar (m)	ماركر
felt-tip pen	'alam fulumaster (m)	قلم فلوماستر
notepad	mozakkera (f)	مذكّرة
agenda (diary)	gadwal el a'māl (m)	جدول الأعمال
ruler	masṭara (f)	مسطرة
calculator	'āla ḥasba (f)	آلة حاسبة
eraser	astīka (f)	استيكة
thumbtack	dabbūs (m)	دبّوس
paper clip	dabbūs wara' (m)	دبوس ورق
glue	ṣamɣ (m)	صمغ
stapler	dabbāsa (f)	دبّاسة
hole punch	χarrāma (m)	خرّامة
pencil sharpener	barrāya (f)	برّاية

116. Various kinds of documents

account (report)	ta'rīr (m)	تقرير
agreement	ettefā' (m)	إتّفاق
application form	estemāret ṭalab (m)	إستمارة طلب
authentic (adj)	aṣly	أصلي
badge (identity tag)	ʃāra (f)	شارة
business card	kart el 'amal (m)	كارت العمل

certificate (~ of quality)	ʃahāda (f)	شهادة
check (e.g., draw a ~)	ʃīk (m)	شيك
check (in restaurant)	ḥesāb (m)	حساب
constitution	dostūr (m)	دستور
contract (agreement)	ʻaʾd (m)	عقد
copy	ṣūra (f)	صورة
copy (of contract, etc.)	nosχa (f)	نسخة
customs declaration	taṣrīḥ gomroky (m)	تصريح جمركي
document	wasīqa (f)	وثيقة
driver's license	roχṣet el qeyāda (f)	رخصة قيادة
addendum	molḥaʾ (m)	ملحق
form	estemāra (f)	استمارة
ID card (e.g., FBI ~)	beṭāʾet el hawiya (f)	بطاقة الهويّة
inquiry (request)	estefsār (m)	إستفسار
invitation card	beṭāʾet daʻwa (f)	بطاقة دعوة
invoice	fatūra (f)	فاتورة
law	qanūn (m)	قانون
letter (mail)	resāla (f)	رسالة
letterhead	tarwīsa (f)	ترويّسة
list (of names, etc.)	qāʾema (f)	قائمة
manuscript	maχṭūṭa (f)	مخطوطة
newsletter	naʃra eχbariya (f)	نشرة إخبارية
note (short letter)	nouta (f)	نوتة
pass (for worker, visitor)	beṭāʾet morūr (f)	بطاقة مرور
passport	basbore (m)	باسبور
permit	roχṣa (f)	رخصة
résumé	sīra zātiya (f)	سيرة ذاتيّة
debt note, IOU	mozakkeret deyn (f)	مذكّرة دين
receipt (for purchase)	eṣāl (m)	إيصال
sales slip, receipt	eṣāl (m)	إيصال
report (mil.)	taʾrīr (m)	تقرير
to show (ID, etc.)	ʾaddem	قدّم
to sign (vt)	waqqaʻ	وقّع
signature	tawqeeʻ (m)	توقيع
seal (stamp)	χetm (m)	ختم
text	noṣṣ (m)	نصّ
ticket (for entry)	tazkara (f)	تذكرة
to cross out	ʃaṭab	شطب
to fill out (~ a form)	mala	ملأ
waybill (shipping invoice)	bolīṣet ʃaḥn (f)	بوليصة شحن
will (testament)	waṣiya (f)	وصيّة

117. Kinds of business

accounting services	χedamāt moḥasba (pl)	خدمات محاسبة
advertising	e'lān (m)	إعلان
advertising agency	wekālet e'lān (f)	وكالة إعلان
air-conditioners	takyīf (m)	تكييف
airline	ʃerket ṭayarān (f)	شركة طيران
alcoholic beverages	maʃrūbāt koḥūliya (pl)	مشروبات كحوليّة
antiques (antique dealers)	toḥaf (pl)	تحف
art gallery (contemporary ~)	ma'raḍ fanny (m)	معرض فنّي
audit services	χedamāt faḥṣ el ḥesābāt (pl)	خدمات فحص الحسابات
banking industry	el qeṭā' el maṣrefy (m)	القطاع المصرفي
bar	bār (m)	بار
beauty parlor	ṣalone tagmīl (m)	صالون تجميل
bookstore	maḥal kotob (m)	محل كتب
brewery	maṣna' bīra (m)	مصنع بيرة
business center	markaz tegāry (m)	مركز تجاري
business school	kolliyet edāret el a'māl (f)	كليّة إدارة الأعمال
casino	kazino (m)	كازينو
construction	benā' (m)	بناء
consulting	esteʃāra (f)	إستشارة
dental clinic	'eyādet asnān (f)	عيادة أسنان
design	taṣmīm (m)	تصميم
drugstore, pharmacy	ṣaydaliya (f)	صيدليّة
dry cleaners	dray klīn (m)	دراي كلين
employment agency	wekālet tawẓīf (f)	وكالة توّظيف
financial services	χedamāt māliya (pl)	خدمات ماليّة
food products	akl (m)	أكل
funeral home	maktab mota'ahhed el dafn (m)	مكتب متعهّد الدفن
furniture (e.g., house ~)	asās (m)	أثاث
clothing, garment	malābes (pl)	ملابس
hotel	fondo' (m)	فندق
ice-cream	'ays krīm (m)	آيس كريم
industry (manufacturing)	ṣenā'a (f)	صناعة
insurance	ta'mīn (m)	تأمين
Internet	internet (m)	إنترنت
investments (finance)	estesmarāt (pl)	إستثمارات
jeweler	ṣā'eɣ (m)	صائغ
jewelry	mogawharāt (pl)	مجوهرات
laundry (shop)	maɣsala (f)	مغسلة
legal advisor	χedamāt qanūniya (pl)	خدمات قانونيّة

light industry	ṣenā'a χafīfa (f)	صناعة خفيفة
magazine	magalla (f)	مجلّة
mail-order selling	bey' be neẓām el barīd (m)	بيع بِنظام البريد
medicine	ṭebb (m)	طِب
movie theater	sinema (f)	سينما
museum	mat-ḥaf (m)	متحف
news agency	wekāla eχbariya (f)	وكالة إخبارية
newspaper	garīda (f)	جريدة
nightclub	malha leyly (m)	ملهى ليّلي
oil (petroleum)	nafṭ (m)	نفط
courier services	χedamāt el ʃaḥn (pl)	خدمات الشحن
pharmaceutics	ṣaydala (f)	صيدلة
printing (industry)	ṭebā'a (f)	طباعة
publishing house	dar el ṭebā'a wel naʃr (f)	دار الطباعة والنشر
radio (~ station)	radio (m)	راديو
real estate	'eqarāt (pl)	عقارات
restaurant	maṭ'am (m)	مطعم
security company	ʃerket amn (f)	شركة أمن
sports	reyāḍa (f)	رياضة
stock exchange	borṣa (f)	بورصة
store	maḥal (m)	محل
supermarket	subermarket (m)	سوبرماركت
swimming pool (public ~)	ḥammām sebāḥa (m)	حمّام سباحة
tailor shop	maḥal χeyāṭa (m)	محل خياطة
television	televizion (m)	تليفزيون
theater	masraḥ (m)	مسرح
trade (commerce)	tegāra (f)	تجارة
transportation	wasā'el el na'l (pl)	وسائل النقل
travel	safar (m)	سفر
veterinarian	doktore beṭary (m)	دكتور بيطري
warehouse	mostawda' (m)	مستوّدع
waste collection	gama' el nefayāt (m)	جمع النفايات

Job. Business. Part 2

118. Show. Exhibition

exhibition, show	maʿraḍ (m)	معرض
trade show	maʿraḍ tegāry (m)	معرض تجاري
participation	eʃterāk (m)	إشتراك
to participate (vi)	ʃārek	شارك
participant (exhibitor)	moʃtarek (m)	مشترك
director	modīr (m)	مدير
organizers' office	maktab el monaẓẓemīn (m)	مكتب المنظّمين
organizer	monazzem (m)	منظّم
to organize (vt)	nazzam	نظّم
participation form	estemāret el eʃterak (f)	إستمارة الإشتراك
to fill out (vt)	mala	ملأ
details	tafaṣīl (pl)	تفاصيل
information	esteʿlamāt (pl)	إستعلامات
price (cost, rate)	seʿr (m)	سعر
including	bema feyh	بما فيه
to include (vt)	taḍamman	تضمّن
to pay (vi, vt)	dafaʿ	دفع
registration fee	rosūm el tasgīl (pl)	رسوم التسجيل
entrance	madχal (m)	مدخل
pavilion, hall	genāḥ (m)	جناح
to register (vt)	saggel	سجّل
badge (identity tag)	ʃāra (f)	شارة
booth, stand	koʃk (m)	كشك
to reserve, to book	ḥagaz	حجز
display case	vatrīna (f)	فترينة
spotlight	kasʃāf el nūr (m)	كشّاف النور
design	taṣmīm (m)	تصميم
to place (put, set)	ḥaṭṭ	حطّ
distributor	mowazzeʿ (m)	موزّع
supplier	mowarred (m)	مورد
country	balad (m)	بلد
foreign (adj)	agnaby	أجنبي
product	montag (m)	منتج

association	gam'iya (f)	جمعيّة
conference hall	qā'et el mo'tamarāt (f)	قاعة المؤتمرات
congress	mo'tamar (m)	مؤتمر
contest (competition)	mosab'a (f)	مسابقة
visitor (attendee)	zā'er (m)	زائر
to visit (attend)	ḥaḍar	حضر
customer	zobūn (m)	زبون

119. Mass Media

newspaper	garīda (f)	جريدة
magazine	magalla (f)	مجلّة
press (printed media)	ṣaḥāfa (f)	صحافة
radio	radio (m)	راديو
radio station	maḥaṭṭet radio (f)	محطّة راديو
television	televizion (m)	تليفزيون
presenter, host	mo'addem (m)	مقدّم
newscaster	mozee' (m)	مذيع
commentator	mo'alleq (m)	معلّق
journalist	ṣaḥafy (m)	صحفي
correspondent (reporter)	morāsel (m)	مراسل
press photographer	moṣawwer ṣaḥafy (m)	مصوّر صحفي
reporter	ṣaḥafy (m)	صحفي
editor	moḥarrer (m)	محرّر
editor-in-chief	ra'īs taḥrīr (m)	رئيس تحرير
to subscribe (to ...)	eʃtarak	إشترك
subscription	eʃterāk (m)	إشتراك
subscriber	moʃtarek (m)	مشترك
to read (vi, vt)	'ara	قرأ
reader	qāre' (m)	قارئ
circulation (of newspaper)	tadāwol (m)	تداول
monthly (adj)	ʃahry	شهري
weekly (adj)	osbū'y	أسبوعي
issue (edition)	'adad (m)	عدد
new (~ issue)	gedīd	جديد
headline	'enwān (m)	عنوان
short article	maqāla saɣīra (f)	مقالة قصيرة
column (regular article)	'amūd (m)	عمود
article	maqāla (f)	مقالة
page	ṣafḥa (f)	صفحة
reportage, report	rebortāʒ (m)	ريبورتاج
event (happening)	ḥadass (m)	حدث

sensation (news)	ḍagga (f)	ضجّة
scandal	feḍīḥa (f)	فضيحة
scandalous (adj)	fāḍeḥ	فاضح
great (~ scandal)	ʃahīr	شهير
show (e.g., cooking ~)	barnāmeg (m)	برنامج
interview	leqā' ṣaḥafy (m)	لقاء صحفي
live broadcast	ezā'a mobāʃera (f)	إذاعة مباشرة
channel	qanah (f)	قناة

120. Agriculture

agriculture	zerā'a (f)	زراعة
peasant (masc.)	fallāḥ (m)	فلّاح
peasant (fem.)	fallāḥa (f)	فلّاحة
farmer	mozāre' (m)	مزارع
tractor (farm ~)	garrār (m)	جرّار
combine, harvester	ḥaṣṣāda (f)	حصّادة
plow	meḥrās (m)	محراث
to plow (vi, vt)	ḥaras	حرث
plowland	ḥaql maḥrūθ (m)	حقل محروث
furrow (in field)	talem (m)	تلم
to sow (vi, vt)	bezr	بذر
seeder	bazzara (f)	بذّارة
sowing (process)	zar' (m)	زرع
scythe	meḥasʃ (m)	محشّ
to mow, to scythe	ḥasʃ	حشّ
spade (tool)	karīk (m)	كريك
to till (vt)	ḥaras	حرث
hoe	magrafa (f)	مجرفة
to hoe, to weed	est'ṣal nabatāt	إستأصل نباتات
weed (plant)	nabāt ṭafayly (m)	نبات طفيّلي
watering can	raʃāʃa (f)	رشّاشة
to water (plants)	sa'a	سقى
watering (act)	sa'y (m)	سقي
pitchfork	mazrāh (f)	مذراة
rake	madamma (f)	مدمّة
fertilizer	semād (m)	سماد
to fertilize (vt)	sammed	سمّد
manure (fertilizer)	semād (m)	سماد
field	ḥaql (m)	حقل

meadow	marag (m)	مرج
vegetable garden	bostān χoḍār (m)	بستان خضار
orchard (e.g., apple ~)	bostān (m)	بستان
to graze (vt)	ra‘a	رعى
herder (herdsman)	rā‘y (m)	راعي
pasture	mar‘a (m)	مرعى
cattle breeding	tarbeya el mawāʃy (f)	تربية المواشي
sheep farming	tarbeya aɣnām (f)	تربية أغنام
plantation	mazra‘a (f)	مزرعة
row (garden bed ~s)	ḥoḍe (m)	حوض
hothouse	dafī’a (f)	دفيئة
drought (lack of rain)	gafāf (m)	جفاف
dry (~ summer)	gāf	جاف
grain	ḥobūb (pl)	حبوب
cereal crops	maḥaṣīl el ḥubūb (pl)	محاصيل الحبوب
to harvest, to gather	ḥaṣad	حصد
miller (person)	ṭaḥḥān (m)	طحّان
mill (e.g., gristmill)	ṭaḥūna (f)	طاحونة
to grind (grain)	ṭaḥn el ḥobūb	طحن الحبوب
flour	de’ī’ (m)	دقيق
straw	’aʃ (m)	قشّ

121. Building. Building process

construction site	arḍ benā’ (f)	أرض بناء
to build (vt)	bana	بنى
construction worker	‘āmel benā’ (m)	عامل بناء
project	maʃrū‘ (m)	مشروع
architect	mohandes me‘māry (m)	مهندس معماري
worker	‘āmel (m)	عامل
foundation (of a building)	asās (m)	أساس
roof	sa’f (m)	سقف
foundation pile	kawmet el asās (f)	كومة الأساس
wall	ḥeyṭa (f)	حيطة
reinforcing bars	ḥadīd taslīḥ (m)	حديد تسليح
scaffolding	sa’’āla (f)	سقّالة
concrete	χarasāna (f)	خرسانة
granite	granīt (m)	جرانيت
stone	ḥagar (m)	حجر
brick	ṭūb (m)	طوب

sand	raml (m)	رمل
cement	asmant (m)	إسمنت
plaster (for walls)	ṭalā' gaṣṣ (m)	طلاء جصّ
to plaster (vt)	ṭala bel gaṣṣ	طلى بالجصّ
paint	dehān (m)	دهان
to paint (~ a wall)	dahhen	دهّن
barrel	barmīl (m)	برميل
crane	rāfe'a (f)	رافعة
to lift, to hoist (vt)	rafa'	رفع
to lower (vt)	nazzel	نزّل
bulldozer	bulldozer (m)	بولدوزر
excavator	ḥaffāra (f)	حفّارة
scoop, bucket	magrafa (f)	مجرفة
to dig (excavate)	ḥafar	حفر
hard hat	χawza (f)	خوذة

122. Science. Research. Scientists

science	'elm (m)	علم
scientific (adj)	'elmy	علمي
scientist	'ālem (m)	عالم
theory	naẓariya (f)	نظريّة
axiom	badīhiya (f)	بديهيّة
analysis	taḥlīl (m)	تحليل
to analyze (vt)	ḥallel	حلّل
argument (strong ~)	borhān (m)	برهان
substance (matter)	madda (f)	مادّة
hypothesis	faraḍiya (f)	فرضيّة
dilemma	mo'ḍela (f)	معضلة
dissertation	resāla 'elmiya (f)	رسالة علميّة
dogma	'aqīda (f)	عقيدة
doctrine	mazhab (m)	مذهب
research	baḥs (m)	بحث
to research (vt)	baḥs	بحث
tests (laboratory ~)	eχtebārāt (pl)	إختبارات
laboratory	moχtabar (m)	مختبر
method	manhag (m)	منهج
molecule	gozaye' (m)	جزيء
monitoring	reqāba (f)	رقابة
discovery (act, event)	ekteʃāf (m)	إكتشاف
postulate	mosallama (f)	مسلّمة
principle	mabda' (m)	مبدأ
forecast	tanabbo' (m)	تنبّؤ

to forecast (vt)	tanabba'	تنبّأ
synthesis	tarkīb (m)	تركيب
trend (tendency)	ettegāh (m)	إتّجاه
theorem	naẓariya (f)	نظريّة
teachings	ta'alīm (pl)	تعاليم
fact	ḥaī'a (f)	حقيقة
expedition	be'sa (f)	بعثة
experiment	tagreba (f)	تجربة
academician	akadīmy (m)	أكاديمي
bachelor (e.g., ~ of Arts)	bakaleryūs (m)	بكالوريوس
doctor (PhD)	doktore (m)	دكتور
Associate Professor	ostāz moʃārek (m)	أستاذ مشارك
Master (e.g., ~ of Arts)	maʒestīr (m)	ماجستير
professor	brofessor (m)	بروفيسور

Professions and occupations

123. Job search. Dismissal

job	'amal (m)	عمل
staff (work force)	kawādir (pl)	كوادر
personnel	ṭāqem el 'āmelīn (m)	طاقم العاملين
career	mehna (f)	مهنة
prospects (chances)	'āfāq (pl)	آفاق
skills (mastery)	maharāt (pl)	مهارات
selection (screening)	exteyār (m)	إختيار
employment agency	wekālet tawẓīf (f)	وكالة توَظيف
résumé	sīra zātiya (f)	سيرة ذاتيَة
job interview	mo'ablet 'amal (f)	مقابلة عمل
vacancy, opening	wazīfa xaleya (f)	وظيفة خالية
salary, pay	morattab (m)	مرتَب
fixed salary	rāteb sābet (m)	راتب ثابت
pay, compensation	ogra (f)	أجرة
position (job)	manṣeb (m)	منصب
duty (of employee)	wāgeb (m)	واجب
range of duties	magmū'a men el wāgebāt (f)	مجموعة من الواجبات
busy (I'm ~)	maʃɣūl	مشغول
to fire (dismiss)	rafad	رفد
dismissal	eqāla (m)	إقالة
unemployment	batāla (f)	بطالة
unemployed (n)	'āṭel (m)	عاطل
retirement	ma'āʃ (m)	معاش
to retire (from job)	oḥīl 'ala el ma'āʃ	أحيل على المعاش

124. Business people

director	modīr (m)	مدير
manager (director)	modīr (m)	مدير
boss	ra'īs (m)	رئيس
superior	motafawweq (m)	متفوَق
superiors	ro'asā' (pl)	رؤساء

president	ra'īs (m)	رئيس
chairman	ra'īs (m)	رئيس
deputy (substitute)	nā'eb (m)	نائب
assistant	mosā'ed (m)	مساعد
secretary	sekerteyr (m)	سكرتير
personal assistant	sekerteyr χāṣ (m)	سكرتير خاص
businessman	ragol a'māl (m)	رجل أعمال
entrepreneur	rā'ed a'māl (m)	رائد أعمال
founder	mo'asses (m)	مؤسّس
to found (vt)	asses	أسّس
incorporator	mo'asses (m)	مؤسّس
partner	ʃerīk (m)	شريك
stockholder	mālek el as-hom (m)	مالك الأسهم
millionaire	millyonīr (m)	مليونير
billionaire	milliardīr (m)	ملياردير
owner, proprietor	ṣāḥeb (m)	صاحب
landowner	ṣāḥeb el arḍ (m)	صاحب الأرض
client	'amīl (m)	عميل
regular client	'amīl dā'em (m)	عميل دائم
buyer (customer)	moʃtary (m)	مشتري
visitor	zā'er (m)	زائر
professional (n)	moḥtaref (m)	محترف
expert	χabīr (m)	خبير
specialist	motaχaṣṣeṣ (m)	متخصّص
banker	ṣāḥeb maṣraf (m)	صاحب مصرف
broker	semsār (m)	سمسار
cashier, teller	'āmel kaʃier (m)	عامل كاشيير
accountant	muḥāseb (m)	محاسب
security guard	ḥāres amn (m)	حارس أمن
investor	mostasmer (m)	مستثمر
debtor	modīn (m)	مدين
creditor	dā'en (m)	دائن
borrower	moqtareḍ (m)	مقترض
importer	mostawred (m)	مستوّرد
exporter	moṣadder (m)	مصدّر
manufacturer	el ʃerka el moṣanne'a (f)	الشركة المصنّعة
distributor	mowazze' (m)	موزّع
middleman	wasīṭ (m)	وسيط
consultant	mostaʃār (m)	مستشار

sales representative	mandūb mabi'āt (m)	مندوب مبيعات
agent	wakīl (m)	وكيل
insurance agent	wakīl el ta'mīn (m)	وكيل التأمين

125. Service professions

cook	ṭabbāχ (m)	طبّاخ
chef (kitchen chef)	el ʃeyf (m)	الشيف
baker	χabbāz (m)	خبّاز
bartender	bārman (m)	بارمان
waiter	garsone (m)	جرسون
waitress	garsona (f)	جرسونة
lawyer, attorney	muḥāmy (m)	محامي
lawyer (legal expert)	muḥāmy χabīr qanūny (m)	محامي خبير قانوني
notary	mowassaq (m)	موثّق
electrician	kahrabā'y (m)	كهربائي
plumber	samkary (m)	سمكري
carpenter	naggār (m)	نجّار
masseur	modallek (m)	مدلّك
masseuse	modalleka (f)	مدلّكة
doctor	doktore (m)	دكتور
taxi driver	sawwā' taksi (m)	سوّاق تاكسي
driver	sawwā' (m)	سوّاق
delivery man	rāgel el delivery (m)	راجل الديلفري
chambermaid	'āmela tandīf ɣoraf (f)	عاملة تنظيف غرف
security guard	ḥāres amn (m)	حارس أمن
flight attendant (fem.)	moḍīfet ṭayarān (f)	مضيفة طيران
schoolteacher	modarres madrasa (m)	مدرّس مدرسة
librarian	amīn maktaba (m)	أمين مكتبة
translator	motargem (m)	مترجم
interpreter	motargem fawwry (m)	مترجم فوّري
guide	morʃed (m)	مرشد
hairdresser	ḥallā' (m)	حلّاق
mailman	sā'y el barīd (m)	ساعي البريد
salesman (store staff)	bayā' (m)	بيّاع
gardener	bostāny (m)	بستاني
domestic servant	χādema (m)	خادمة
maid (female servant)	χadema (f)	خادمة
cleaner (cleaning lady)	'āmela tandīf (f)	عاملة تنظيف

126. Military professions and ranks

private	gondy (m)	جندي
sergeant	raqīb tāny (m)	رقيب تاني
lieutenant	molāzem tāny (m)	ملازم تاني
captain	naqīb (m)	نقيب
major	rā'ed (m)	رائد
colonel	'aqīd (m)	عقيد
general	ʒenerāl (m)	جنرال
marshal	marʃāl (m)	مارشال
admiral	amerāl (m)	أميرال
military (n)	'askary (m)	عسكري
soldier	gondy (m)	جندي
officer	ḍābeṭ (m)	ضابط
commander	qā'ed (m)	قائد
border guard	ḥaras ḥodūd (m)	حرس حدود
radio operator	'āmel lāselky (m)	عامل لاسلكي
scout (searcher)	rā'ed mostakʃef (m)	رائد مستكشف
pioneer (sapper)	mohandes 'askary (m)	مهندس عسكري
marksman	rāmy (m)	رامي
navigator	mallāḥ (m)	ملاّح

127. Officials. Priests

king	malek (m)	ملك
queen	maleka (f)	ملكة
prince	amīr (m)	أمير
princess	amīra (f)	أميرة
czar	qayṣar (m)	قيصر
czarina	qayṣara (f)	قيصرة
president	ra'īs (m)	رئيس
Secretary (minister)	wazīr (m)	وزير
prime minister	ra'īs wozarā' (m)	رئيس وزراء
senator	'oḍw magles el ʃoyūχ (m)	عضو مجلس الشيوخ
diplomat	deblomāsy (m)	دبلوماسي
consul	qonṣol (m)	قنصل
ambassador	safīr (m)	سفير
counsilor (diplomatic officer)	mostaʃār (m)	مستشار
official, functionary (civil servant)	mowaẓẓaf (m)	موظّف

prefect	ra'īs edāret el ḥayī (m)	رئيس إدارة الحي
mayor	ra'īs el baladiya (m)	رئيس البلديّة
judge	qāḍy (m)	قاضي
prosecutor (e.g., district attorney)	el na'eb el 'ām (m)	النائب العام
missionary	mobasʃer (m)	مبشّر
monk	rāheb (m)	راهب
abbot	ra'īs el deyr (m)	رئيس الدير
rabbi	ḥaχām (m)	حاخام
vizier	wazīr (m)	وزير
shah	ʃāh (m)	شاه
sheikh	ʃɛyχ (m)	شيخ

128. Agricultural professions

beekeeper	naḥḥāl (m)	نحّال
herder, shepherd	rā'y (m)	راعي
agronomist	mohandes zerā'y (m)	مهندس زراعي
cattle breeder	morabby el mawāʃy (m)	مربّي المواشي
veterinarian	doktore beṭary (m)	دكتور بيطري
farmer	mozāre' (m)	مزارع
winemaker	ṣāne' el χamr (m)	صانع الخمر
zoologist	χabīr fe 'elm el ḥayawān (m)	خبير في علم الحيوان
cowboy	rā'y el ba'ar (m)	راعي البقر

129. Art professions

actor	momassel (m)	ممثّل
actress	momassela (f)	ممثّلة
singer (masc.)	moṭreb (m)	مطرب
singer (fem.)	moṭreba (f)	مطربة
dancer (masc.)	rāqeṣ (m)	راقص
dancer (fem.)	ra'āṣa (f)	راقصة
performer (masc.)	fannān (m)	فنّان
performer (fem.)	fannāna (f)	فنّانة
musician	'āzef (m)	عازف
pianist	'āzef biano (m)	عازف بيانو
guitar player	'āzef guitar (m)	عازف جيتار
conductor (orchestra ~)	qā'ed orkestra (m)	قائد أوركسترا

composer	molaḥḥen (m)	ملحّن
impresario	modīr fer'a (m)	مدير فرقة
film director	moχreg aflām (m)	مخرج أفلام
producer	monteg (m)	منتج
scriptwriter	kāteb senario (m)	كاتب سيناريو
critic	nāqed (m)	ناقد
writer	kāteb (m)	كاتب
poet	ʃā'er (m)	شاعر
sculptor	naḥḥāt (m)	نحّات
artist (painter)	rassām (m)	رسّام
juggler	bahlawān (m)	بهلوان
clown	aragoze (m)	أراجوز
acrobat	bahlawān (m)	بهلوان
magician	sāḥer (m)	ساحر

130. Various professions

doctor	doktore (m)	دكتور
nurse	momarreḍa (f)	ممرّضة
psychiatrist	doktore nafsāny (m)	دكتور نفساني
dentist	doktore asnān (m)	دكتور أسنان
surgeon	garrāḥ (m)	جرّاح
astronaut	rā'ed faḍā' (m)	رائد فضاء
astronomer	'ālem falak (m)	عالم فلك
pilot	ṭayār (m)	طيّار
driver (of taxi, etc.)	sawwā' (m)	سوّاق
engineer (train driver)	sawwā' (m)	سوّاق
mechanic	mikanīky (m)	ميكانيكي
miner	'āmel mangam (m)	عامل منجم
worker	'āmel (m)	عامل
locksmith	'affāl (m)	قفّال
joiner (carpenter)	naggār (m)	نجّار
turner (lathe machine operator)	χarrāṭ (m)	خرّاط
construction worker	'āmel benā' (m)	عامل بناء
welder	laḥḥām (m)	لحّام
professor (title)	brofessor (m)	بروفيسور
architect	mohandes me'māry (m)	مهندس معماري
historian	mo'arreχ (m)	مؤرّخ
scientist	'ālem (m)	عالم
physicist	fizyā'y (m)	فيزيائي
chemist (scientist)	kemyā'y (m)	كيميائي
archeologist	'ālem'āsār (m)	عالم آثار

geologist	ʒeoloʒy (m)	جيولوجي
researcher (scientist)	bāḥes (m)	باحث
babysitter	dāda (f)	دادة
teacher, educator	mo'allem (m)	معلّم
editor	moḥarrer (m)	محرّر
editor-in-chief	ra'īs taḥrīr (m)	رئيس تحرير
correspondent	morāsel (m)	مراسل
typist (fem.)	kāteba 'ala el 'āla el kāteba (f)	كاتبة على الآلة الكاتبة
designer	moṣammem (m)	مصمّم
computer expert	motaχaṣṣeṣ bel kombuter (m)	متخصص بالكمبيوتر
programmer	mobarmeg (m)	مبرمج
engineer (designer)	mohandes (m)	مهندس
sailor	baḥḥār (m)	بحّار
seaman	baḥḥār (m)	بحّار
rescuer	monqez (m)	منقذ
fireman	rāgel el maṭāfy (m)	راجل المطافئ
police officer	ʃorṭy (m)	شرطي
watchman	ḥāres (m)	حارس
detective	moḥaqqeq (m)	محقّق
customs officer	mowazzaf el gamārek (m)	موظّف الجمارك
bodyguard	ḥāres ʃaχṣy (m)	حارس شخصي
prison guard	ḥāres segn (m)	حارس سجن
inspector	mofatteʃ (m)	مفتّش
sportsman	reyāḍy (m)	رياضي
trainer, coach	modarreb (m)	مدرّب
butcher	gazzār (m)	جزّار
cobbler (shoe repairer)	eskāfy (m)	إسكافي
merchant	tāger (m)	تاجر
loader (person)	ʃayāl (m)	شيّال
fashion designer	moṣammem azyā' (m)	مصمّم أزياء
model (fem.)	modeyl (f)	موديل

131. Occupations. Social status

schoolboy	talmīz (m)	تلميذ
student (college ~)	ṭāleb (m)	طالب
philosopher	faylasūf (m)	فيلسوف
economist	eqtiṣādy (m)	إقتصادي
inventor	moχtare' (m)	مخترع

unemployed (n)	‘āṭel (m)	عاطل
retiree	motaqā‘ed (m)	متقاعد
spy, secret agent	gasūs (m)	جاسوس
prisoner	sagīn (m)	سجين
striker	moḍrab (m)	مضرب
bureaucrat	buroqrāṭy (m)	بيروقراطي
traveler (globetrotter)	raḥḥāla (m)	رحّالة
gay, homosexual (n)	ʃāz (m)	شاذ
hacker	haker (m)	هاكر
hippie	hippi (m)	هيبي
bandit	qāṭe‘ ṭarī’ (m)	قاطع طريق
hit man, killer	qātel ma’gūr (m)	قاتل مأجور
drug addict	modmen moχaddarāt (m)	مدمن مخدّرات
drug dealer	tāger moχaddarāt (m)	تاجر مخدّرات
prostitute (fem.)	mommos (f)	مومّس
pimp	qawwād (m)	قوّاد
sorcerer	sāḥer (m)	ساحر
sorceress (evil ~)	sāḥera (f)	ساحرة
pirate	’orṣān (m)	قرصان
slave	‘abd (m)	عبد
samurai	samuray (m)	ساموراي
savage (primitive)	motawaḥḥeʃ (m)	متوحّش

Sports

132. Kinds of sports. Sportspersons

sportsman	reyāḍy (m)	رياضي
kind of sports	nū‘ men el reyāḍa (m)	نوع من الرياضة
basketball	koret el salla (f)	كرة السلّة
basketball player	lā‘eb korat el salla (m)	لاعب كرة السلّة
baseball	baseball (m)	بيسبول
baseball player	lā‘eb basebāl (m)	لاعب بيسبول
soccer	koret el qadam (f)	كرة القدم
soccer player	lā‘eb korat qadam (m)	لاعب كرة القدم
goalkeeper	ḥāres el marma (m)	حارس المرمى
hockey	hoky (m)	هوكي
hockey player	lā‘eb hoky (m)	لاعب هوكي
volleyball	voliball (m)	فولي بول
volleyball player	lā‘eb volly bal (m)	لاعب فولي بول
boxing	molakma (f)	ملاكمة
boxer	molākem (m)	ملاكم
wrestling	moṣar‘a (f)	مصارعة
wrestler	moṣāre‘ (m)	مصارع
karate	karate (m)	كاراتيه
karate fighter	lā‘eb karateyh (m)	لاعب كاراتيه
judo	ʒudo (m)	جودو
judo athlete	lā‘eb ʒudo (m)	لاعب جودو
tennis	tennis (m)	تنسَ
tennis player	lā‘eb tennis (m)	لاعب تنس
swimming	sebāḥa (f)	سباحة
swimmer	sabbāḥ (m)	سبّاح
fencing	mobarza (f)	مبارزة
fencer	mobārez (m)	مبارز
chess	ʃaṭarang (m)	شطرنج
chess player	lā‘eb ʃaṭarang (m)	لاعب شطرنج

alpinism	tasalloq el gebāl (m)	تسلّق الجبال
alpinist	motasalleq el gebāl (m)	متسلّق الجبال
running	garyī (m)	جريَ
runner	'addā' (m)	عدّاء
athletics	al'āb el qowa (pl)	ألعاب القوى
athlete	lā'eb reyāḍy (m)	لاعب رياضي
horseback riding	reyāḍa el forūsiya (f)	رياضة الفروسيّة
horse rider	fāres (m)	فارس
figure skating	tazallog fanny 'alal galīd (m)	تزلّج فنّي على الجليد
figure skater (masc.)	motazalleg rāqeṣ (m)	متزلّج راقص
figure skater (fem.)	motazallega rāqeṣa (f)	متزلّجة راقصة
powerlifting	raf' el asqāl (m)	رفع الأثقال
powerlifter	rāfe' el asqāl (m)	رافع الأثقال
car racing	sebā' el sayarāt (m)	سباق السيارات
racing driver	sawwā' sebā' (m)	سائق سباق
cycling	rokūb el darragāt (m)	ركوب الدرّاجات
cyclist	lā'eb el darrāga (m)	لاعب الدرّاجة
broad jump	el qafz el 'āly (m)	القفز العالي
pole vault	el qafz bel 'aṣa (m)	القفز بالعصا
jumper	qāfez (m)	قافز

133. Kinds of sports. Miscellaneous

football	koret el qadam (f)	كرة القدم
badminton	el rīʃa (m)	الريشة
biathlon	el biatlon (m)	البياتلون
billiards	bilyardo (m)	بليادو
bobsled	zalāga gama'iya (f)	زلاجة جماعية
bodybuilding	body building (m)	بادي بيلدنج
water polo	koret el maya (f)	كرة الميّة
handball	koret el yad (f)	كرة اليد
golf	golf (m)	جولف
rowing, crew	tagdīf (m)	تجديف
scuba diving	ɣoṣe (m)	غوص
cross-country skiing	reyāḍa el ski (f)	رياضة الإسكي
table tennis (ping-pong)	koret el ṭawla (f)	كرة الطاولة
sailing	reyāḍa ebḥār el marākeb (f)	رياضة إبحارالمراكب
rally racing	sebā' el sayarāt (m)	سباق السيارات

rugby	rugby (m)	رجبي
snowboarding	el tazallog 'lal galīd (m)	التزلّج على الجليد
archery	remāya (f)	رماية

134. Gym

barbell	bār ḥadīd (m)	بار حديد
dumbbells	dumbbells (m)	دمبلز
training machine	gehāz tadrīb (m)	جهاز تدريب
exercise bicycle	'agalet tadrīb (f)	عجلة تدريب
treadmill	trīdmil (f)	تريد ميل
horizontal bar	'o'la (f)	عقلة
parallel bars	el motawaziyīn (pl)	المتوازيين
vault (vaulting horse)	manaṣṣet el qafz (f)	منصّة القفز
mat (exercise ~)	ḥaṣīra (f)	حصيرة
jump rope	ḥabl el naṭṭ (m)	حبل النطّ
aerobics	aerobiks (m)	ايروبيكس
yoga	yoga (f)	يوجا

135. Hockey

hockey	hoky (m)	هوكي
hockey player	lā'eb hoky (m)	لاعب هوكي
to play hockey	le'eb el hoky	لعب الهوكي
ice	galīd (m)	جليد
puck	'orṣ el hoky (m)	قرص الهوكي
hockey stick	maḍrab el hoky (m)	مضرب الهوكي
ice skates	zallagāt (pl)	زلّاجات
board (ice hockey rink ~)	ḥalabet el hokky (f)	حلبة الهوكي
shot	ramya (f)	رمية
goaltender	ḥāres el marma (m)	حارس المرمى
goal (score)	hadaf (m)	هدف
to score a goal	gāb hadaf	جاب هدف
period	ʃoṭe (m)	شوط
second period	el ʃoṭe el tāni (m)	الشوط التاني
substitutes bench	dekket el eḥtiāṭy (f)	دكّة الإحتياطي

136. Soccer

soccer	koret el qadam (f)	كرة القدم
soccer player	lā'eb korat qadam (m)	لاعب كرة القدم

to play soccer	leʿeb korret el qadam	لعب كرة القدم
major league	el dawry el kebīr (m)	الدوري الكبير
soccer club	nādy koret el qadam (m)	نادي كرة القدم
coach	modarreb (m)	مدرب
owner, proprietor	ṣāḥeb (m)	صاحب
team	farīʾ (m)	فريق
team captain	kabten el farīʾ (m)	كابتن الفريق
player	lāʿeb (m)	لاعب
substitute	lāʿeb eḥteyāṭy (m)	لاعب إحتياطي
forward	lāʿeb hogūm (m)	لاعب هجوم
center forward	wasaṭ el hogūm (m)	وسط الهجوم
scorer	haddāf (m)	هدّاف
defender, back	modāfeʿ (m)	مدافع
midfielder, halfback	lāʿeb χaṭṭ wasaṭ (m)	لاعب خطّ وسط
match	mobarā (f)	مباراة
to meet (vi, vt)	ʾābel	قابل
final	mobarāh nehaʾiya (f)	مباراة نهائيّة
semi-final	el dore el neṣf el nehāʾy (m)	الدور النصف النهائي
championship	boṭūla (f)	بطولة
period, half	ʃoṭe (m)	شوط
first period	el ʃoṭe el awwal (m)	الشوط الأوّل
half-time	beyn el ʃoṭeyn	بين الشوطين
goal	marma (m)	مرمى
goalkeeper	ḥāres el marma (m)	حارس المرمى
goalpost	ʿārḍa (f)	عارضة
crossbar	ʿārḍa (f)	عارضة
net	ʃabaka (f)	شبكة
to concede a goal	samaḥ be eṣābet el hadaf	سمح بإصابة الهدف
ball	kora (f)	كرة
pass	tamrīra (f)	تمريرة
kick	ḍarba (f)	ضربة
to kick (~ the ball)	ʃāt	شات
free kick (direct ~)	ḍarba ḥorra (f)	ضربة حرّة
corner kick	ḍarba rokniya (f)	ضربة ركنيّة
attack	hogūm (m)	هجوم
counterattack	hagma moḍāda (f)	هجمة مضادّة
combination	tarkīb (m)	تركيب
referee	ḥakam (m)	حكم
to blow the whistle	ṣaffar	صفّر
whistle (sound)	ṣoffāra (f)	صفّارة
foul, misconduct	moχalfa (f)	مخالفة
to commit a foul	χālef	خالف
to send off	ṭarad men el malʿab	طرد من الملعب
yellow card	el kart el aṣfar (m)	الكارت الأصفر

red card	el kart el aḥmar (m)	الكارت الأحمر
disqualification	ḥermān (m)	حرمان
to disqualify (vt)	ḥaram	حرم
penalty kick	ḍarbet gazā' (f)	ضربة جزاء
wall	ḥā'eṭ (m)	حائط
to score (vi, vt)	gāb hadaf	جاب هدف
goal (score)	hadaf (m)	هدف
to score a goal	gāb hadaf	جاب هدف
substitution	tabdīl (m)	تبديل
to replace (a player)	baddal	بدّل
rules	qawā'ed (pl)	قواعد
tactics	taktīk (m)	تكتيك
stadium	mal'ab (m)	ملعب
stand (bleachers)	modarrag (m)	مدرّج
fan, supporter	moʃagge' (m)	مشجّع
to shout (vi)	ṣarraχ	صرّخ
scoreboard	lawḥet el natīga (f)	لوحة النتيجة
score	natīga (f)	نتيجة
defeat	hazīma (f)	هزيمة
to lose (not win)	χeser	خسر
tie	ta'ādol (m)	تعادل
to tie (vi)	ta'ādal	تعادل
victory	foze (m)	فوز
to win (vi, vt)	fāz	فاز
champion	baṭal (m)	بطل
best (adj)	aḥsan	أحسن
to congratulate (vt)	hanna	هنّأ
commentator	mo'alleq (m)	معلّق
to commentate (vt)	'alla'	علّق
broadcast	ezā'a (f)	إذاعة

137. Alpine skiing

skis	zallagāt (pl)	زلّاجات
to ski (vi)	tazallag	تزلّج
mountain-ski resort	montaga' gabaly lel tazaḥloq (m)	منتجع جبلي للتزلج
ski lift	meṣ'ad (m)	مصعد
ski poles	'eṣyān el tazallog (pl)	عصيان التزلّج
slope	monḥadar (m)	منحدر
slalom	el tazallog el mota'arreg (m)	التزلّج المتعرّج

138. Tennis. Golf

golf	golf (m)	جولف
golf club	nādy golf (m)	نادي جولف
golfer	lā'eb golf (m)	لاعب جولف
hole	tagwīf (m)	تجويف
club	maḍrab (m)	مضرب
golf trolley	'araba lel golf (f)	عربة للجولف
tennis	tennis (m)	تنسّ
tennis court	mal'ab tennis (m)	ملعب تنسّ
serve	monawla (f)	مناولة
to serve (vt)	nāwel	ناول
racket	maḍrab (m)	مضرب
net	ʃabaka (f)	شبكة
ball	kora (f)	كرة

139. Chess

chess	ʃaṭarang (m)	شطرنج
chessmen	aḥgār el ʃaṭarang (pl)	أحجار الشطرنج
chess player	lā'eb ʃaṭarang (m)	لاعب شطرنج
chessboard	lawḥet el ʃaṭarang (f)	لوحة الشطرنج
chessman	ḥagar (m)	حجر
White (white pieces)	aḥgār bayḍā' (pl)	أحجار بيضاء
Black (black pieces)	aḥgār sawdā' (pl)	أحجار سوداء
pawn	bayda' (m)	بيدق
bishop	fīl (m)	فيل
knight	ḥoṣān (m)	حصان
rook	rakχ (m)	رخّ
queen	el maleka (f)	الملكة
king	el malek (m)	الملك
move	χaṭwa (f)	خطوة
to move (vi, vt)	ḥarrak	حرّك
to sacrifice (vt)	ḍaḥḥa	ضحّى
castling	χaṭwa el raχ wel ʃah (f)	خطوة الرخ والشاه
check	kesʃ	كشّ
checkmate	kesʃ malek	كشّ ملك
chess tournament	boṭūlet ʃaṭarang (f)	بطولة شطرنج
Grand Master	grand master (m)	جراند ماستر
combination	tarkīb (m)	تركيب
game (in chess)	dore (m)	دور
checkers	dama (f)	داما

140. Boxing

boxing	molakma (f)	ملاكمة
fight (bout)	molakma (f)	ملاكمة
boxing match	mobarāt molakma (f)	مباراة ملاكمة
round (in boxing)	gawla (f)	جولة
ring	ḥalaba (f)	حلبة
gong	naqūs (m)	ناقوس
punch	ḍarba (f)	ضربة
knockdown	ḍarba ḥasema (f)	ضربة حاسمة
knockout	ḍarba 'āḍya (f)	ضربة قاضية
to knock out	ḍarab ḍarba qāḍiya	ضرب ضربة قاضية
boxing glove	qoffāz el molakma (m)	قفّاز الملاكمة
referee	ḥakam (m)	حكم
lightweight	el wazn el χafīf (m)	الوزن الخفيف
middleweight	el wazn el motawasseṭ (m)	الوزن المتوسط
heavyweight	el wazn el te'īl (m)	الوزن الثقيل

141. Sports. Miscellaneous

Olympic Games	al'āb olombiya (pl)	ألعاب أولمبيّة
winner	fā'ez (m)	فائز
to be winning	fāz	فاز
to win (vi)	fāz	فاز
leader	za'īm (m)	زعيم
to lead (vi)	ta'addam	تقدّم
first place	el martaba el ūla (f)	المرتبة الأولى
second place	el martaba el tanya (f)	المرتبة الثانية
third place	el martaba el talta (f)	المرتبة الثالثة
medal	medalya (f)	ميدالية
trophy	ka's (f)	كأس
prize cup (trophy)	ka's (f)	كأس
prize (in game)	gayza (f)	جائزة
main prize	akbar gayza (f)	أكبر جائزة
record	raqam qeyāsy (m)	رقم قياسي
to set a record	fāz be raqam qeyāsy	فاز برقم قياسي
final	mobarāh neha'iya (f)	مباراة نهائيّة
final (adj)	nehā'y	نهائي
champion	baṭal (m)	بطل
championship	boṭūla (f)	بطولة

stadium	malʿab (m)	ملعب
stand (bleachers)	modarrag (m)	مدرّج
fan, supporter	moʃaggeʿ (m)	مشجّع
opponent, rival	ʿadeww (m)	عدوّ
start (start line)	χaṭṭ el bedāya (m)	خطّ البداية
finish line	χaṭṭ el nehāya (m)	خطّ النهاية
defeat	hazīma (f)	هزيمة
to lose (not win)	χeser	خسر
referee	ḥakam (m)	حكم
jury (judges)	hay'et el ḥokm (f)	هيئة الحكم
score	natīga (f)	نتيجة
tie	taʿādol (m)	تعادل
to tie (vi)	taʿādal	تعادل
point	no'ṭa (f)	نقطة
result (final score)	natīga neha'iya (f)	نتيجة نهائية
period	ʃoṭe (m)	شوط
half-time	beyn el ʃoṭeyn	بين الشوطين
doping	monasʃeṭāt (pl)	منشّطات
to penalize (vt)	ʿāqab	عاقب
to disqualify (vt)	ḥaram	حرم
apparatus	adah (f)	أداة
javelin	remḥ (m)	رمح
shot (metal ball)	kora maʿdaniya (f)	كرة معدنية
ball (snooker, etc.)	kora (f)	كرة
aim (target)	hadaf (m)	هدف
target	hadaf (m)	هدف
to shoot (vi)	ḍarab bel nār	ضرب بالنار
accurate (~ shot)	maḍbūṭ	مضبوط
trainer, coach	modarreb (m)	مدرّب
to train (sb)	darrab	درّب
to train (vi)	etdarrab	إتدرّب
training	tadrīb (m)	تدريب
gym	gīm (m)	جيم
exercise (physical)	tamrīn (m)	تمرين
warm-up (athlete ~)	tasχīn (m)	تسخين

Education

142. School

school	madrasa (f)	مدرسة
principal (headmaster)	modīr el madrasa (m)	مدير المدرسة
pupil (boy)	talmīz (m)	تلميذ
pupil (girl)	telmīza (f)	تلميذة
schoolboy	talmīz (m)	تلميذ
schoolgirl	telmīza (f)	تلميذة
to teach (sb)	ʿallem	علّم
to learn (language, etc.)	taʿallam	تعلّم
to learn by heart	ḥafaẓ	حفظ
to learn (~ to count, etc.)	taʿallam	تعلّم
to be in school	daras	درس
to go to school	rāḥ el madrasa	راح المدرسة
alphabet	abgadiya (f)	أبجدية
subject (at school)	madda (f)	مادّة
classroom	faṣl (m)	فصل
lesson	dars (m)	درس
recess	estrāḥa (f)	إستراحة
school bell	garas el madrasa (m)	جرس المدرسة
school desk	disk el madrasa (m)	ديسك المدرسة
chalkboard	sabbūra (f)	سبّورة
grade	daraga (f)	درجة
good grade	daraga kewayesa (f)	درجة كويسة
bad grade	daraga meʃ kewayesa (f)	درجة مش كويسة
to give a grade	edda daraga	إدّى درجة
mistake, error	χaṭa' (m)	خطأ
to make mistakes	aχṭa'	أخطأ
to correct (an error)	ṣaḥḥaḥ	صحّح
cheat sheet	berʃām (m)	برشام
homework	wāgeb (m)	واجب
exercise (in education)	tamrīn (m)	تمرين
to be present	ḥaḍar	حضر
to be absent	ɣāb	غاب
to miss school	taɣeyyab ʿan el madrasa	تغيّب عن المدرسة

to punish (vt)	ʻāqab	عاقب
punishment	ʻeqāb (m)	عقاب
conduct (behavior)	solūk (m)	سلوك
report card	el taqrīr el madrasy (m)	التقرير المدرسي
pencil	ʼalam roṣāṣ (m)	قلم رصاص
eraser	astīka (f)	استيكة
chalk	ṭabaʃīr (m)	طباشير
pencil case	maʼlama (f)	مقلمة
schoolbag	ʃanṭet el madrasa (f)	شنطة المدرسة
pen	ʼalam (m)	قلم
school notebook	daftar (m)	دفتر
textbook	ketāb taʻlīm (m)	كتاب تعليم
compasses	bargal (m)	برجل
to make technical drawings	rasam rasm teqany	رسم رسم تقني
technical drawing	rasm teqany (m)	رسم تقني
poem	ʼaṣīda (f)	قصيدة
by heart (adv)	ʻan ẓahr qalb	عن ظهر قلب
to learn by heart	ḥafaẓ	حفظ
school vacation	agāza (f)	أجازة
to be on vacation	ʻando agāza	عنده أجازة
to spend one's vacation	ʼaḍa el agāza	قضى الأجازة
test (written math ~)	emteḥān (m)	إمتحان
essay (composition)	enʃāʼ (m)	إنشاء
dictation	emlāʼ (m)	إملاء
exam (examination)	emteḥān (m)	إمتحان
to take an exam	ʻamal emteḥān	عمل إمتحان
experiment (e.g., chemistry ~)	tagreba (f)	تجربة

143. College. University

academy	akademiya (f)	أكاديميّة
university	gamʻa (f)	جامعة
faculty (e.g., ~ of Medicine)	kolliya (f)	كلّيّة
student (masc.)	ṭāleb (m)	طالب
student (fem.)	ṭāleba (f)	طالبة
lecturer (teacher)	muḥāḍer (m)	محاضر
lecture hall, room	modarrag (m)	مدرّج
graduate	motaχarreg (m)	متخرج
diploma	dibloma (f)	دبلومة

dissertation	resāla 'elmiya (f)	رسالة علميّة
study (report)	derāsa (f)	دراسة
laboratory	moχtabar (m)	مختبر
lecture	moḥaḍra (f)	محاضرة
coursemate	zamīl fel ṣaff (m)	زميل في الصفّ
scholarship	menḥa derāsiya (f)	منحة دراسيّة
academic degree	daraga 'elmiya (f)	درجة علميّة

144. Sciences. Disciplines

mathematics	reyāḍīāt (pl)	رياضيّات
algebra	el gabr (m)	الجبر
geometry	handasa (f)	هندسة
astronomy	'elm el falak (m)	علم الفلك
biology	al aḥya' (m)	الأحياء
geography	goɣrafia (f)	جغرافيا
geology	ʒeoloʒia (f)	جيولوجيا
history	tarīχ (m)	تاريخ
medicine	ṭebb (m)	طبّ
pedagogy	tarbeya (f)	تربية
law	qanūn (m)	قانون
physics	fezya' (f)	فيزياء
chemistry	kemya' (f)	كيمياء
philosophy	falsafa (f)	فلسفة
psychology	'elm el nafs (m)	علم النفس

145. Writing system. Orthography

grammar	el naḥw wel ṣarf (m)	النحو والصرف
vocabulary	mofradāt el loɣa (pl)	مفردات اللغة
phonetics	ṣawtīāt (pl)	صوتيات
noun	esm (m)	اسم
adjective	ṣefa (f)	صفة
verb	fe'l (m)	فعل
adverb	ẓarf (m)	ظرف
pronoun	ḍamīr (m)	ضمير
interjection	oslūb el ta'aggob (m)	أسلوب التعجّب
preposition	ḥarf el garr (m)	حرف الجرّ
root	gezr el kelma (m)	جذر الكلمة
ending	nehāya (f)	نهاية
prefix	sabaeqa (f)	سابقة

syllable	maqṭa' lafzy (m)	مقطع لفظي
suffix	lāḥeqa (f)	لاحقة
stress mark	nabra (f)	نبرة
apostrophe	'alāmet ḥazf (f)	علامة حذف
period, dot	no'ṭa (f)	نقطة
comma	faṣla (f)	فاصلة
semicolon	no'ṭa w faṣla (f)	نقطة وفاصلة
colon	no'ṭeteyn (pl)	نقطتين
ellipsis	talat no'aṭ (pl)	ثلاث نقط
question mark	'alāmet estefhām (f)	علامة إستفهام
exclamation point	'alāmet ta'aggob (f)	علامة تعجّب
quotation marks	'alamāt el eqtebās (pl)	علامات الإقتباس
in quotation marks	beyn 'alamaty el eqtebās	بين علامتي الاقتباس
parenthesis	qoseyn (du)	قوسين
in parenthesis	beyn el qoseyn	بين القوسين
hyphen	'alāmet waṣl (f)	علامة وصل
dash	ʃorṭa (f)	شرطة
space (between words)	farāɣ (m)	فراغ
letter	ḥarf (m)	حرف
capital letter	ḥarf kebīr (m)	حرف كبير
vowel (n)	ḥarf ṣauty (m)	حرف صوتي
consonant (n)	ḥarf sāken (m)	حرف ساكن
sentence	gomla (f)	جملة
subject	fā'el (m)	فاعل
predicate	mosnad (m)	مسند
line	saṭr (m)	سطر
on a new line	men bedāyet el saṭr	من بداية السطر
paragraph	faqra (f)	فقرة
word	kelma (f)	كلمة
group of words	magmū'a men el kelamāt (pl)	مجموعة من الكلمات
expression	moṣṭalaḥ (m)	مصطلح
synonym	morādef (m)	مرادف
antonym	motaḍād loɣawy (m)	متضاد لغوي
rule	qa'eda (f)	قاعدة
exception	estesnā' (m)	إستثناء
correct (adj)	ṣaḥīḥ	صحيح
conjugation	ṣarf (m)	صرف
declension	taṣrīf el asmā' (m)	تصريف الأسماء
nominal case	ḥāla esmiya (f)	حالة أسمية

question	so'āl (m)	سؤال
to underline (vt)	ḥaṭṭ ẖaṭṭ taḥt	حطّ خطّ تحت
dotted line	ẖaṭṭ mena''aṭ (m)	خطّ منقّط

146. Foreign languages

language	loɣa (f)	لغة
foreign (adj)	agnaby	أجنبيّ
foreign language	loɣa agnabiya (f)	لغة أجنبية
to study (vt)	daras	درس
to learn (language, etc.)	ta'allam	تعلّم
to read (vi, vt)	'ara	قرأ
to speak (vi, vt)	kallem	كلّم
to understand (vt)	fehem	فهم
to write (vt)	katab	كتب
fast (adv)	bosor'a	بسرعة
slowly (adv)	bo boṭ'	ببطء
fluently (adv)	beṭalāqa	بطلاقة
rules	qawā'ed (pl)	قواعد
grammar	el naḥw wel ṣarf (m)	النحو والصرف
vocabulary	mofradāt el loɣa (pl)	مفردات اللغة
phonetics	ṣawtīāt (pl)	صوتيات
textbook	ketāb ta'līm (m)	كتاب تعليم
dictionary	qamūs (m)	قاموس
teach-yourself book	ketāb ta'līm zāty (m)	كتاب تعليم ذاتي
phrasebook	ketāb lel 'ebarāt el ʃā'e'a (m)	كتاب للعبارت الشائعة
cassette, tape	kasett (m)	كاسيت
videotape	ʃerī't video (m)	شريط فيديو
CD, compact disc	sidī (m)	سي دي
DVD	dividī (m)	دي في دي
alphabet	abgadiya (f)	أبجدية
to spell (vt)	tahagga	تهجّى
pronunciation	noṭ' (m)	نطق
accent	lahga (f)	لهجة
with an accent	be lahga	بـ لهجة
without an accent	men ɣeyr lahga	من غير لهجة
word	kelma (f)	كلمة
meaning	ma'na (m)	معنى
course (e.g., a French ~)	dawra (f)	دورة
to sign up	saggel esmo	سجّل إسمه

teacher	modarres (m)	مدرّس
translation (process)	targama (f)	ترجمة
translation (text, etc.)	targama (f)	ترجمة
translator	motargem (m)	مترجم
interpreter	motargem fawwry (m)	مترجم فوّري
polyglot	'alīm be'eddet loɣāt (m)	عليم بعدّة لغات
memory	zākera (f)	ذاكرة

147. Fairy tale characters

Santa Claus	baba neweyl (m)	بابا نويل
Cinderella	sindrīla	سيندريلا
mermaid	'arūset el baḥr (f)	عروسة البحر
Neptune	nibtūn (m)	نبتون
magician, wizard	sāḥer (m)	ساحر
fairy	genniya (f)	جنّيّة
magic (adj)	seḥry	سحري
magic wand	el 'aṣāya el seḥriya (f)	العصاية السحرية
fairy tale	ḥekāya χayaliya (f)	حكاية خيالية
miracle	mo'geza (f)	معجزة
dwarf	qazam (m)	قزم
to turn into ...	taḥawwal ela ...	تحوّل إلى...
ghost	ʃabaḥ (m)	شبح
phantom	ʃabaḥ (m)	شبح
monster	waḥʃ (m)	وحش
dragon	tennīn (m)	تنّين
giant	'emlāq (m)	عملاق

148. Zodiac Signs

Aries	borg el ḥaml (m)	برج الحمل
Taurus	borg el sore (m)	برج الثور
Gemini	borg el gawzā' (m)	برج الجوزاء
Cancer	borg el saraṭān (m)	برج السرطان
Leo	borg el asad (m)	برج الأسد
Virgo	borg el 'azrā' (m)	برج العذراء
Libra	borg el mezān (m)	برج الميزان
Scorpio	borg el 'a'rab (m)	برج العقرب
Sagittarius	borg el qose (m)	برج القوس
Capricorn	borg el gady (m)	برج الجدي
Aquarius	borg el dalw (m)	برج الدلو
Pisces	borg el ḥūt (m)	برج الحوت
character	ʃaχṣiya (f)	شخصية

character traits	el ṣefāt el ʃaχṣiya (pl)	الصفات الشخصية
behavior	solūk (m)	سلوك
to tell fortunes	ʾara el ṭāleʿ	قرأ الطالع
fortune-teller	ʿarrāfa (f)	عرّافة
horoscope	tawaqqoʿāt el abrāg (pl)	توقّعات الأبراج

Arts

149. Theater

theater	masraḥ (m)	مسرح
opera	obra (f)	أوبرا
operetta	obrette (f)	أوبريت
ballet	baleyh (m)	باليه
theater poster	molṣaq (m)	ملصق
troupe (theatrical company)	fer'a (f)	فرقة
tour	gawlet fananīn (f)	جولة فنّانين
to be on tour	tagawwal	تجوّل
to rehearse (vi, vt)	'amal brova	عمل بروفة
rehearsal	brova (f)	بروفة
repertoire	barnāmeg el masraḥ (m)	برنامج المسرح
performance	adā' (m)	أداء
theatrical show	'arḍ masraḥy (m)	عرض مسرحي
play	masraḥiya (f)	مسرحيّة
ticket	tazkara (f)	تذكرة
box office (ticket booth)	ʃebbāk el tazāker (m)	شبّاك التذاكر
lobby, foyer	ṣāla (f)	صالة
coat check (cloakroom)	ɣorfet īdā' el ma'āṭef (f)	غرفة إيداع المعاطف
coat check tag	beṭā'et edā' el ma'aṭef (f)	بطاقة إيداع المعاطف
binoculars	naḍḍāra mo'aẓẓema lel obera (f)	نظارة معظمة للأوبرا
usher	ḥāgeb el sinema (m)	حاجب السينما
orchestra seats	karāsy el orkestra (pl)	كراسي الأوركسترا
balcony	balakona (f)	بلكونة
dress circle	ʃorfa (f)	شرفة
box	log (m)	لوج
row	ṣaff (m)	صفّ
seat	meq'ad (m)	مقعد
audience	gomhūr (m)	جمهور
spectator	moʃāhed (m)	مشاهد
to clap (vi, vt)	ṣaffa'	صفّق
applause	taṣfī' (m)	تصفيق
ovation	taṣfī' ḥār (m)	تصفيق حار
stage	χaʃabet el masraḥ (f)	خشبة المسرح
curtain	setāra (f)	ستارة

scenery	dekor (m)	ديكور
backstage	kawalīs (pl)	كواليس
scene (e.g., the last ~)	maʃ-had (m)	مشهد
act	faṣl (m)	فصل
intermission	estrāḥa (f)	استراحة

150. Cinema

actor	momassel (m)	ممثل
actress	momassela (f)	ممثلة
movies (industry)	el aflām (m)	الأفلام
movie	film (m)	فيلم
episode	goz' (m)	جزء
detective movie	film bolīsy (m)	فيلم بوليسي
action movie	film akʃen (m)	فيلم أكشن
adventure movie	film moɣamarāt (m)	فيلم مغامرات
science fiction movie	film χayāl 'elmy (m)	فيلم خيال علمي
horror movie	film ro'b (m)	فيلم رعب
comedy movie	film komedia (f)	فيلم كوميديا
melodrama	melodrama (m)	ميلودراما
drama	drama (f)	دراما
fictional movie	film χayāly (m)	فيلم خيالي
documentary	film wasā'eqy (m)	فيلم وثائقي
cartoon	kartōn (m)	كرتون
silent movies	sinema ṣāmeta (f)	سينما صامتة
role (part)	dore (m)	دور
leading role	dore ra'īsy (m)	دور رئيسي
to play (vi, vt)	massel	مثّل
movie star	negm senamā'y (m)	نجم سينمائي
well-known (adj)	ma'rūf	معروف
famous (adj)	maʃ-hūr	مشهور
popular (adj)	maḥbūb	محبوب
script (screenplay)	senario (m)	سيناريو
scriptwriter	kāteb senario (m)	كاتب سيناريو
movie director	moχreg (m)	مخرج
producer	monteg (m)	منتج
assistant	mosā'ed (m)	مساعد
cameraman	moṣawwer (m)	مصوّر
stuntman	mo'addy maʃāhed χaṭīra (m)	مؤدي مشاهد خطيرة
double (stuntman)	momassel badīl (m)	ممثّل بديل
to shoot a movie	ṣawwar film	صوّر فيلم
audition, screen test	tagreba adā' (f)	تجربة أداء

shooting	taṣwīr (m)	تصوير
movie crew	ṭāqem el film (m)	طاقم الفيلم
movie set	mante'et taṣwīr (f)	منطقة التصوير
camera	kamera (f)	كاميرا
movie theater	sinema (f)	سينما
screen (e.g., big ~)	ʃāʃa (f)	شاشة
to show a movie	'araḍ film	عرض فيلم
soundtrack	mosīqa taṣweriya (f)	موسيقي تصويرية
special effects	mo'asserāt χāṣa (pl)	مؤثّرات خاصّة
subtitles	targamet el ḥewār (f)	ترجمة الحوار
credits	ʃāret el nehāya (f)	شارة النهاية
translation	targama (f)	ترجمة

151. Painting

art	fann (m)	فنّ
fine arts	fonūn gamīla (pl)	فنون جميلة
art gallery	ma'raḍ fonūn (m)	معرض فنون
art exhibition	ma'raḍ fanny (m)	معرض فنّي
painting (art)	lawḥa (f)	لوحة
graphic art	fann taṣwīry (m)	فنّ تصويري
abstract art	fann tagrīdy (m)	فنّ تجريدي
impressionism	el enṭebā'iya (f)	الإنطباعيّة
picture (painting)	lawḥa (f)	لوحة
drawing	rasm (m)	رسم
poster	boster (m)	بوستر
illustration (picture)	rasm tawḍīḥy (m)	رسم توضيحي
miniature	ṣūra moṣagχara (f)	صورة مصغّرة
copy (of painting, etc.)	nosχa (f)	نسخة
reproduction	nosχa ṭeb' el aṣl (f)	نسخة طبق الأصل
mosaic	fosayfesā' (f)	فسيفساء
stained glass window	ʃebbāk 'ezāz mlawwen (m)	شبّاك قزاز ملوّن
fresco	taṣwīr gaṣṣy (m)	تصوير جصي
engraving	na'ʃ (m)	نقش
bust (sculpture)	temsāl neṣfy (m)	تمثال نصفي
sculpture	naḥt (m)	نحت
statue	temsāl (m)	تمثال
plaster of Paris	gibss (m)	جبس
plaster (as adj)	men el gebs	من الجبس
portrait	bortreyh (m)	بورتريه
self-portrait	bortreyh ʃaχṣy (m)	بورتريه شخصي
landscape painting	lawḥet manzar ṭabee'y (f)	لوحة منظر طبيعي

still life	ṭabee'a ṣāmeta (f)	طبيعة صامتة
caricature	ṣūra karikatoriya (f)	صورة كاريكاتورية
sketch	rasm tamhīdy (m)	رسم تمهيدي
paint	lone (m)	لون
watercolor paint	alwān maya (m)	ألوان ميّة
oil (paint)	zeyt (m)	زيت
pencil	'alam roṣāṣ (m)	قلم رصاص
India ink	ḥebr hendy (m)	حبر هندي
charcoal	faḥm (m)	فحم
to draw (vi, vt)	rasam	رسم
to paint (vi, vt)	rasam	رسم
to pose (vi)	'a'ad	قعد
artist's model (masc.)	modeyl ḥayī amām el rassām (m)	موديل حيّ أمام الرسّام
artist's model (fem.)	modeyl ḥayī amām el rassām (m)	موديل حيّ أمام الرسّام
artist (painter)	rassām (m)	رسّام
work of art	'amal fanny (m)	عمل فنّي
masterpiece	toḥfa faniya (f)	تحفة فنية
studio (artist's workroom)	warʃa (f)	ورشة
canvas (cloth)	kanava (f)	كانفا
easel	masnad el loḥe (m)	مسند اللوح
palette	lawḥet el alwān (f)	لوحة الألوان
frame (picture ~, etc.)	eṭār (m)	إطار
restoration	tarmīm (m)	ترميم
to restore (vt)	rammem	رمّم

152. Literature & Poetry

literature	adab (m)	أدب
author (writer)	mo'allef (m)	مؤلّف
pseudonym	esm mosta'ār (m)	اسم مستعار
book	ketāb (m)	كتاب
volume	mogallad (m)	مجلّد
table of contents	gadwal el moḥtawayāt (m)	جدوّل المحتويات
page	ṣafḥa (f)	صفحة
main character	el ʃaχṣiya el ra'esiya (f)	الشخصية الرئيسية
autograph	tawqee' el mo'allef (m)	توقيع المؤلّف
short story	qeṣṣa 'aṣīra (f)	قصّة قصيرة
story (novella)	'oṣṣa (f)	قصّة
novel	rewāya (f)	رواية
work (writing)	mo'allef (m)	مؤلّف
fable	ḥekāya (f)	حكاية

detective novel	rewāya bolesiya (f)	رواية بوليسية
poem (verse)	'aṣīda (f)	قصيدة
poetry	ʃe'r (m)	شعر
poem (epic, ballad)	'aṣīda (f)	قصيدة
poet	ʃā'er (m)	شاعر
fiction	χayāl (m)	خيال
science fiction	χayāl 'elmy (m)	خيال علمي
adventures	adab el moɣamrāt (m)	أدب المغامرات
educational literature	adab tarbawy (m)	أدب تربوي
children's literature	adab el aṭfāl (m)	أدب الأطفال

153. Circus

circus	serk (m)	سيرك
traveling circus	serk motana''el (m)	سيرك متنقّل
program	barnāmeg (m)	برنامج
performance	adā' (m)	أداء
act (circus ~)	'arḍ (m)	عرض
circus ring	ḥalabet el serk (f)	حلبة السيرك
pantomime (act)	momassel īmā'y (m)	ممثّل إيمائي
clown	aragoze (m)	أراجوز
acrobat	bahlawān (m)	بهلوان
acrobatics	al'ab bahlawaniya (f)	ألعاب بهلوانية
gymnast	lā'eb gombāz (m)	لاعب جمباز
gymnastics	gombāz (m)	جمباز
somersault	ḥarakāt ʃa'laba (pl)	حركات شقلبة
athlete (strongman)	el ragl el qawy (m)	الرجل القوي
tamer (e.g., lion ~)	morawweḍ (m)	مروّض
rider (circus horse ~)	fāres (m)	فارس
assistant	mosā'ed (m)	مساعد
stunt	ḥeyla (f)	حيلة
magic trick	χed'a seḥriya (f)	خدعة سحرية
conjurer, magician	sāḥer (m)	ساحر
juggler	bahlawān (m)	بهلوان
to juggle (vi, vt)	le'eb be korāt 'adīda	لعب بكرات عديدة
animal trainer	modarreb ḥayawanāt (m)	مدرّب حيوانات
animal training	tadrīb el ḥayawanāt (m)	تدريب الحيوانات
to train (animals)	darrab	درّب

154. Music. Pop music

music	mosīqa (f)	موسيقى
musician	'āzef (m)	عازف

musical instrument	ʾāla moseqiya (f)	آلة موسيقيّة
to play ...	ʿazaf ...	عزف...
guitar	guitar (m)	جيتار
violin	kamān (m)	كمان
cello	el tʃello (m)	التشيلو
double bass	kamān kebīr (m)	كمان كبير
harp	qesār (m)	قيثار
piano	biano (m)	بيانو
grand piano	biano kebīr (m)	بيانو كبير
organ	arɣan (m)	أرغن
wind instruments	ʾālāt el nafχ (pl)	آلات النفخ
oboe	mezmār (m)	مزمار
saxophone	saksofon (m)	ساكسوفون
clarinet	klarinet (m)	كلارنيت
flute	flute (m)	فلوت
trumpet	būʾ (m)	بوق
accordion	okordiōn (m)	أكورديون
drum	ṭabla (f)	طبلة
duo	sonāʾy (m)	ثنائي
trio	solāsy (m)	ثلاثي
quartet	robāʿy (m)	رباعي
choir	korale (m)	كورال
orchestra	orkestra (f)	أوركسترا
pop music	mosīqa el bob (f)	موسيقى البوب
rock music	mosīqa el rok (f)	موسيقى الروك
rock group	ferʾet el rokk (f)	فرقة الروك
jazz	ʒāzz (m)	جاز
idol	maʿbūd (m)	معبود
admirer, fan	moʿgab (m)	معجب
concert	ḥafla mūsiqiya (f)	حفلة موسيقيّة
symphony	semfoniya (f)	سمفونيّة
composition	ʾeṭʿa mosiqiya (f)	قطعة موسيقيّة
to compose (write)	allaf	ألّف
singing (n)	ɣenāʾ (m)	غناء
song	oɣniya (f)	أغنيّة
tune (melody)	laḥn (m)	لحن
rhythm	eqāʿ (m)	إيقاع
blues	mosīqa el blues (f)	موسيقى البلوز
sheet music	notāt (pl)	نوتات
baton	ʿaṣa el maystro (m)	عصا المايسترو
bow	qose (m)	قوس
string	watar (m)	وتر
case (e.g., guitar ~)	ʃanṭa (f)	شنطة

Rest. Entertainment. Travel

155. Trip. Travel

tourism, travel	seyāḥa (f)	سياحة
tourist	sā'eḥ (m)	سائح
trip, voyage	reḥla (f)	رحلة
adventure	moɣamra (f)	مغامرة
trip, journey	reḥla (f)	رحلة
vacation	agāza (f)	أجازة
to be on vacation	kān fi agāza	كان في أجازة
rest	estrāḥa (f)	إستراحة
train	qeṭār, 'aṭṭr (m)	قطار
by train	bel qeṭār - bel aṭṭr	بالقطار
airplane	ṭayāra (f)	طيّارة
by airplane	bel ṭayāra	بالطيّارة
by car	bel sayāra	بالسيّارة
by ship	bel safīna	بالسفينة
luggage	el ʃonaṭ (pl)	الشنط
suitcase	ʃanṭa (f)	شنطة
luggage cart	'arabet ʃonaṭ (f)	عربة شنط
passport	basbore (m)	باسبور
visa	ta'ʃīra (f)	تأشيرة
ticket	tazkara (f)	تذكرة
air ticket	tazkara ṭayarān (f)	تذكرة طيران
guidebook	dalīl (m)	دليل
map (tourist ~)	χarīṭa (f)	خريطة
area (rural ~)	mante'a (f)	منطقة
place, site	makān (m)	مكان
exotica (n)	ɣarāba (f)	غرابة
exotic (adj)	ɣarīb	غريب
amazing (adj)	mod-heʃ	مدهش
group	magmū'a (f)	مجموعة
excursion, sightseeing tour	gawla (f)	جولة
guide (person)	morʃed (m)	مرشد

156. Hotel

hotel	fondo' (m)	فندق
motel	motel (m)	موتيل
three-star (~ hotel)	talat nogūm	ثلاث نجوم
five-star	χamas nogūm	خمس نجوم
to stay (in a hotel, etc.)	nezel	نزل
room	oḍa (f)	أوضة
single room	owḍa le ʃaχṣ wāḥed (f)	أوضة لشخص واحد
double room	oḍa le ʃaχṣeyn (f)	أوضة لشخصين
to book a room	ḥagaz owḍa	حجز أوضة
half board	wagbeteyn fel yome (du)	وجبتين في اليوم
full board	talat wagabāt fel yome	ثلاث وجبات في اليوم
with bath	bel banyo	بـ البانيو
with shower	bel doʃ	بالدوش
satellite television	televizion be qanawāt faḍā'iya (m)	تليفزيون بقنوات فضائية
air-conditioner	takyīf (m)	تكييف
towel	fūṭa (f)	فوطة
key	meftāḥ (m)	مفتاح
administrator	modīr (m)	مدير
chambermaid	'āmela tanḍīf ɣoraf (f)	عاملة تنظيف غرف
porter, bellboy	ʃayāl (m)	شيّال
doorman	bawwāb (m)	بوّاب
restaurant	maṭ'am (m)	مطعم
pub, bar	bār (m)	بار
breakfast	foṭūr (m)	فطور
dinner	'aʃā' (m)	عشاء
buffet	bofeyh (m)	بوفيه
lobby	rad-ha (f)	ردهة
elevator	asanseyr (m)	اسانسير
DO NOT DISTURB	nargu 'adam el ez'āg	نرجو عدم الإزعاج
NO SMOKING	mamnū' el tadχīn	ممنوع التدخين

157. Books. Reading

book	ketāb (m)	كتاب
author	mo'allef (m)	مؤلّف
writer	kāteb (m)	كاتب
to write (~ a book)	allaf	ألّف
reader	qāre' (m)	قارئ

to read (vi, vt)	'ara	قرأ
reading (activity)	qerā'a (f)	قراءة
silently (to oneself)	beṣamt	بصمت
aloud (adv)	beṣote 'āly	بصوت عالي
to publish (vt)	naʃar	نشر
publishing (process)	naʃr (m)	نشر
publisher	nāʃer (m)	ناشر
publishing house	dar el ṭebā'a wel naʃr (f)	دار الطباعة والنشر
to come out (be released)	ṣadar	صدر
release (of a book)	ṣodūr (m)	صدور
print run	'adad el nosaχ (m)	عدد النسخ
bookstore	maḥal kotob (m)	محل كتب
library	maktaba (f)	مكتبة
story (novella)	'oṣṣa (f)	قصّة
short story	qeṣṣa 'aṣīra (f)	قصّة قصيرة
novel	rewāya (f)	رواية
detective novel	rewāya bolesiya (f)	رواية بوليسية
memoirs	mozakkerāt (pl)	مذكّرات
legend	osṭūra (f)	أسطورة
myth	χorāfa (f)	خرافة
poetry, poems	ʃe'r (m)	شعر
autobiography	sīret ḥayah (f)	سيرة حياة
selected works	muχtarāt (pl)	مختارات
science fiction	χayāl 'elmy (m)	خيال علمي
title	'enwān (m)	عنوان
introduction	moqaddema (f)	مقدّمة
title page	ṣafḥet 'enwān (f)	صفحة العنوان
chapter	faṣl (m)	فصل
extract	χolāṣa (f)	خلاصة
episode	maʃ-had (m)	مشهد
plot (storyline)	ḥabka (f)	حبكة
contents	moḥtawayāt (pl)	محتويات
table of contents	gadwal el moḥtawayāt (m)	جدوّل المحتويات
main character	el ʃaχṣiya el ra'esiya (f)	الشخصية الرئيسية
volume	mogallad (m)	مجلّد
cover	ɣelāf (m)	غلاف
binding	taglīd (m)	تجليد
bookmark	ʃerī'ṭ (m)	شريط
page	ṣafḥa (f)	صفحة
to page through	'alleb el ṣafaḥāt	قلّب الصفحات

margins	hāmeʃ (m)	هامش
annotation (marginal note, etc.)	molaḥza (f)	ملاحظة
footnote	molaḥza (f)	ملاحظة
text	noṣṣ (m)	نصّ
type, font	nū' el xaṭṭ (m)	نوع الخطّ
misprint, typo	xaṭa' maṭba'y (m)	خطأ مطبعيّ
translation	targama (f)	ترجمة
to translate (vt)	targem	ترجم
original (n)	aṣliya (f)	أصلية
famous (adj)	maʃ-hūr	مشهور
unknown (not famous)	meʃ ma'rūf	مش معروف
interesting (adj)	moʃawweq	مشوّق
bestseller	aktar mabee'an (m)	أكثر مبيعاً
dictionary	qamūs (m)	قاموس
textbook	ketāb ta'līm (m)	كتاب تعليم
encyclopedia	ensayklopedia (f)	إنسيكلوبيديا

158. Hunting. Fishing

hunting	ṣeyd (m)	صيد
to hunt (vi, vt)	eṣṭād	إصطاد
hunter	ṣayād (m)	صيّاد
to shoot (vi)	ḍarab bel nār	ضرب بالنار
rifle	bondoqiya (f)	بندقيّة
bullet (shell)	roṣāṣa (f)	رصاصة
shot (lead balls)	'eyār (m)	عيار
steel trap	maṣyada (f)	مصيّدة
snare (for birds, etc.)	fakx (m)	فخّ
to fall into the steel trap	we'e' fe fakx	وقع في فخّ
to lay a steel trap	naṣb fakx	نصب فخّ
poacher	sāre' el ṣeyd (m)	سارق الصيد
game (in hunting)	ṣeyd (m)	صيد
hound dog	kalb ṣeyd (m)	كلب صيد
safari	safāry (m)	سفاري
mounted animal	ḥayawān moḥannaṭ (m)	حيوان محنّط
fisherman, angler	ṣayād el samak (m)	صيّاد السمك
fishing (angling)	ṣeyd el samak (m)	صيد السمك
to fish (vi)	eṣṭād samak	إصطاد سمك
fishing rod	ṣennāra (f)	صنّارة
fishing line	xeyṭ (m)	خيط

hook	ʃaṣ el garīma (m)	شص الصيد
float, bobber	ʿawwāma (f)	عوّامة
bait	ṭaʿm (m)	طعم
to cast a line	ṭaraḥ el ṣennāra	طرح الصنّارة
to bite (ab. fish)	ʿaḍḍ	عضّ
catch (of fish)	el samak el moṣṭād (m)	السمك المصطاد
ice-hole	fat-ḥa fel galīd (f)	فتحة في الجليد
fishing net	ʃabaket el ṣeyd (f)	شبكة الصيد
boat	markeb (m)	مركب
to net (to fish with a net)	eṣṭād bel ʃabaka	إصطاد بالشبكة
to cast[throw] the net	rama ʃabaka	رمى شبكة
to haul the net in	aχrag ʃabaka	أخرج شبكة
to fall into the net	weʾeʿ fe ʃabaka	وقع في شبكة
whaler (person)	ṣayād el ḥūt (m)	صيّاد الحوت
whaleboat	safīna ṣeyd ḥitān (f)	سفينة صيد الحيتان
harpoon	ḥerba (f)	حربة

159. Games. Billiards

billiards	bilyardo (m)	بلياردو
billiard room, hall	qāʿa bilyardo (m)	قاعة بلياردو
ball (snooker, etc.)	kora (f)	كرة
to pocket a ball	dakχal kora	دخّل كرة
cue	ʿaṣāyet bilyardo (f)	عصاية بلياردو
pocket	geyb bilyardo (m)	جيب بلياردو

160. Games. Playing cards

diamonds	el dinary (m)	الديناري
spades	el bastūny (m)	البستوني
hearts	el koba (f)	الكوبة
clubs	el sebāty (m)	السباتي
ace	ʾāss (m)	آس
king	malek (m)	ملك
queen	maleka (f)	ملكة
jack, knave	walad (m)	ولد
playing card	waraʾa (f)	ورقة
cards	waraʾ (m)	ورق
trump	waraʾa rābeḥa (f)	ورقة رابحة
deck of cards	desta waraʾ ʿenab (f)	دستة ورق اللعب
point	nuʾṭa (f)	نقطة
to deal (vi, vt)	farraʾ	فرّق

to shuffle (cards)	χalaṭ	خلط
lead, turn (n)	dore (m)	دور
cardsharp	moḥtāl fel 'omār (m)	محتال في القمار

161. Casino. Roulette

casino	kazino (m)	كازينو
roulette (game)	rulett (m)	روليت
bet	rahān (m)	رهان
to place bets	qāmar	قامر
red	aḥmar (m)	أحمر
black	aswad (m)	أسود
to bet on red	rāhen 'ala el aḥmar	راهن على الأحمر
to bet on black	rāhen 'ala el aswad	راهن على الأسود
croupier (dealer)	mowazzaf nādy el 'omār (m)	موظّف نادى القمار
to spin the wheel	dawwar el 'agala	دوّر العجلة
rules (of game)	qawā'ed (pl)	قواعد
chip	fīʃa (f)	فيشة
to win (vi, vt)	keseb	كسب
win (winnings)	rebḥ (m)	ربح
to lose (~ 100 dollars)	χeser	خسر
loss (losses)	χesāra (f)	خسارة
player	lā'eb (m)	لاعب
blackjack (card game)	blɛkdʒɛk (m)	بلاك جاك
craps (dice game)	le'bet el nard (f)	لعبة النرد
dice (a pair of ~)	zahr el nard (m)	زهر النرد
slot machine	'ālet qomār (f)	آلة قمار

162. Rest. Games. Miscellaneous

to stroll (vi, vt)	tamasʃa	تمشّى
stroll (leisurely walk)	tamʃeya (f)	تمشيّة
car ride	gawla bel sayāra (f)	جولة بالسيّارة
adventure	moɣamra (f)	مغامرة
picnic	nozha (f)	نزهة
game (chess, etc.)	le'ba (f)	لعبة
player	lā'eb (m)	لاعب
game (one ~ of chess)	dore (m)	دور
collector (e.g., philatelist)	gāme' (m)	جامِع
to collect (stamps, etc.)	gamma'	جمّع

collection	magmūʻa (f)	مجموعة
crossword puzzle	kalemāt motaqaṭʻa (pl)	كلمات متقاطعة
racetrack (horse racing venue)	ḥalabet el sebā' (f)	حلبة السباق
disco (discotheque)	disko (m)	ديسكو
sauna	sauna (f)	ساونا
lottery	yanaṣīb (m)	يانصيب
camping trip	reḥlet taχyīm (f)	رحلة تخييم
camp	moχayam (m)	مخيّم
tent (for camping)	χeyma (f)	خيمة
compass	boṣla (f)	بوصلة
camper	moχayam (m)	مخيّم
to watch (movie, etc.)	ʃāhed	شاهد
viewer	moʃāhed (m)	مشاهد
TV show (TV program)	barnāmeg televiziony (m)	برنامج تليفزيوني

163. Photography

camera (photo)	kamera (f)	كاميرا
photo, picture	ṣūra (f)	صورة
photographer	moṣawwer (m)	مصوّر
photo studio	estudio taṣwīr (m)	إستوديو تصوير
photo album	albūm el ṣewar (m)	ألبوم الصور
camera lens	ʻadaset kamera (f)	عدسة الكاميرا
telephoto lens	ʻadasa teleskopiya (f)	عدسة تلسكوبيّة
filter	filter (m)	فلتر
lens	ʻadasa (f)	عدسة
optics (high-quality ~)	baṣrīāt (pl)	بصريات
diaphragm (aperture)	saddāda (f)	سدّادة
exposure time (shutter speed)	moddet el taʻarroḍ (f)	مدّة التعرض
viewfinder	el ʻeyn el faḥeṣa (f)	العين الفاحصة
digital camera	kamera diʒital (f)	كاميرا ديجيتال
tripod	tribod (m)	ترايبود
flash	flāʃ (m)	فلاش
to photograph (vt)	ṣawwar	صوّر
to take pictures	ṣawwar	صوّر
to have one's picture taken	etṣawwar	إتصوّر
focus	tarkīz (m)	تركيز
to focus	rakkez	ركّز
sharp, in focus (adj)	ḥādda	حادّة

sharpness	ḥedda (m)	حدّة
contrast	tabāyon (m)	تباين
contrast (as adj)	motabāyen	متباين
picture (photo)	ṣūra (f)	صورة
negative (n)	el nosχa el salba (f)	النسخة السالبة
film (a roll of ~)	film (m)	فيلم
frame (still)	eṭār (m)	إطار
to print (photos)	ṭaba'	طبع

164. Beach. Swimming

beach	ʃāṭe' (m)	شاطئ
sand	raml (m)	رمل
deserted (beach)	mahgūr	مهجور
suntan	esmerār el baʃra (m)	إسمرار البشرة
to get a tan	etʃammes	إتشمّس
tan (adj)	asmar	أسمر
sunscreen	krīm wāqy men el ʃams (m)	كريم واقي من الشمس
bikini	bikini (m)	بكيني
bathing suit	mayo (m)	مايّوه
swim trunks	mayo regāly (m)	مايّوه رجالي
swimming pool	ḥammām sebāḥa (m)	حمّام سباحة
to swim (vi)	'ām, sabaḥ	عام, سبح
shower	doʃ (m)	دوش
to change (one's clothes)	ɣayar lebso	غيّر لبسه
towel	fūṭa (f)	فوطة
boat	markeb (m)	مركب
motorboat	lunʃ (m)	لنش
water ski	tazallog 'alal mā' (m)	تزلّج على الماء
paddle boat	el baddāl (m)	البدّال
surfing	surfing (m)	سيرفينج
surfer	rākeb el amwāg (m)	راكب الأمواج
scuba set	gehāz el tanaffos (m)	جهاز التنفّس
flippers (swim fins)	za'ānef el sebāḥa (pl)	زعانف السباحة
mask (diving ~)	kamāma (f)	كمامة
diver	ɣawwāṣ (m)	غوّاص
to dive (vi)	ɣāṣ	غاص
underwater (adv)	taḥt el maya	تحت المايّة
beach umbrella	ʃamsiya (f)	شمسيّة
sunbed (lounger)	korsy blāʒ (m)	كرسي بلاج
sunglasses	naḍḍāret ʃams (f)	نضّارة شمس
air mattress	martaba hawa'iya (f)	مرتبة هوائية

to play (amuse oneself)	le'eb	لعب
to go for a swim	sebeḥ	سبح
beach ball	koret ʃaṭṭ (f)	كرة شطّ
to inflate (vt)	nafaχ	نفخ
inflatable, air (adj)	qābel lel nafχ	قابل للنفخ
wave	mouga (f)	موجة
buoy (line of ~s)	ʃamandūra (f)	شمندورة
to drown (ab. person)	ɣere'	غرق
to save, to rescue	anqaz	أنقذ
life vest	sotret nagah (f)	سترة نجاة
to observe, to watch	rāqab	راقب
lifeguard	ḥāres ʃāṭe' (m)	حارس شاطئ

TECHNICAL EQUIPMENT. TRANSPORTATION

Technical equipment

165. Computer

computer	kombuter (m)	كمبيوتر
notebook, laptop	lab tob (m)	لابتوب
to turn on	fataḥ, ʃagɣal	فتح, شغّل
to turn off	ṭaffa	طفّى
keyboard	lawḥet el mafatīḥ (f)	لوحة المفاتيح
key	meftāḥ (m)	مفتاح
mouse	maws (m)	ماوس
mouse pad	maws bād (m)	ماوس باد
button	zerr (m)	زرّ
cursor	mo'asʃer (m)	مؤشّر
monitor	ʃāʃa (f)	شاشة
screen	ʃāʃa (f)	شاشة
hard disk	hard disk (m)	هارد ديسك
hard disk capacity	se'et el hard disk (f)	سعة الهارد ديسك
memory	zākera (f)	ذاكرة
random access memory	zākerat el woṣūl el 'aʃwā'y (f)	ذاكرة الوصول العشوائي
file	malaff (m)	ملفّ
folder	ḥāfeza (m)	حافظة
to open (vt)	fataḥ	فتح
to close (vt)	'afal	قفل
to save (vt)	ḥafaẓ	حفظ
to delete (vt)	masaḥ	مسح
to copy (vt)	nasax	نسخ
to sort (vt)	ṣannaf	صنّف
to transfer (copy)	na'al	نقل
program	barnāmeg (m)	برنامج
software	barmagīāt (pl)	برمجيات
programmer	mobarmeg (m)	مبرمج
to program (vt)	barmag	برمج
hacker	haker (m)	هاكر

password	kelmet el serr (f)	كلمة السرّ
virus	virūs (m)	فيروس
to find, to detect	la'a	لقى
byte	byte (m)	بايت
megabyte	megabayt (m)	ميجا بايت
data	bayanāt (pl)	بيانات
database	qa'edet bayanāt (f)	قاعدة بيانات
cable (USB, etc.)	kabl (m)	كابل
to disconnect (vt)	faṣal	فصل
to connect (sth to sth)	waṣṣal	وصّل

166. Internet. E-mail

Internet	internet (m)	إنترنت
browser	motaṣaffeḥ (m)	متصفّح
search engine	moḥarrek baḥs (m)	محرك بحث
provider	ʃerket el internet (f)	شركة الإنترنت
webmaster	modīr el mawqe' (m)	مدير الموقع
website	mawqe' elektrony (m)	موقع الكتروني
webpage	ṣafḥet web (f)	صفحة ويب
address (e-mail ~)	'enwān (m)	عنوان
address book	daftar el 'anawīn (m)	دفتر العناوين
mailbox	ṣandū' el barīd (m)	صندوق البريد
mail	barīd (m)	بريد
full (adj)	mumtali'	ممتلىء
message	resāla (f)	رسالة
incoming messages	rasa'el wārda (pl)	رسائل واردة
outgoing messages	rasa'el ṣādra (pl)	رسائل صادرة
sender	morsel (m)	مرسل
to send (vt)	arsal	أرسل
sending (of mail)	ersāl (m)	إرسال
receiver	morsel elayh (m)	مرسل إليه
to receive (vt)	estalam	إستلم
correspondence	morasla (f)	مراسلة
to correspond (vi)	tarāsal	تراسل
file	malaff (m)	ملفّ
to download (vt)	ḥammel	حمّل
to create (vt)	'amal	عمل
to delete (vt)	masaḥ	مسح
deleted (adj)	mamsūḥ	ممسوح

connection (ADSL, etc.)	etteṣāl (m)	إتّصال
speed	sor'a (f)	سرعة
modem	modem (m)	مودم
access	woṣūl (m)	وصول
port (e.g., input ~)	maχrag (m)	مخرج
connection (make a ~)	etteṣāl (m)	إتّصال
to connect to ... (vi)	yuwṣel	يوصل
to select (vt)	eχtār	إختار
to search (for ...)	baḥs	بحث

167. Electricity

electricity	kahraba' (m)	كهرباء
electric, electrical (adj)	kahrabā'y	كهربائي
electric power plant	maḥaṭṭa kahraba'iya (f)	محطة كهربائيّة
energy	ṭāqa (f)	طاقة
electric power	ṭāqa kahraba'iya (f)	طاقة كهربائيّة
light bulb	lammba (f)	لمّبة
flashlight	kasʃāf el nūr (m)	كشّاف النور
street light	'amūd el nūr (m)	عمود النور
light	nūr (m)	نور
to turn on	fataḥ, ʃagɣal	فتح, شغّل
to turn off	ṭaffa	طفّى
to turn off the light	ṭaffa el nūr	طفّى النور
to burn out (vi)	eṭṭafa	إتّطفى
short circuit	dayra kahraba'iya 'aṣīra (f)	دائرة كهربائية قصيرة
broken wire	selk ma'ṭū' (m)	سلك مقطوع
contact (electrical ~)	talāmos (m)	تلامس
light switch	meftāḥ el nūr (m)	مفتاح النور
wall socket	bareza el kaharaba' (f)	بريزة الكهرباء
plug	fiʃet el kahraba' (f)	فيشة الكهرباء
extension cord	selk tawṣīl (m)	سلك توصيل
fuse	fetīl (m)	فتيل
cable, wire	selk (m)	سلك
wiring	aslāk (pl)	أسلاك
ampere	ambere (m)	أمبير
amperage	ʃeddet el tayār (f)	شدّة التيّار
volt	volt (m)	فولت
voltage	el gohd el kaharab'y (m)	الجهد الكهربائي
electrical device	gehāz kahrabā'y (m)	جهاز كهربائي
indicator	mo'asʃer (m)	مؤشّر

electrician	kahrabā'y (m)	كهربائي
to solder (vt)	laḥam	لحم
soldering iron	adat laḥm (f)	إداة لحم
electric current	tayār kahrabā'y (m)	تيّاركهربائي

168. Tools

tool, instrument	adah (f)	أداة
tools	adawāt (pl)	أدوات
equipment (factory ~)	mo'eddāt (pl)	معدّات
hammer	ʃakūʃ (m)	شاكوش
screwdriver	mefakk (m)	مفكّ
ax	fa's (m)	فأس
saw	monʃār (m)	منشار
to saw (vt)	naʃar	نشر
plane (tool)	mesḥāg (m)	مسحاج
to plane (vt)	saḥag	سحج
soldering iron	adat laḥm (f)	إداة لحم
to solder (vt)	laḥam	لحم
file (tool)	mabrad (m)	مبرد
carpenter pincers	kamʃa (f)	كمشة
lineman's pliers	zardiya (f)	زرديّة
chisel	ezmīl (m)	إزميل
drill bit	mesqāb (m)	مثقاب
electric drill	drill kahrabā'y (m)	دريل كهربائي
to drill (vi, vt)	ḥafar	حفر
knife	sekkīna (f)	سكّينة
pocket knife	sekkīnet gīb (m)	سكّينة جيب
blade	ʃafra (f)	شفرة
sharp (blade, etc.)	ḥād	حاد
dull, blunt (adj)	telma	تلمة
to get blunt (dull)	kānet telma	كانت تلمة
to sharpen (vt)	sann	سنّ
bolt	mesmār 'alawoze (m)	مسمار قلاووظ
nut	ṣamūla (f)	صامولة
thread (of a screw)	χaʃχana (f)	خشخنة
wood screw	'alawūz (m)	قلاووظ
nail	mesmār (m)	مسمار
nailhead	rās el mesmār (m)	رأس المسمار
ruler (for measuring)	masṭara (f)	مسطرة
tape measure	ʃerī'ṭ el 'eyās (m)	شريط القياس

spirit level	mizān el maya (m)	ميزان الميّة
magnifying glass	'adasa mokabbera (f)	عدسة مكبّرة
measuring instrument	gehāz 'eyās (m)	جهاز قياس
to measure (vt)	'ās	قاس
scale (of thermometer, etc.)	me'yās (m)	مقياس
readings	qerā'a (f)	قراءة
compressor	kombressor (m)	كومبرسور
microscope	mikroskob (m)	ميكروسكوب
pump (e.g., water ~)	ṭolommba (f)	طلمّبة
robot	robot (m)	روبوت
laser	laser (m)	ليزر
wrench	meftāḥ rabṭ (m)	مفتاح ربط
adhesive tape	laz' (m)	لزق
glue	ṣamɣ (m)	صمغ
sandpaper	wara' ṣanfara (m)	ورق صنفرة
spring	sosta (f)	سوستة
magnet	meɣnaṭīs (m)	مغنطيس
gloves	gwanty (m)	جوانتي
rope	ḥabl (m)	حبل
cord	selk (m)	سلك
wire (e.g., telephone ~)	selk (m)	سلك
cable	kabl (m)	كابل
sledgehammer	marzaba (f)	مرزبة
prybar	'atala (f)	عتلة
ladder	sellem (m)	سلّم
stepladder	sellem na'āl (m)	سلّم نقال
to screw (tighten)	aḥkam el ʃadd	أحكم الشدّ
to unscrew (lid, filter, etc.)	fataḥ	فتح
to tighten (e.g., with a clamp)	kamaʃ	كمش
to glue, to stick	alṣaq	ألصق
to cut (vt)	'aṭa'	قطع
malfunction (fault)	'oṭl (m)	عطل
repair (mending)	taṣlīḥ (m)	تصليح
to repair, to fix (vt)	ṣallaḥ	صلّح
to adjust (machine, etc.)	ḍabaṭ	ضبط
to check (to examine)	eχtabar	إختبر
checking	faḥṣ (m)	فحص
readings	qerā'a (f)	قراءة
reliable, solid (machine)	matīn	متين
complex (adj)	morakkab	مركّب

to rust (get rusted)	ṣada’	صدئ
rusty, rusted (adj)	meṣaddy	مصدّي
rust	ṣada’ (m)	صدأ

Transportation

169. Airplane

airplane	ṭayāra (f)	طيّارة
air ticket	tazkara ṭayarān (f)	تذكرة طيران
airline	ʃerket ṭayarān (f)	شركة طيران
airport	maṭār (m)	مطار
supersonic (adj)	χāreq lel ṣote	خارق للصوت
captain	kabten (m)	كابتن
crew	ṭa'm (m)	طقم
pilot	ṭayār (m)	طيّار
flight attendant (fem.)	moḍīfet ṭayarān (f)	مضيفة طيران
navigator	mallāḥ (m)	ملاّح
wings	agneḥa (pl)	أجنحة
tail	deyl (m)	ذيل
cockpit	kabīna (f)	كابينة
engine	motore (m)	موتور
undercarriage (landing gear)	'agalāt el hobūṭ (pl)	عجلات الهبوط
turbine	torbīna (f)	توربينة
propeller	marwaḥa (f)	مروّحة
black box	mosaggel el ṭayarān (m)	مسجّل الطيران
yoke (control column)	moqawwed el ṭayāra (m)	مقوّد الطيّارة
fuel	woqūd (m)	وقود
safety card	beṭā'et el salāma (f)	بطاقة السلامة
oxygen mask	mask el oksyʒīn (m)	ماسك الاوكسيجين
uniform	zayī muwaḥḥad (m)	زيّ موحّد
life vest	sotret nagah (f)	سترة نجاة
parachute	baraʃot (m)	باراشوت
takeoff	eqlā' (m)	إقلاع
to take off (vi)	aqla'et	أقلعت
runway	modarrag el ṭa'erāṭ (m)	مدرّج الطائرات
visibility	ro'ya (f)	رؤية
flight (act of flying)	ṭayarān (m)	طيران
altitude	ertefā' (m)	إرتفاع
air pocket	geyb hawā'y (m)	جيب هوائي
seat	meq'ad (m)	مقعد
headphones	samma'āt ra'siya (pl)	سمّاعات رأسية

folding tray (tray table)	ṣeniya qabela lel ṭayī (f)	صينية قابلة للطيّ
airplane window	ʃebbāk el ṭayāra (m)	شبّاك الطيّارة
aisle	mamarr (m)	ممرّ

170. Train

train	qeṭār, 'aṭṭr (m)	قطار
commuter train	qeṭār rokkāb (m)	قطار ركّاب
express train	qeṭār saree' (m)	قطار سريع
diesel locomotive	qāṭeret dīzel (f)	قاطرة ديزل
steam locomotive	qāṭera boχariya (f)	قاطرة بخاريّة
passenger car	'araba (f)	عربة
dining car	'arabet el ṭa'ām (f)	عربة الطعام
rails	qoḍbān (pl)	قضبان
railroad	sekka ḥadīdiya (f)	سكّة حديديّة
railway tie	'āreḍa sekket ḥadīd (f)	عارضة سكّة الحديد
platform (railway ~)	raṣīf (m)	رصيف
track (~ 1, 2, etc.)	χaṭṭ (m)	خطّ
semaphore	semafore (m)	سيمافور
station	maḥaṭṭa (f)	محطّة
engineer (train driver)	sawwā' (m)	سوّاق
porter (of luggage)	ʃayāl (m)	شيّال
car attendant	mas'ūl 'arabet el qeṭār (m)	مسؤول عربة القطار
passenger	rākeb (m)	راكب
conductor (ticket inspector)	kamsary (m)	كمسري
corridor (in train)	mamarr (m)	ممرّ
emergency brake	farāmel el ṭawāre' (pl)	فرامل الطوارئ
compartment	ɣorfa (f)	غرفة
berth	serīr (m)	سرير
upper berth	serīr 'olwy (m)	سرير علوّي
lower berth	serīr sofly (m)	سرير سفلي
bed linen, bedding	aɣṭeyet el serīr (pl)	أغطيّة السرير
ticket	tazkara (f)	تذكرة
schedule	gadwal (m)	جدوَل
information display	lawḥet ma'lomāt (f)	لوحة معلومات
to leave, to depart	ɣādar	غادر
departure (of train)	moɣadra (f)	مغادرة
to arrive (ab. train)	weṣel	وصل
arrival	woṣūl (m)	وصول
to arrive by train	weṣel bel qeṭār	وصل بالقطار
to get on the train	rekeb el qeṭār	ركب القطار

to get off the train	nezel men el qeṭār	نزل من القطار
train wreck	ḥeṭām qeṭār (m)	حطام قطار
to derail (vi)	xarag 'an xaṭṭ sīru	خرج عن خطّ سيره
steam locomotive	qāṭera boxariya (f)	قاطرة بخاريّة
stoker, fireman	'atʃagy (m)	عطشجي
firebox	forn el moḥarrek (m)	فرن المحرّك
coal	faḥm (m)	فحم

171. Ship

ship	safīna (f)	سفينة
vessel	safīna (f)	سفينة
steamship	baxera (f)	باخرة
riverboat	baxera nahriya (f)	باخرة نهرية
cruise ship	safīna seyaḥiya (f)	سفينة سياحيّة
cruiser	ṭarrād safīna baḥariya (m)	طرّاد سفينة بحريّة
yacht	yaxt (m)	يخت
tugboat	qāṭera baḥariya (f)	قاطرة بحريّة
barge	ṣandal (m)	صندل
ferry	'abbāra (f)	عبّارة
sailing ship	safīna ʃera'iya (m)	سفينة شراعيّة
brigantine	markeb ʃerā'y (m)	مركب شراعي
ice breaker	moḥaṭṭemet galīd (f)	محطّمة جليد
submarine	ɣawwāṣa (f)	غوّاصة
boat (flat-bottomed ~)	markeb (m)	مركب
dinghy	zawra' (m)	زورق
lifeboat	qāreb nagah (m)	قارب نجاة
motorboat	lunʃ (m)	لنش
captain	'obṭān (m)	قبطان
seaman	baḥḥār (m)	بحّار
sailor	baḥḥār (m)	بحّار
crew	ṭāqem (m)	طاقم
boatswain	rabbān (m)	ربّان
ship's boy	ṣaby el safīna (m)	صبي السفينة
cook	ṭabbāx (m)	طبّاخ
ship's doctor	ṭabīb el safīna (m)	طبيب السفينة
deck	saṭ-ḥ el safīna (m)	سطح السفينة
mast	sāreya (f)	سارية
sail	ʃerā' (m)	شراع
hold	'anbar (m)	عنبر
bow (prow)	mo'addema (m)	مقدّمة

stern	mo'aχeret el safīna (f)	مؤخّرة السفينة
oar	megdāf (m)	مجذاف
screw propeller	marwaḥa (f)	مروَحة
cabin	kabīna (f)	كابينة
wardroom	ɣorfet el ṭa'ām wel rāḥa (f)	غرفة الطعام والراحة
engine room	qesm el 'ālāt (m)	قسم الآلات
bridge	borg el qeyāda (m)	برج القيادة
radio room	ɣorfet el lāselky (f)	غرفة اللاسلكي
wave (radio)	mouga (f)	موجة
logbook	segel el safīna (m)	سجل السفينة
spyglass	monzār (m)	منظار
bell	garas (m)	جرس
flag	'alam (m)	علم
hawser (mooring ~)	ḥabl (m)	حبل
knot (bowline, etc.)	'o'da (f)	عقدة
deckrails	drabzīn saṭ-ḥ el safīna (m)	درابزين سطح السفينة
gangway	sellem (m)	سلّم
anchor	marsāh (f)	مرساة
to weigh anchor	rafa' morsah	رفع مرساة
to drop anchor	rasa	رسا
anchor chain	selselet morsah (f)	سلسلة مرساة
port (harbor)	minā' (m)	ميناء
quay, wharf	marsa (m)	مرسى
to berth (moor)	rasa	رسا
to cast off	aqla'	أقلع
trip, voyage	reḥla (f)	رحلة
cruise (sea trip)	reḥla baḥariya (f)	رحلة بحريّة
course (route)	masār (m)	مسار
route (itinerary)	ṭarī' (m)	طريق
fairway (safe water channel)	magra melāḥy (m)	مجرى ملاحيّ
shallows	meyāh ḍaḥla (f)	مياه ضحلة
to run aground	ganaḥ	جنح
storm	'āṣefa (f)	عاصفة
signal	eʃara (f)	إشارة
to sink (vi)	ɣere'	غرق
Man overboard!	sa'aṭ rāgil min el sefīna!	سقط راجل من السفينة!
SOS (distress signal)	nedā' eɣāsa (m)	نداء إغاثة
ring buoy	ṭo'e nagah (m)	طوق نجاة

172. Airport

airport	maṭār (m)	مطار
airplane	ṭayāra (f)	طيّارة
airline	ʃerket ṭayarān (f)	شركة طيران
air traffic controller	marākeb el ḥaraka el gawiya (m)	مراكب الحركة الجويّة
departure	moɣadra (f)	مغادرة
arrival	woṣūl (m)	وصول
to arrive (by plane)	weṣel	وصل
departure time	wa't el moɣadra (m)	وقت المغادرة
arrival time	wa't el woṣūl (m)	وقت الوصول
to be delayed	ta'akχar	تأخّر
flight delay	ta'aχor el reḥla (m)	تأخّر الرحلة
information board	lawḥet el ma'lomāt (f)	لوحة المعلومات
information	este'lamāt (pl)	إستعلامات
to announce (vt)	a'lan	أعلن
flight (e.g., next ~)	reḥlet ṭayarān (f)	رحلة طيران
customs	gamārek (pl)	جمارك
customs officer	mowazzaf el gamārek (m)	موظّف الجمارك
customs declaration	taṣrīḥ gomroky (m)	تصريح جمركي
to fill out (vt)	mala	ملا
to fill out the declaration	mala el taṣrīḥ	ملأ التصريح
passport control	taftīʃ el gawazāt (m)	تفتيش الجوازات
luggage	el ʃonaṭ (pl)	الشنط
hand luggage	ʃonaṭ el yad (pl)	شنط اليد
luggage cart	'arabet ʃonaṭ (f)	عربة شنط
landing	hobūṭ (m)	هبوط
landing strip	mamarr el hobūṭ (m)	ممرّ الهبوط
to land (vi)	habaṭ	هبط
airstairs	sellem el ṭayāra (m)	سلّم الطيّارة
check-in	tasgīl (m)	تسجيل
check-in counter	makān tasgīl (m)	مكان تسجيل
to check-in (vi)	saggel	سجّل
boarding pass	beṭāqet el rokūb (f)	بطاقة الركوب
departure gate	bawwābet el moɣadra (f)	بوّابة المغادرة
transit	tranzīt (m)	ترانزيت
to wait (vt)	estanna	إستنّى
departure lounge	ṣālet el moɣadra (f)	صالة المغادرة
to see off	wadda'	ودّع
to say goodbye	wadda'	ودّع

173. Bicycle. Motorcycle

bicycle	beskeletta (f)	بيسكلتّة
scooter	fezba (f)	فزبة
motorcycle, bike	motosekl (m)	موتوسيكل
to go by bicycle	rāḥ bel beskeletta	راحِ بالبسكلتّة
handlebars	moqawwed (m)	مقوِد
pedal	dawwāsa (f)	دوّاسة
brakes	farāmel (pl)	فرامل
bicycle seat (saddle)	korsy (m)	كرسي
pump	ṭolommba (f)	طلمّبة
luggage rack	raff el amte'a (m)	رفّ الأمتعة
front lamp	el meṣbāḥ el amāmy (m)	المصباح الأمامي
helmet	χawza (f)	خوذة
wheel	'agala (f)	عجلة
fender	refrāf (m)	رفراف
rim	eṭār (m)	إطار
spoke	mekbaḥ el 'agala (m)	مكبح العجلة

Cars

174. Types of cars

automobile, car	sayāra (f)	سيّارة
sports car	sayāra reyāḍiya (f)	سيّارة رياضيّة
limousine	limozīn (m)	ليموزين
off-road vehicle	sayāret ṭoro' wa'ra (f)	سيّارة طرق وعرة
convertible (n)	kabryoleyh (m)	كابريوليه
minibus	mikrobāṣ (m)	ميكروباص
ambulance	es'āf (m)	إسعاف
snowplow	garrāfet talg (f)	جرّافة ثلج
truck	ʃāḥena (f)	شاحنة
tanker truck	nāqelet betrūl (f)	ناقلة بترول
van (small truck)	'arabiyet na'l (f)	عربيّة نقل
road tractor (trailer truck)	garrār (m)	جرّار
trailer	ma'ṭūra (f)	مقطورة
comfortable (adj)	morīḥ	مريح
used (adj)	mosta'mal	مستعمل

175. Cars. Bodywork

hood	kabbūt (m)	كبوّت
fender	refrāf (m)	رفراف
roof	sa'f (m)	سقف
windshield	ezāz amāmy (f)	إزاز أمامي
rear-view mirror	merāya daχeliya (f)	مراية داخليّة
windshield washer	monazzef el ezāz el amāmy (m)	منظّف الإزاز الأمامي
windshield wipers	massāḥāt (pl)	مسّاحات
side window	ʃebbāk gāneby (m)	شبّاك جانبي
window lift (power window)	ezāz kahrabā'y (m)	إزاز كهربائي
antenna	hawā'y (m)	هوائي
sunroof	fat-ḥet el sa'f (f)	فتحة السقف
bumper	ekṣedām (m)	اكصدام
trunk	ʃanṭet el 'arabiya (f)	شنطة العربيّة
roof luggage rack	raff sa'f el 'arabiya (m)	رفّ سقف العربيّة

door	bāb (m)	باب
door handle	okret el bāb (f)	اوكرة الباب
door lock	'efl el bāb (m)	قفل الباب
license plate	lawḥet raqam el sayāra (f)	لوحة رقم السيارة
muffler	kātem lel ṣote (m)	كاتم للصوت
gas tank	χazzān el banzīn (m)	خزّان البنزين
tailpipe	anbūb el 'ādem (m)	أنبوب العادم
gas, accelerator	ɣāz (m)	غاز
pedal	dawwāsa (f)	دوّاسة
gas pedal	dawwāset el banzīn (f)	دوّاسة البنزين
brake	farāmel (pl)	فرامل
brake pedal	dawwāset el farāmel (m)	دوّاسة الفرامل
to brake (use the brake)	farmel	فرمل
parking brake	farāmel el enteẓār (pl)	فرامل الإنتظار
clutch	klatʃ (m)	كلتش
clutch pedal	dawwāset el klatʃ (f)	دوّاسة الكلتش
clutch disc	'orṣ el klatʃ (m)	قرص الكلتش
shock absorber	momtaṣṣ lel ṣadamāt (m)	ممتصّ للصدمات
wheel	'agala (f)	عجلة
spare tire	'agala eḥteyāṭy (f)	عجلة إحتياطية
tire	eṭār (m)	إطار
hubcap	ṭīs (m)	طيس
driving wheels	'agalāt el qeyāda (pl)	عجلات القيادة
front-wheel drive (as adj)	daf' amāmy (m)	دفع أمامي
rear-wheel drive (as adj)	daf' χalfy (m)	دفع خلفي
all-wheel drive (as adj)	daf' kāmel (m)	دفع كامل
gearbox	gearboks (m)	جير بوكس
automatic (adj)	otomatīky	أوتوماتيكي
mechanical (adj)	mikanīky	ميكانيكي
gear shift	meqbaḍ nāqel lel ḥaraka (m)	مقبض ناقل الحركة
headlight	el meṣbāḥ el amāmy (m)	المصباح الأمامي
headlights	el maṣabīḥ el amamiya (pl)	المصابيح الأمامية
low beam	nūr mo'aʃer monχafeḍ (pl)	نور مؤشر منخفض
high beam	nūr mo'asʃer 'āly (m)	نور مؤشر عالي
brake light	nūr el farāmel (m)	نور الفرامل
parking lights	lambet el enteẓār (f)	لمبة الإنتظار
hazard lights	eʃārāt el taḥzīr (pl)	إشارات التحذير
fog lights	kasʃāf el ḍabāb (m)	كشّاف الضباب
turn signal	eʃāret el en'eṭāf (f)	إشارة الإنعطاف
back-up light	ḍū' el rogū' lel χalf (m)	ضوء الرجوع للخلف

176. Cars. Passenger compartment

car inside (interior)	ṣalone el sayāra (m)	صالون السيارة
leather (as adj)	men el geld	من الجلد
velour (as adj)	men el moχmal	من المخمل
upholstery	tangīd (m)	تنجيد
instrument (gage)	gehāz (m)	جهاز
dashboard	lawḥet ag-heza (f)	لوحة أجهزة
speedometer	me'yās sor'a (m)	مقياس سرعة
needle (pointer)	mo'asʃer (m)	مؤشّر
odometer	'addād el mesafāt (m)	عدّاد المسافات
indicator (sensor)	'addād (m)	عدّاد
level	mostawa (m)	مستوى
warning light	lammbet enzār (f)	لمّبة إنذار
steering wheel	moqawwed (m)	مقوّد
horn	kalaks (m)	كلاكس
button	zerr (m)	زر
switch	nāqel, meftāḥ (m)	ناقل, مفتاح
seat	korsy (m)	كرسي
backrest	masnad el ḍahr (m)	مسند الظهر
headrest	masnad el ra's (m)	مسند الرأس
seat belt	ḥezām el amān (m)	حزام الأمان
to fasten the belt	rabaṭ el ḥezām	ربط الحزام
adjustment (of seats)	ḍabṭ (m)	ضبط
airbag	wesāda hawa'iya (f)	وسادة هوائية
air-conditioner	takyīf (m)	تكييف
radio	radio (m)	راديو
CD player	moʃagɣel sidi (m)	مشغّل سي دي
to turn on	fataḥ, ʃagɣal	فتح, شغّل
antenna	hawā'y (m)	هوائي
glove box	dorg (m)	درج
ashtray	ṭa'ṭū'a (f)	طقطوقة

177. Cars. Engine

engine	moḥarrek (m)	محرّك
motor	motore (m)	موتور
diesel (as adj)	'alal diesel	على الديزل
gasoline (as adj)	'alal banzīn	على البنزين
engine volume	ḥagm el moḥarrek (m)	حجم المحرّك
power	'owwa (f)	قوّة
horsepower	ḥoṣān (m)	حصان

piston	mekbas (m)	مكبس
cylinder	esṭewāna (f)	أسطوانة
valve	ṣamām (m)	صمام
injector	baχāχa (f)	بخّاخة
generator (alternator)	mowalled (m)	مولّد
carburetor	karburetor (m)	كاربراتير
motor oil	zeyt el moḥarrek (m)	زيت المحرّك
radiator	radiator (m)	رادياتير
coolant	mobarred (m)	مبرّد
cooling fan	marwaḥa (f)	مروّحة
battery (accumulator)	baṭṭariya (f)	بطّاريّة
starter	meftāḥ el taʃɣīl (m)	مفتاح التشغيل
ignition	nezām taʃɣīl (m)	نظام تشغيل
spark plug	ʃam'et el eḥterāq (f)	شمعة الإحتراق
terminal (of battery)	ṭaraf tawṣīl (m)	طرف توصيل
positive terminal	ṭaraf muwgeb (m)	طرف موجب
negative terminal	ṭaraf sāleb (m)	طرف سالب
fuse	fetīl (m)	فتيل
air filter	ṣaffāyet el hawā' (f)	صفّاية الهواء
oil filter	ṣaffāyet el zeyt (f)	صفّاية الزيت
fuel filter	ṣaffāyet el banzīn (f)	صفّاية البنزين

178. Cars. Crash. Repair

car crash	ḥadset sayāra (f)	حادثة سيارة
traffic accident	ḥādes morūry (m)	حادث مروري
to crash (into the wall, etc.)	χabaṭ	خبط
to get smashed up	daʃdaʃ	دشدش
damage	χesāra (f)	خسارة
intact (unscathed)	salīm	سليم
to break down (vi)	ta'aṭṭal	تعطّل
towrope	ḥabl el saḥb	حبل السحب
puncture	soqb (m)	ثقب
to be flat	fasʃ	فشّ
to pump up	nafaχ	نفخ
pressure	ḍaɣṭ (m)	ضغط
to check (to examine)	eχtabar	إختبر
repair	taṣlīḥ (m)	تصليح
auto repair shop	warʃet taṣlīḥ 'arabīāt (f)	ورشة تصليح عربيات
spare part	'eṭ'et ɣeyār (f)	قطعة غيار
part	'eṭ'a (f)	قطعة

bolt (with nut)	mesmār 'alawoze (m)	مسمار قلاووظ
screw (fastener)	mesmār (m)	مسمار
nut	ṣamūla (f)	صامولة
washer	warda (f)	وردة
bearing	maḥmal (m)	محمل
tube	anbūba (f)	أنبوبة
gasket (head ~)	'az'a (f)	عزقة
cable, wire	selk (m)	سلك
jack	'afrīṭa (f)	عفريطة
wrench	meftāḥ rabṭ (m)	مفتاح ربط
hammer	ʃakūʃ (m)	شاكوش
pump	ṭolommba (f)	طلمبّة
screwdriver	mefakk (m)	مفكّ
fire extinguisher	ṭaffayet ḥarī' (f)	طفّاية حريق
warning triangle	eʃāret taḥzīr (f)	إشارة تحذير
to stall (vi)	et'aṭṭal	إتعطّل
stall (n)	tawaqqof (m)	توقّف
to be broken	kān maksūr	كان مكسور
to overheat (vi)	soχn aktar men el lāzem	سخن أكثر من اللازم
to be clogged up	kān masdūd	كان مسدود
to freeze up (pipes, etc.)	etgammed	إتجمّد
to burst (vi, ab. tube)	enqaṭa' - ett'aṭṭa'	إنقطع
pressure	ḍaγṭ (m)	ضغط
level	mostawa (m)	مستوى
slack (~ belt)	ḍa'īf	ضعيف
dent	ṭa'ga (f)	طعجة
knocking noise (engine)	da'' (m)	دقّ
crack	ʃa'' (m)	شقّ
scratch	χadʃ (m)	خدش

179. Cars. Road

road	ṭarī' (m)	طريق
highway	ṭarī' saree' (m)	طريق سريع
freeway	otostrad (m)	اوتوستراد
direction (way)	ettegāh (m)	إتّجاه
distance	masāfa (f)	مسافة
bridge	kobry (m)	كبري
parking lot	maw'ef el 'arabeyāt (m)	موقف العربيات
square	medān (m)	ميدان
interchange	taqāṭo' ṭoro' (m)	تقاطع طرق
tunnel	nafa' (m)	نفق

gas station	maḥaṭṭet banzīn (f)	محطّة بنزين
parking lot	maw'ef el 'arabeyāt (m)	موقف العربيات
gas pump (fuel dispenser)	maḍaχet banzīn (f)	مضخّة بنزين
auto repair shop	warʃet taṣlīḥ 'arabīāt (f)	ورشة تصليح عربيات
to get gas (to fill up)	mala banzīn	ملى بنزين
fuel	woqūd (m)	وقود
jerrycan	ʒerken (m)	جركن
asphalt	asfalt (m)	اسفلت
road markings	'alamāt el ṭarī' (pl)	علامات الطريق
curb	bardora (f)	بردورة
guardrail	sūr (m)	سور
ditch	ter'a (f)	ترعة
roadside (shoulder)	ḥaffet el ṭarī' (f)	حافّة الطريق
lamppost	'amūd nūr (m)	عمود نور
to drive (a car)	sā'	ساق
to turn (e.g., ~ left)	ḥād	حاد
to make a U-turn	laff fe u-turn	لفّ في يو تيرن
reverse (~ gear)	ḥaraka ela al warā' (f)	حركة إلى الوراء
to honk (vi)	zammar	زمّر
honk (sound)	kalaks (m)	كلاكس
to get stuck (in the mud, etc.)	ɣaraz	غرز
to spin the wheels	dawwar	دوّر
to cut, to turn off (vt)	awqaf	أوقف
speed	sor'a (f)	سرعة
to exceed the speed limit	'adda el sor'a	عدّى السرعة
to give a ticket	faraḍ ɣarāma	فرض غرامة
traffic lights	eʃārāt el morūr (pl)	إشارات المرور
driver's license	roχṣet el qeyāda (f)	رخصة قيادة
grade crossing	ma'bar (m)	معبر
intersection	taqāṭo' (m)	تقاطع
crosswalk	ma'bar (m)	معبر
bend, curve	mon'aṭaf (m)	منعطف
pedestrian zone	mante'a lel moʃāh (f)	منطقة للمشاة

180. Traffic signs

rules of the road	qawā'ed el ṭarī' (pl)	قواعد الطريق
road sign (traffic sign)	'alāma (f)	علامة
passing (overtaking)	tagāwuz (m)	تجاوز
curve	mon'aṭaf (m)	منعطف
U-turn	malaff (m)	ملفّ
traffic circle	dawarān morūry (m)	دوّران مروري
No entry	mamnū' el doχūl	ممنوع الدخول
No vehicles allowed	mamnū' morūr el sayārāt	ممنوع مرور السيارات

No passing	mamnūʿ el morūr	ممنوع المرور
No parking	mamnūʿ el woʾūf	ممنوع الوقوف
No stopping	mamnūʿ el woʾūf	ممنوع الوقوف
dangerous bend	monʿaṭaf χaṭar (m)	منعطف خطر
steep descent	monḥadar ʃedīd (m)	منحدر شديد
one-way traffic	ṭarīʾ etegāh wāḥed	طريق إتجاه واحد
crosswalk	maʿbar (m)	معبر
slippery road	ṭarīʾ zaleq (m)	طريق زلق
YIELD	eʃāret el awlawiya	إشارة الأولوية

PEOPLE. LIFE EVENTS

Life events

181. Holidays. Event

celebration, holiday	ʿīd (m)	عيد
national day	ʿīd waṭany (m)	عيد وطني
public holiday	agāza rasmiya (f)	أجازة رسميّة
to commemorate (vt)	eḥtafal be zekra	إحتفل بذكرى
event (happening)	ḥadass (m)	حدث
event (organized activity)	monasba (f)	مناسبة
banquet (party)	walīma (f)	وليمة
reception (formal party)	ḥaflet esteʾbāl (f)	حفلة إستقبال
feast	walīma (f)	وليمة
anniversary	zekra sanawiya (f)	ذكرى سنوية
jubilee	yobeyl (m)	يوبيل
to celebrate (vt)	eḥtafal	إحتفل
New Year	raʾs el sanna (m)	رأس السنة
Happy New Year!	koll sana wenta ṭayeb!	كلّ سنة وأنت طيّب!
Santa Claus	baba neweyl (m)	بابا نويل
Christmas	ʿīd el melād (m)	عيد الميلاد
Merry Christmas!	ʿīd melād saʿīd!	عيد ميلاد سعيد!
Christmas tree	ʃagaret el kresmas (f)	شجرة الكريسمس
fireworks (fireworks show)	alʿāb nāriya (pl)	ألعاب ناريّة
wedding	faraḥ (m)	فرح
groom	ʿarīs (m)	عريس
bride	ʿarūsa (f)	عروسة
to invite (vt)	ʿazam	عزم
invitation card	beṭāʾet daʿwa (f)	بطاقة دعوة
guest	ḍeyf (m)	ضيف
to visit (~ your parents, etc.)	zār	زار
to meet the guests	estaʾbal ḍoyūf	إستقبل ضيوف
gift, present	hediya (f)	هديّة
to give (sth as present)	edda	إدّى
to receive gifts	estalam hadāya	إستلم هدايا

bouquet (of flowers)	bokeyh (f)	بوكيه
congratulations	tahne'a (f)	تهنئة
to congratulate (vt)	hanna	هنّأ
greeting card	beṭā'et tahne'a (f)	بطاقة تهنئة
to send a postcard	ba'at beṭā'et tahne'a	بعت بطاقة تهنئة
to get a postcard	estalam beṭā'a tahne'a	استلم بطاقة تهنئة
toast	naχab (m)	نخب
to offer (a drink, etc.)	ḍayaf	ضيّف
champagne	ʃambania (f)	شمبانيا
to enjoy oneself	estamta'	إستمتع
merriment (gaiety)	bahga (f)	بهجة
joy (emotion)	sa'āda (f)	سعادة
dance	ra'ṣa (f)	رقصة
to dance (vi, vt)	ra'aṣ	رقص
waltz	valles (m)	فالس
tango	tango (m)	تانجو

182. Funerals. Burial

cemetery	maqbara (f)	مقبرة
grave, tomb	'abr (m)	قبر
cross	ṣalīb (m)	صليب
gravestone	ḥagar el ma''bara (m)	حجر المقبرة
fence	sūr (m)	سور
chapel	kenīsa saɣīra (f)	كنيسة صغيرة
death	mote (m)	موت
to die (vi)	māt	مات
the deceased	el motawaffy (m)	المتوفّي
mourning	ḥedād (m)	حداد
to bury (vt)	dafan	دفن
funeral home	maktab mota'ahhed el dafn (m)	مكتب متعهّد الدفن
funeral	ganāza (f)	جنازة
wreath	eklīl (m)	إكليل
casket, coffin	tabūt (m)	تابوت
hearse	na'ʃ (m)	نعش
shroud	kafan (m)	كفن
funeral procession	ganāza (f)	جنازة
funerary urn	garra gana'eziya (f)	جرّة جنائزية
crematory	maḥra'et gosas el mawta (f)	محرقة جثث الموتى

obituary	segel el wafīāt (m)	سجل الوفيات
to cry (weep)	baka	بكى
to sob (vi)	nawwaḥ	نوّح

183. War. Soldiers

platoon	faṣīla (f)	فصيلة
company	serriya (f)	سريّة
regiment	foge (m)	فوج
army	geyʃ (m)	جيش
division	fer'a (f)	فرقة
section, squad	weḥda (f)	وحدة
host (army)	geyʃ (m)	جيش
soldier	gondy (m)	جنّدي
officer	ḍābeṭ (m)	ضابط
private	gondy (m)	جنّدي
sergeant	raqīb tāny (m)	رقيب تاني
lieutenant	molāzem tāny (m)	ملازم تاني
captain	naqīb (m)	نقيب
major	rā'ed (m)	رائد
colonel	'aqīd (m)	عقيد
general	ʒenerāl (m)	جنرال
sailor	baḥḥār (m)	بحّار
captain	'obṭān (m)	قبطان
boatswain	rabbān (m)	ربّان
artilleryman	gondy fe selāḥ el madfa'iya (m)	جنّدي في سلاح المدفعيّة
paratrooper	selāḥ el maẓallāt (m)	سلاح المظلّلات
pilot	ṭayār (m)	طيّار
navigator	mallāḥ (m)	ملاّح
mechanic	mikanīky (m)	ميكانيكي
pioneer (sapper)	mohandes 'askary (m)	مهندس عسكري
parachutist	gondy el baraʃot (m)	جنّدي الباراشوت
reconnaissance scout	kaʃāfet el esteṭlā' (f)	كشّافة الإستطلاع
sniper	qannāṣ (m)	قنّاص
patrol (group)	dawriya (f)	دوريّة
to patrol (vt)	'ām be dawriya	قام بدوريّة
sentry, guard	ḥāres (m)	حارس
warrior	muḥāreb (m)	محارب
patriot	waṭany (m)	وطني
hero	baṭal (m)	بطل
heroine	baṭala (f)	بطلة

traitor	χāyen (m)	خاين
to betray (vt)	χān	خان
deserter	hāreb men el gondiya (m)	هارب من الجنديّة
to desert (vi)	farr men el geyʃ	فرّ من الجيش
mercenary	ma'gūr (m)	مأجور
recruit	gondy gedīd (m)	جنّدي جديد
volunteer	motaṭawweʿ (m)	متطوّع
dead (n)	'atīl (m)	قتيل
wounded (n)	garīḥ (m)	جريح
prisoner of war	asīr ḥarb (m)	أسير حرب

184. War. Military actions. Part 1

war	ḥarb (f)	حرب
to be at war	ḥārab	حارب
civil war	ḥarb ahliya (f)	حرب أهليّة
treacherously (adv)	ɣadran	غدراً
declaration of war	eʿlān ḥarb (m)	إعلان حرب
to declare (~ war)	aʿlan	أعلن
aggression	ʿedwān (m)	عدوان
to attack (invade)	hagam	هجم
to invade (vt)	eḥtall	إحتلّ
invader	moḥtell (m)	محتلّ
conqueror	fāteḥ (m)	فاتح
defense	defāʿ (m)	دفاع
to defend (a country, etc.)	dāfaʿ	دافع
to defend (against ...)	dāfaʿ ʿan ...	دافع عن ...
enemy	ʿadeww (m)	عدوّ
foe, adversary	χeṣm (m)	خصم
enemy (as adj)	ʿadeww	عدوّ
strategy	estrateʒiya (f)	إستراتيجيّة
tactics	taktīk (m)	تكتيك
order	amr (m)	أمر
command (order)	amr (m)	أمر
to order (vt)	amar	أمر
mission	mohemma (f)	مهمّة
secret (adj)	serry	سرّي
battle	maʿraka (f)	معركة
combat	'etāl (m)	قتال
attack	hogūm (m)	هجوم
charge (assault)	enqeḍāḍ (m)	إنقضاض

to storm (vt)	enqaḍḍ	إنقضّ
siege (to be under ~)	ḥeṣār (m)	حصار
offensive (n)	hogūm (m)	هجوم
to go on the offensive	hagam	هجم
retreat	ensehāb (m)	إنسحاب
to retreat (vi)	ensaḥab	إنسحب
encirclement	eḥāṭa (f)	إحاطة
to encircle (vt)	aḥāṭ	أحاط
bombing (by aircraft)	ʾaṣf (m)	قصف
to drop a bomb	asqaṭ qonbola	أسقط قنبلة
to bomb (vt)	ʾaṣaf	قصف
explosion	enfegār (m)	إنفجار
shot	ṭalʾa (f)	طلقة
to fire (~ a shot)	aṭlaq el nār	أطلق النار
firing (burst of ~)	eṭlāq nār (m)	إطلاق نار
to aim (to point a weapon)	ṣawwab ʿala …	... صوّب على
to point (a gun)	ṣawwab	صوّب
to hit (the target)	aṣāb el hadaf	أصاب الهدف
to sink (~ a ship)	aɣraʾ	أغرق
hole (in a ship)	soqb (m)	ثقب
to founder, to sink (vi)	ɣereʾ	غرق
front (war ~)	gabha (f)	جبهة
evacuation	eχlāʾ (m)	إخلاء
to evacuate (vt)	aχla	أخلى
trench	χondoq (m)	خندق
barbwire	aslāk ʃāʾeka (pl)	أسلاك شائكة
barrier (anti tank ~)	ḥāgez (m)	حاجز
watchtower	borg moraʾba (m)	برج مراقبة
military hospital	mostaʃfa ʿaskary (m)	مستشفى عسكري
to wound (vt)	garaḥ	جرح
wound	garḥ (m)	جرح
wounded (n)	garīḥ (m)	جريح
to be wounded	oṣīb bel garḥ	أصيب بالجرح
serious (wound)	χaṭīr	خطير

185. War. Military actions. Part 2

captivity	asr (m)	أسر
to take captive	asar	أسر
to be held captive	etʾasar	أتأسر

to be taken captive	we'e' fel asr	وقع في الأسر
concentration camp	mo'askar e'teqāl (m)	معسكر إعتقال
prisoner of war	asīr ḥarb (m)	أسير حرب
to escape (vi)	hereb	هرب
to betray (vt)	χān	خان
betrayer	χāyen (m)	خاين
betrayal	χeyāna (f)	خيانة
to execute (by firing squad)	a'dam ramyan bel roṣāṣ	أعدم رمياً بالرصاص
execution (by firing squad)	e'dām ramyan bel roṣāṣ (m)	إعدام رمياً بالرصاص
equipment (military gear)	el 'etād el 'askary (m)	العتاد العسكري
shoulder board	kattāfa (f)	كتافة
gas mask	qenā' el ɣāz (m)	قناع الغاز
field radio	gehāz lāselky (m)	جهاز لاسلكي
cipher, code	ʃafra (f)	شفرة
secrecy	serriya (f)	سريّة
password	kelmet el morūr (f)	كلمة مرور
land mine	loɣz arāḍy (m)	لغم أرضي
to mine (road, etc.)	lagɣam	لغّم
minefield	ḥaql alɣām (m)	حقل ألغام
air-raid warning	enzār gawwy (m)	إنذار جوّي
alarm (alert signal)	enzār (m)	إنذار
signal	eʃara (f)	إشارة
signal flare	eʃāra moḍī'a (f)	إشارة مضيئة
headquarters	maqarr (m)	مقرّ
reconnaissance	kaʃāfet el esteṭlā' (f)	كشّافة الإستطلاع
situation	ḥāla (f), waḍ' (m)	حالة, وضع
report	ta'rīr (m)	تقرير
ambush	kamīn (m)	كمين
reinforcement (of army)	emdadāt 'askariya (pl)	إمدادات عسكريّة
target	hadaf (m)	هدف
proving ground	arḍ eχtebār (m)	أرض إختبار
military exercise	monawrāt 'askariya (pl)	مناورات عسكريّة
panic	zo'r (m)	ذعر
devastation	damār (m)	دمار
destruction, ruins	ḥeṭām (pl)	حطام
to destroy (vt)	dammar	دمّر
to survive (vi, vt)	negy	نجي
to disarm (vt)	garrad men el selāḥ	جرّد من السلاح
to handle (~ a gun)	esta'mel	إستعمل
Attention!	entebāh!	إنتباه!

At ease!	estareḥ!	!إسترح
act of courage	ma'sara (f)	مأثرة
oath (vow)	qasam (m)	قسم
to swear (an oath)	aqsam	أقسم
decoration (medal, etc.)	wesām (m)	وسام
to award (give medal to)	manaḥ	منح
medal	medalya (f)	ميدالية
order (e.g., ~ of Merit)	wesām 'askary (m)	وسام عسكري
victory	enteṣār - foze (m)	إنتصار, فوز
defeat	hazīma (f)	هزيمة
armistice	hodna (f)	هدنة
standard (battle flag)	rāyet el ma'raka (f)	راية المعركة
glory (honor, fame)	magd (m)	مجد
parade	mawkeb (m)	موكب
to march (on parade)	sār	سار

186. Weapons

weapons	asleḥa (pl)	أسلحة
firearms	asleḥa nāriya (pl)	أسلحة ناريّة
cold weapons (knives, etc.)	asleḥa bayḍā' (pl)	أسلحة بيضاء
chemical weapons	asleḥa kemawiya (pl)	أسلحة كيماويّة
nuclear (adj)	nawawy	نوويّ
nuclear weapons	asleḥa nawawiya (pl)	أسلحة نوويّة
bomb	qonbela (f)	قنبلة
atomic bomb	qonbela nawawiya (f)	قنبلة نوويّة
pistol (gun)	mosaddas (m)	مسدّس
rifle	bondoqiya (f)	بندقيّة
submachine gun	mosaddas rasʃāʃ (m)	مسدّس رشّاش
machine gun	rasʃāʃ (m)	رشّاش
muzzle	fawha (f)	فوهة
barrel	anbūba (f)	أنبوبة
caliber	'eyār (m)	عيار
trigger	zanād (m)	زناد
sight (aiming device)	moṣawweb (m)	مصوّب
magazine	maχzan (m)	مخزن
butt (shoulder stock)	'aqab el bondo'iya (m)	عقب البندقيّة
hand grenade	qonbela yadawiya (f)	قنبلة يدويّة
explosive	mawād motafaggera (pl)	مواد متفجّرة
bullet	roṣāṣa (f)	رصاصة

cartridge	xarṭūʃa (f)	خرطوشة
charge	ḥaʃwa (f)	حشوة
ammunition	zaxīra (f)	ذخيرة
bomber (aircraft)	qazefet qanābel (f)	قاذفة قنابل
fighter	ṭayāra muqātela (f)	طيّارة مقاتلة
helicopter	heliokobter (m)	هليكوبتر
anti-aircraft gun	madfaʿ moḍād lel ṭaʾerāṭ (m)	مدفع مضاد للطائرات
tank	dabbāba (f)	دبّابة
tank gun	madfaʿ el dabbāba (m)	مدفع الدبّابة
artillery	madfaʿiya (f)	مدفعيّة
gun (cannon, howitzer)	madfaʿ (m)	مدفع
to lay (a gun)	ṣawwab	صوّب
shell (projectile)	qazīfa (f)	قذيفة
mortar bomb	qonbela hawn (f)	قنبلة هاون
mortar	hawn (m)	هاون
splinter (shell fragment)	ʃazya (f)	شظية
submarine	ɣawwāṣa (f)	غوّاصة
torpedo	ṭorbīd (m)	طوربيد
missile	ṣarūx (m)	صاروخ
to load (gun)	ʿammar	عمّر
to shoot (vi)	ḍarab bel nār	ضرب بالنار
to point at (the cannon)	ṣawwab ʿala …	صوّب على ...
bayonet	ḥerba (f)	حربة
rapier	seyf zu ḥaddeyn (m)	سيف ذو حدّين
saber (e.g., cavalry ~)	seyf monḥany (m)	سيف منحني
spear (weapon)	remḥ (m)	رمح
bow	qose (m)	قوس
arrow	sahm (m)	سهم
musket	musket (m)	مسكيت
crossbow	qose mostaʿraḍ (m)	قوس مستعرض

187. Ancient people

primitive (prehistoric)	bedāʾy	بدائي
prehistoric (adj)	ma qabl el tarīx	ما قبل التاريخ
ancient (~ civilization)	ʾadīm	قديم
Stone Age	el ʿaṣr el ḥagary (m)	العصر الحجري
Bronze Age	el ʿaṣr el bronzy (m)	العصر البرونزي
Ice Age	el ʿaṣr el galīdy (m)	العصر الجليدي
tribe	qabīla (f)	قبيلة
cannibal	ʾākel loḥūm el baʃar (m)	آكل لحوم البشر

hunter	ṣayād (m)	صيّاد
to hunt (vi, vt)	eṣṭād	إصطاد
mammoth	mamūθ (m)	ماموث
cave	kahf (m)	كهف
fire	nār (f)	نار
campfire	nār moχayem (m)	نار مخيّم
cave painting	rasm fel kahf (m)	رسم في الكهف
tool (e.g., stone ax)	adah (f)	أداة
spear	remḥ (m)	رمح
stone ax	fa's ḥagary (m)	فأس حجري
to be at war	ḥārab	حارب
to domesticate (vt)	esta'nas	استئنس
idol	ṣanam (m)	صنم
to worship (vt)	'abad	عبد
superstition	χorāfa (f)	خرافة
rite	mansak (m)	منسك
evolution	taṭṭawwor (m)	تطوّر
development	nomoww (m)	نموّ
disappearance (extinction)	enqerāḍ (m)	إنقراض
to adapt oneself	takayaf (ma')	تكيّف (مع)
archeology	'elm el 'āsār (m)	علم الآثار
archeologist	'ālem āsār (m)	عالم آثار
archeological (adj)	asary	أثري
excavation site	mawqe' ḥafr (m)	موقع حفر
excavations	tanqīb (m)	تنقيب
find (object)	ekteʃāf (m)	إكتشاف
fragment	'eṭ'a (f)	قطعة

188. Middle Ages

people (ethnic group)	ʃa'b (m)	شعب
peoples	ʃo'ūb (pl)	شعوب
tribe	qabīla (f)	قبيلة
tribes	qabā'el (pl)	قبائل
barbarians	el barabra (pl)	البرابرة
Gauls	el ɣaliyūn (pl)	الغاليّون
Goths	el qūṭiyūn (pl)	القوطيون
Slavs	el selāf (pl)	السلاف
Vikings	el viking (pl)	الفايكينج
Romans	el romān (pl)	الرومان
Roman (adj)	romāny	روماني
Byzantines	bizanṭiyūn (pl)	بيزنطيون

Byzantium	bīzanṭa (f)	بيزنطة
Byzantine (adj)	bīzanṭy	بيزنطي
emperor	embraṭore (m)	إمبراطور
leader, chief (tribal ~)	za'īm (m)	زعيم
powerful (~ king)	gabbār	جبّار
king	malek (m)	ملك
ruler (sovereign)	ḥākem (m)	حاكم
knight	fāres (m)	فارس
feudal lord	eqṭā'y (m)	إقطاعي
feudal (adj)	eqṭā'y	إقطاعي
vassal	ḥākem tābe' (m)	حاكم تابع
duke	dū' (m)	دوق
earl	earl (m)	ايرل
baron	barūn (m)	بارون
bishop	asqof (m)	أسقف
armor	der' (m)	درع
shield	der' (m)	درع
sword	seyf (m)	سيف
visor	ḥaffa amamiya lel χoza (f)	حافة أماميّة للخوذة
chainmail	der' el zard (m)	درع الزرد
Crusade	ḥamla ṣalībiya (f)	حملة صليبيّة
crusader	ṣalīby (m)	صليبي
territory	arḍ (f)	أرض
to attack (invade)	hagam	هجم
to conquer (vt)	fataḥ	فتح
to occupy (invade)	eḥtall	إحتلّ
siege (to be under ~)	ḥeṣār (m)	حصار
besieged (adj)	moḥāṣar	محاصر
to besiege (vt)	ḥāṣar	حاصر
inquisition	maḥākem el taftīʃ (pl)	محاكم التفتيش
inquisitor	mofatteʃ (m)	مفتّش
torture	ta'zīb (m)	تعذيب
cruel (adj)	waḥʃy	وحشي
heretic	moharṭeq (m)	مهرطق
heresy	harṭa'a (f)	هرطقة
seafaring	el safar bel baḥr (m)	السفر بالبحر
pirate	'orṣān (m)	قرصان
piracy	'arṣana (f)	قرصنة
boarding (attack)	mohagmet safīna (f)	مهاجمة سفينة
loot, booty	ɣanīma (f)	غنيمة
treasures	konūz (pl)	كنوز
discovery	ekteʃāf (m)	إكتشاف
to discover (new land, etc.)	ektaʃaf	إكتشف

expedition	beʻsa (f)	بعثة
musketeer	fāres (m)	فارس
cardinal	kardinal (m)	كاردينال
heraldry	ʃeʻārāt el nabāla (pl)	شعارات النبالة
heraldic (adj)	χāṣṣ be ʃeʻarāt el nebāla	خاصّ بشعارات النبالة

189. Leader. Chief. Authorities

king	malek (m)	ملك
queen	maleka (f)	ملكة
royal (adj)	malaky	ملكي
kingdom	mamlaka (f)	مملكة
prince	amīr (m)	أمير
princess	amīra (f)	أميرة
president	raʾīs (m)	رئيس
vice-president	nāʾeb el raʾīs (m)	نائب الرئيس
senator	ʻoḍw magles el ʃoyūχ (m)	عضو مجلس الشيوخ
monarch	ʻāhel (m)	عاهل
ruler (sovereign)	ḥākem (m)	حاكم
dictator	dektatore (m)	ديكتاتور
tyrant	ṭāɣeya (f)	طاغية
magnate	raʾsmāly kebīr (m)	رأسمالي كبير
director	modīr (m)	مدير
chief	raʾīs (m)	رئيس
manager (director)	modīr (m)	مدير
boss	raʾīs (m)	رئيس
owner	ṣāḥeb (m)	صاحب
leader	zaʻīm (m)	زعيم
head (~ of delegation)	raʾīs (m)	رئيس
authorities	solṭāt (pl)	سلطات
superiors	roʾasāʾ (pl)	رؤساء
governor	muḥāfeẓ (m)	محافظ
consul	qonṣol (m)	قنصل
diplomat	deblomāsy (m)	دبلوماسي
mayor	raʾīs el baladiya (m)	رئيس البلديّة
sheriff	ʃerīf (m)	شريف
emperor	embraṭore (m)	إمبراطور
tsar, czar	qayṣar (m)	قيصر
pharaoh	ferʻone (m)	فرعون
khan	χān (m)	خان

190. Road. Way. Directions

road	ṭarī' (m)	طريق
way (direction)	ṭarī' (m)	طريق
freeway	otostrad (m)	اوتوستراد
highway	ṭarī' saree' (m)	طريق سريع
interstate	ṭarī' waṭany (m)	طريق وطني
main road	ṭarī' ra'īsy (m)	طريق رئيسي
dirt road	ṭarī' torāby (m)	طريق ترابي
pathway	mamarr (m)	ممرّ
footpath (troddenpath)	mamarr (m)	ممرّ
Where?	feyn?	فين؟
Where (to)?	feyn?	فين؟
From where?	meneyn?	منين؟
direction (way)	ettegāh (m)	إتّجاه
to point (~ the way)	ʃāwer	شاور
to the left	lel ʃemāl	للشمال
to the right	lel yemīn	لليمين
straight ahead (adv)	'ala ṭūl	على طول
back (e.g., to turn ~)	wara'	وراء
bend, curve	mon'aṭaf (m)	منعطف
to turn (e.g., ~ left)	ḥād	حاد
to make a U-turn	laff fe u-turn	لفّ في يو تيرن
to be visible (mountains, castle, etc.)	ẓahar	ظهر
to appear (come into view)	ẓahar	ظهر
stop, halt (e.g., during a trip)	estrāḥa ṭawīla (f)	إستراحة طويلة
to rest, to pause (vi)	rayaḥ	ريّح
rest (pause)	rāḥa (f)	راحة
to lose one's way	tāh	تاه
to lead to ... (ab. road)	adda ela ...	أدّى إلى...
to come out (e.g., on the highway)	weṣel ela ...	وصل إلى...
stretch (of road)	emtedād (m)	إمتداد
asphalt	asfalt (m)	اسفلت
curb	bardora (f)	بردورة
ditch	ter'a (f)	ترعة
manhole	fat-ḥa (f)	فتحة
roadside (shoulder)	ḥaffet el ṭarī' (f)	حافّة الطريق

pit, pothole	ḥofra (f)	حفرة
to go (on foot)	meʃy	مشى
to pass (overtake)	egtāz	إجتاز
step (footstep)	χaṭwa (f)	خطوة
on foot (adv)	maʃyī	مشيّ
to block (road)	sadd	سدّ
boom gate	ḥāgez ṭarī' (m)	حاجز طريق
dead end	ṭarī' masdūd (m)	طريق مسدود

191. Breaking the law. Criminals. Part 1

bandit	qāṭe' ṭarī' (m)	قاطع طريق
crime	garīma (f)	جريمة
criminal (person)	mogrem (m)	مجرم
thief	sāre' (m)	سارق
to steal (vi, vt)	sara'	سرق
stealing, theft	ser'a (f)	سرقة
to kidnap (vt)	χaṭaf	خطف
kidnapping	χaṭf (m)	خطف
kidnapper	χāṭef (m)	خاطف
ransom	fedya (f)	فدية
to demand ransom	ṭalab fedya	طلب فدية
to rob (vt)	nahab	نهب
robbery	nahb (m)	نهب
robber	nahhāb (m)	نهّاب
to extort (vt)	balṭag	بلطج
extortionist	balṭagy (m)	بلطجي
extortion	balṭaga (f)	بلطجة
to murder, to kill	'atal	قتل
murder	'atl (m)	قتل
murderer	qātel (m)	قاتل
gunshot	ṭal'et nār (f)	طلقة نار
to fire (~ a shot)	aṭlaq el nār	أطلق النار
to shoot to death	'atal bel roṣāṣ	قتل بالرصاص
to shoot (vi)	ḍarab bel nār	ضرب بالنار
shooting	ḍarb nār (m)	ضرب نار
incident (fight, etc.)	ḥādes (m)	حادث
fight, brawl	χenā'a (f)	خناقة
Help!	sā'idni	ساعدني!
victim	ḍaḥiya (f)	ضحيّة

to damage (vt)	χarrab	خرّب
damage	χesāra (f)	خسارة
dead body, corpse	gossa (f)	جثّة
grave (~ crime)	χaṭīra	خطيرة
to attack (vt)	hagam	هجم
to beat (to hit)	ḍarab	ضرب
to beat up	ḍarab	ضرب
to take (rob of sth)	salab	سلب
to stab to death	ṭa'an ḥatta el mote	طعن حتّى الموت
to maim (vt)	ʃawwah	شوّه
to wound (vt)	garaḥ	جرح
blackmail	ebtezāz (m)	إبتزاز
to blackmail (vt)	ebtazz	إبتزّ
blackmailer	mobtazz (m)	مبتزّ
protection racket	balṭaga (f)	بلطجة
racketeer	mobtazz (m)	مبتزّ
gangster	ragol 'eṣāba (m)	رجل عصابة
mafia, Mob	mafia (f)	مافيا
pickpocket	nasʃāl (m)	نشّال
burglar	leṣṣ beyūt (m)	لص بيوت
smuggling	tahrīb (m)	تهريب
smuggler	moharreb (m)	مهرّب
forgery	tazwīr (m)	تزوير
to forge (counterfeit)	zawwar	زوّر
fake (forged)	mozawwara	مزوّرة

192. Breaking the law. Criminals. Part 2

rape	eɣteṣāb (m)	إغتصاب
to rape (vt)	eɣtaṣab	إغتصب
rapist	moɣtaṣeb (m)	مغتصب
maniac	mahwūs (m)	مهووس
prostitute (fem.)	mommos (f)	مومّس
prostitution	da'āra (f)	دعارة
pimp	qawwād (m)	قوّاد
drug addict	modmen moχaddarāt (m)	مدمن مخدّرات
drug dealer	tāger moχaddarāt (m)	تاجر مخدّرات
to blow up (bomb)	faggar	فجّر
explosion	enfegār (m)	إنفجار
to set fire	aʃ'al el nār	أشعل النار
arsonist	moʃ'el ḥarīq 'an 'amd (m)	مشعل حريق عن عمد
terrorism	erhāb (m)	إرهاب

terrorist	erhāby (m)	إرهابي
hostage	rahīna (m)	رهينة
to swindle (deceive)	eḥtāl	إحتال
swindle, deception	eḥteyāl (m)	إحتيال
swindler	moḥtāl (m)	محتال
to bribe (vt)	raʃa	رشا
bribery	erteʃā' (m)	إرتشاء
bribe	raʃwa (f)	رشوة
poison	semm (m)	سمّ
to poison (vt)	sammem	سمّم
to poison oneself	sammem nafsoh	سمّم نفسه
suicide (act)	enteḥār (m)	إنتحار
suicide (person)	montaḥer (m)	منتحر
to threaten (vt)	hadded	هدّد
threat	tahdīd (m)	تهديد
to make an attempt	ḥāwel eɣteyāl	حاول إغتيال
attempt (attack)	moḥawlet eɣteyāl (f)	محاولة إغتيال
to steal (a car)	sara'	سرق
to hijack (a plane)	eχtaṭaf	إختطف
revenge	enteqām (m)	إنتقام
to avenge (get revenge)	entaqam	إنتقم
to torture (vt)	'azzeb	عذّب
torture	ta'zīb (m)	تعذيب
to torment (vt)	'azzeb	عذّب
pirate	'orṣān (m)	قرصان
hooligan	wabaʃ (m)	وبش
armed (adj)	mosallaḥ	مسلّح
violence	'onf (m)	عنف
illegal (unlawful)	meʃ qanūniy	مش قانونيّ
spying (espionage)	tagassas (m)	تجسّس
to spy (vi)	tagassas	تجسّس

193. Police. Law. Part 1

justice	qaḍā' (m)	قضاء
court (see you in ~)	maḥkama (f)	محكمة
judge	qāḍy (m)	قاضي
jurors	moḥallafīn (pl)	محلّفين
jury trial	qaḍā' el muḥallafīn (m)	قضاء المحلّفين

to judge (vt)	ḥakam	حكم
lawyer, attorney	muḥāmy (m)	محامي
defendant	modda'y 'aleyh (m)	مدّعي عليه
dock	'afaṣ el ettehām (m)	قفص الإتّهام
charge	ettehām (m)	إتّهام
accused	mottaham (m)	متّهم
sentence	ḥokm (m)	حكم
to sentence (vt)	ḥakam	حكم
guilty (culprit)	gāny (m)	جاني
to punish (vt)	'āqab	عاقب
punishment	'eqāb (m)	عقاب
fine (penalty)	ɣarāma (f)	غرامة
life imprisonment	segn mada el ḥayah (m)	سجن مدى الحياة
death penalty	'oqūbet 'e'dām (f)	عقوبة إعدام
electric chair	el korsy el kaharabā'y (m)	الكرسي الكهربائي
gallows	maʃna'a (f)	مشنقة
to execute (vt)	a'dam	أعدم
execution	e'dām (m)	إعدام
prison, jail	segn (m)	سجن
cell	zenzāna (f)	زنزانة
escort	ḥerāsa (f)	حراسة
prison guard	ḥāres segn (m)	حارس سجن
prisoner	sagīn (m)	سجين
handcuffs	kalabʃāt (pl)	كلابشات
to handcuff (vt)	kalbeʃ	كلبش
prison break	horūb men el segn (m)	هروب من السجن
to break out (vi)	hereb	هرب
to disappear (vi)	eχtafa	إختفى
to release (from prison)	aχla sabīl	أخلى سبيل
amnesty	'afw 'ām (m)	عفو عام
police	ʃorṭa (f)	شرطة
police officer	ʃorṭy (m)	شرطي
police station	qesm ʃorṭa (m)	قسم شرطة
billy club	'aṣāya maṭṭāṭiya (f)	عصاية مطّاطية
bullhorn	bū' (m)	بوق
patrol car	'arabiyet dawrīāt (f)	عربيّة دوريات
siren	sarīna (f)	سرينة
to turn on the siren	walla' el sarīna	ولّع السرينة
siren call	ṣote sarīna (m)	صوت سرينة
crime scene	masraḥ el garīma (m)	مسرح الجريمة
witness	ʃāhed (m)	شاهد

freedom	ḥorriya (f)	حرّيّة
accomplice	ʃerīk fel garīma (m)	شريك في الجريمة
to flee (vi)	hereb	هرب
trace (to leave a ~)	asar (m)	أثر

194. Police. Law. Part 2

search (investigation)	baḥs (m)	بحث
to look for ...	dawwar ʿala	دوّر على
suspicion	ʃobha (f)	شبهة
suspicious (e.g., ~ vehicle)	maʃbūh	مشبوه
to stop (cause to halt)	awqaf	أوقّف
to detain (keep in custody)	eʿtaqal	إعتقل
case (lawsuit)	ʾaḍiya (f)	قضيّة
investigation	taḥʾīʾ (m)	تحقيق
detective	moḥaqqeq (m)	محقّق
investigator	mofatteʃ (m)	مفتّش
hypothesis	rewāya (f)	رواية
motive	dāfeʿ (m)	دافع
interrogation	estegwāb (m)	إستجواب
to interrogate (vt)	estagweb	إستجوّب
to question (~ neighbors, etc.)	estanṭaʾ	إستنطق
check (identity ~)	faḥṣ (m)	فحص
round-up	gamʿ (m)	جمع
search (~ warrant)	taftīʃ (m)	تفتيش
chase (pursuit)	moṭarda (f)	مطاردة
to pursue, to chase	ṭārad	طارد
to track (a criminal)	tatabbaʿ	تتبّع
arrest	eʿteqāl (m)	إعتقال
to arrest (sb)	eʿtaqal	اعتقل
to catch (thief, etc.)	ʾabaḍ ʿala	قبض على
capture	ʾabḍ (m)	قبض
document	wasīqa (f)	وثيقة
proof (evidence)	dalīl (m)	دليل
to prove (vt)	asbat	أثبت
footprint	baṣma (f)	بصّمة
fingerprints	baṣamāt el aṣābeʿ (pl)	بصمات الأصابع
piece of evidence	ʾeṭʿa men el adella (f)	قطعة من الأدلّة
alibi	ḥegget ɣeyāb (f)	حجّة غياب
innocent (not guilty)	barīʾ	بريء
injustice	ẓolm (m)	ظلم
unjust, unfair (adj)	meʃ ʿādel	مش عادل
criminal (adj)	mogrem	مجرم

to confiscate (vt)	ṣādar	صادر
drug (illegal substance)	moχaddarāt (pl)	مخدّرات
weapon, gun	selāḥ (m)	سلاح
to disarm (vt)	garrad men el selāḥ	جرّد من السلاح
to order (command)	amar	أمر
to disappear (vi)	eχtafa	إختفى
law	qanūn (m)	قانون
legal, lawful (adj)	qanūny	قانوني
illegal, illicit (adj)	meʃ qanūny	مش قانوني
responsibility (blame)	mas'oliya (f)	مسؤوليّة
responsible (adj)	mas'ūl (m)	مسؤول

NATURE

The Earth. Part 1

195. Outer space

space	faḍā' (m)	فضاء
space (as adj)	faḍā'y	فضائي
outer space	el faḍā' el χāregy (m)	الفضاء الخارجي
world	'ālam (m)	عالم
universe	el kōn (m)	الكون
galaxy	el magarra (f)	المجرّة
star	negm (m)	نجم
constellation	borg (m)	برج
planet	kawwkab (m)	كوّكب
satellite	'amar ṣenā'y (m)	قمر صناعي
meteorite	nayzek (m)	نيّزك
comet	mozannab (m)	مذنّب
asteroid	kowaykeb (m)	كويكب
orbit	madār (m)	مدار
to revolve (~ around the Earth)	dār	دار
atmosphere	el ɣelāf el gawwy (m)	الغلاف الجوّي
the Sun	el ʃams (f)	الشمس
solar system	el magmū'a el ʃamsiya (f)	المجموعة الشمسيّة
solar eclipse	kosūf el ʃams (m)	كسوف الشمس
the Earth	el arḍ (f)	الأرض
the Moon	el 'amar (m)	القمر
Mars	el marrīχ (m)	المّريخ
Venus	el zahra (f)	الزهرة
Jupiter	el moʃtary (m)	المشتري
Saturn	zoḥḥol (m)	زحل
Mercury	'aṭāred (m)	عطارد
Uranus	uranus (m)	اورانوس
Neptune	nibtūn (m)	نبتون
Pluto	bluto (m)	بلوتو
Milky Way	darb el tebbāna (m)	درب التبّانة
Great Bear (Ursa Major)	el dobb el akbar (m)	الدب الأكبر

North Star	negm el 'oṭb (m)	نجم القطب
Martian	sāken el marrīχ (m)	ساكن المرّيخ
extraterrestrial (n)	faḍā'y (m)	فضائي
alien	kā'en faḍā'y (m)	كائن فضائي
flying saucer	ṭaba' ṭā'er (m)	طبق طائر
spaceship	markaba faḍa'iya (f)	مركبة فضائية
space station	maḥaṭṭet faḍā' (f)	محطّة فضاء
blast-off	enṭelāq (m)	إنطلاق
engine	motore (m)	موتور
nozzle	manfaθ (m)	منفث
fuel	woqūd (m)	وقود
cockpit, flight deck	kabīna (f)	كابينة
antenna	hawā'y (m)	هوائي
porthole	kowwa mostadīra (f)	كوّة مستديرة
solar panel	lawḥa ʃamsiya (f)	لوحة شمسيّة
spacesuit	badlet el faḍā' (f)	بدلة الفضاء
weightlessness	en'edām wazn (m)	إنعدام الوزن
oxygen	oksiʒīn (m)	أوكسجين
docking (in space)	rasw (m)	رسو
to dock (vi, vt)	rasa	رسى
observatory	marṣad (m)	مرصد
telescope	teleskop (m)	تلسكوب
to observe (vt)	rāqab	راقب
to explore (vt)	estakʃef	إستكشف

196. The Earth

the Earth	el arḍ (f)	الأرض
the globe (the Earth)	el kora el arḍiya (f)	الكرة الأرضيّة
planet	kawwkab (m)	كوكب
atmosphere	el ɣelāf el gawwy (m)	الغلاف الجوّي
geography	goɣrafia (f)	جغرافيا
nature	ṭabee'a (f)	طبيعة
globe (table ~)	namūzag lel kora el arḍiya (m)	نموذج للكرة الأرضيّة
map	χarīṭa (f)	خريطة
atlas	aṭlas (m)	أطلس
Europe	orobba (f)	أوروبّا
Asia	asya (f)	آسيا
Africa	afreqia (f)	أفريقيا
Australia	ostorālya (f)	أستراليا

America	amrīka (f)	أمريكا
North America	amrīka el ʃamaliya (f)	أمريكا الشماليّة
South America	amrīka el ganūbiya (f)	أمريكا الجنوبيّة
Antarctica	el qoṭb el ganūby (m)	القطب الجنوبي
the Arctic	el qoṭb el ʃamāly (m)	القطب الشمالي

197. Cardinal directions

north	ʃemāl (m)	شمال
to the north	lel ʃamāl	للشمال
in the north	fel ʃamāl	في الشمال
northern (adj)	ʃamāly	شمالي
south	ganūb (m)	جنوب
to the south	lel ganūb	للجنوب
in the south	fel ganūb	في الجنوب
southern (adj)	ganūby	جنوبي
west	ɣarb (m)	غرب
to the west	lel ɣarb	للغرب
in the west	fel ɣarb	في الغرب
western (adj)	ɣarby	غربي
east	ʃarʾ (m)	شرق
to the east	lel ʃarʾ	للشرق
in the east	fel ʃarʾ	في الشرق
eastern (adj)	ʃarʾy	شرقي

198. Sea. Ocean

sea	baḥr (m)	بحر
ocean	moḥīṭ (m)	محيط
gulf (bay)	χalīg (m)	خليج
straits	maḍīq (m)	مضيق
land (solid ground)	barr (m)	برّ
continent (mainland)	qārra (f)	قارّة
island	gezīra (f)	جزيرة
peninsula	ʃebh gezeyra (f)	شبه جزيرة
archipelago	magmūʿet gozor (f)	مجموعة جزر
bay, cove	χalīg (m)	خليج
harbor	mināʾ (m)	ميناء
lagoon	lagūn (m)	لاجون
cape	raʾs (m)	رأس
atoll	gezīra morganiya estwaʾiya (f)	جزيزة مرجانيةَ إستوائيّة

reef	ʃoʻāb (pl)	شعاب
coral	morgān (m)	مرجان
coral reef	ʃoʻāb morganiya (pl)	شعاب مرجانية
deep (adj)	ʻamīq	عميق
depth (deep water)	ʻomq (m)	عمق
abyss	el ʻomq el saḥīq (m)	العمق السحيق
trench (e.g., Mariana ~)	χondoq (m)	خندق
current (Ocean ~)	tayār (m)	تيّار
to surround (bathe)	ḥāṭ	حاط
shore	sāḥel (m)	ساحل
coast	sāḥel (m)	ساحل
flow (flood tide)	tayār (m)	تيّار
ebb (ebb tide)	gozor (m)	جزر
shoal	meyāh ḍaḥla (f)	مياه ضحلة
bottom (~ of the sea)	qāʻ (m)	قاع
wave	mouga (f)	موجة
crest (~ of a wave)	qemma (f)	قمّة
spume (sea foam)	zabad el baḥr (m)	زبد البحر
storm (sea storm)	ʻāṣefa (f)	عاصفة
hurricane	eʻṣār (m)	إعصار
tsunami	tsunāmy (m)	تسونامي
calm (dead ~)	hodūʼ (m)	هدوء
quiet, calm (adj)	hady	هادئ
pole	ʼoṭb (m)	قطب
polar (adj)	ʼoṭby	قطبي
latitude	ʻarḍ (m)	عرض
longitude	χaṭṭ ṭūl (m)	خطّ طول
parallel	motawāz (m)	متواز
equator	χaṭṭ el estewāʼ (m)	خطّ الإستواء
sky	samāʼ (f)	سماء
horizon	ofoq (m)	أفق
air	hawāʼ (m)	هواء
lighthouse	manāra (f)	منارة
to dive (vi)	ɣāṣ	غاص
to sink (ab. boat)	ɣereʼ	غرق
treasures	konūz (pl)	كنوز

199. Seas' and Oceans' names

Atlantic Ocean	el moḥeyṭ el aṭlanṭy (m)	المحيط الأطلنطي
Indian Ocean	el moḥeyṭ el hendy (m)	المحيط الهندي

Pacific Ocean	el moḥeyṭ el hādy (m)	المحيط الهادي
Arctic Ocean	el moḥeyṭ el motagammed el ʃamāly (m)	المحيط المتجمّد الشمالي
Black Sea	el baḥr el aswad (m)	البحر الأسود
Red Sea	el baḥr el aḥmar (m)	البحر الأحمر
Yellow Sea	el baḥr el aṣfar (m)	البحر الأصفر
White Sea	el baḥr el abyaḍ (m)	البحر الأبيض
Caspian Sea	baḥr qazwīn (m)	بحر قزوين
Dead Sea	el baḥr el mayet (m)	البحر الميّت
Mediterranean Sea	el baḥr el abyaḍ el motawasseṭ (m)	البحر الأبيض المتوسطّ
Aegean Sea	baḥr eygah (m)	بحر إيجة
Adriatic Sea	el baḥr el adreyatīky (m)	البحر الأدرياتيكي
Arabian Sea	baḥr el ʿarab (m)	بحر العرب
Sea of Japan	baḥr el yabān (m)	بحر اليابان
Bering Sea	baḥr bering (m)	بحر بيرينغ
South China Sea	baḥr el ṣeyn el ganūby (m)	بحر الصين الجنوبي
Coral Sea	baḥr el morgān (m)	بحر المرجان
Tasman Sea	baḥr tazman (m)	بحر تسمان
Caribbean Sea	el baḥr el karību (m)	البحر الكاريبي
Barents Sea	baḥr barents (m)	بحر بارنتس
Kara Sea	baḥr kara (m)	بحر كارا
North Sea	baḥr el ʃamāl (m)	بحر الشمال
Baltic Sea	baḥr el balṭīq (m)	بحر البلطيق
Norwegian Sea	baḥr el nerwīg (m)	بحر النرويج

200. Mountains

mountain	gabal (m)	جبل
mountain range	selselet gebāl (f)	سلسلة جبال
mountain ridge	notūʾ el gabal (m)	نتوء الجبل
summit, top	qemma (f)	قمّة
peak	qemma (f)	قمّة
foot (~ of the mountain)	asfal (m)	أسفل
slope (mountainside)	monḥadar (m)	منحدر
volcano	borkān (m)	بركان
active volcano	borkān naʃeṭ (m)	بركان نشط
dormant volcano	borkān χāmed (m)	بركان خامد
eruption	sawarān (m)	ثوّران
crater	fawhet el borkān (f)	فوهة البركان

magma	magma (f)	ماجما
lava	ḥomam borkāniya (pl)	حمم بركانية
molten (~ lava)	monṣahera	منصهرة
canyon	wādy ḍaye' (m)	وادي ضيّق
gorge	mamarr ḍaye' (m)	ممرّ ضيّق
crevice	ʃa'' (m)	شقّ
abyss (chasm)	hāwya (f)	هاوية
pass, col	mamarr gabaly (m)	ممرّ جبلي
plateau	haḍaba (f)	هضبة
cliff	garf (m)	جرف
hill	tall (m)	تلّ
glacier	nahr galīdy (m)	نهر جليدي
waterfall	ʃallāl (m)	شلّال
geyser	nab' maya ḥāra (m)	نبع ميّة حارة
lake	boḥeyra (f)	بحيرة
plain	sahl (m)	سهل
landscape	manzar ṭabee'y (m)	منظر طبيعي
echo	ṣada (m)	صدى
alpinist	motasalleq el gebāl (m)	متسلّق الجبال
rock climber	motasalleq ṣoxūr (m)	متسلّق صخور
to conquer (in climbing)	taɣallab 'ala	تغلّب على
climb (an easy ~)	tasalloq (m)	تسلّق

201. Mountains names

The Alps	gebāl el alb (pl)	جبال الألب
Mont Blanc	mōn blōn (m)	مون بلون
The Pyrenees	gebāl el barānes (pl)	جبال البرانس
The Carpathians	gebāl el karbāt (pl)	جبال الكاربات
The Ural Mountains	gebāl el urāl (pl)	جبال الأورال
The Caucasus Mountains	gebāl el qoqāz (pl)	جبال القوقاز
Mount Elbrus	gabal elbrus (m)	جبل إلبروس
The Altai Mountains	gebāl altāy (pl)	جبال ألتاي
The Tian Shan	gebāl tian ʃan (pl)	جبال تيان شان
The Pamir Mountains	gebāl bamir (pl)	جبال بامير
The Himalayas	himalāya (pl)	هيمالايا
Mount Everest	gabal everest (m)	جبل افرست
The Andes	gebāl el andīz (pl)	جبال الأنديز
Mount Kilimanjaro	gabal kilimanʒaro (m)	جبل كليمنجارو

202. Rivers

river	nahr (m)	نهر
spring (natural source)	'eyn (m)	عين
riverbed (river channel)	magra el nahr (m)	مجرى النهر
basin (river valley)	ḥoḍe (m)	حوض
to flow into …	ṣabb fe …	صبّ في...
tributary	rāfed (m)	رافد
bank (of river)	ḍaffa (f)	ضفّة
current (stream)	tayār (m)	تيّار
downstream (adv)	ma' ettigāh magra el nahr	مع إتّجاه مجرى النهر
upstream (adv)	ḍed el tayār	ضد التيار
inundation	ɣamr (m)	غمر
flooding	fayaḍān (m)	فيضان
to overflow (vi)	fāḍ	فاض
to flood (vt)	ɣamar	غمر
shallow (shoal)	meyāh ḍaḥla (f)	مياه ضحلة
rapids	monḥadar el nahr (m)	منحدر النهر
dam	sadd (m)	سدّ
canal	qanah (f)	قناة
reservoir (artificial lake)	χazzān mā'y (m)	خزّان مائي
sluice, lock	bawwāba qanṭara (f)	بوّابة قنطرة
water body (pond, etc.)	berka (f)	بركة
swamp (marshland)	mostanqa' (m)	مستنقع
bog, marsh	mostanqa' (m)	مستنقع
whirlpool	dawwāma (f)	دوّامة
stream (brook)	gadwal (m)	جدوّل
drinking (ab. water)	el ʃorb	الشرب
fresh (~ water)	'azb	عذب
ice	galīd (m)	جليد
to freeze over (ab. river, etc.)	etgammed	إتجمّد

203. Rivers' names

Seine	el seyn (m)	السين
Loire	el lua:r (m)	اللوار
Thames	el teymz (m)	التيمز
Rhine	el rayn (m)	الراين
Danube	el danūb (m)	الدانوب

Volga	el volga (m)	الفولغا
Don	el done (m)	الدون
Lena	lena (m)	لينا
Yellow River	el nahr el aṣfar (m)	النهر الأصفر
Yangtze	el yangesty (m)	اليانغستي
Mekong	el mekong (m)	الميكونغ
Ganges	el ɣang (m)	الغانج
Nile River	el nīl (m)	النيل
Congo River	el kongo (m)	الكونغو
Okavango River	okavango (m)	أوكافانجو
Zambezi River	el zambizi (m)	الزمبيزي
Limpopo River	limbobo (m)	ليمبوبو
Mississippi River	el mississibbi (m)	الميسيسيبي

204. Forest

forest, wood	ɣāba (f)	غابة
forest (as adj)	ɣāba	غابة
thick forest	ɣāba kasīfa (f)	غابة كثيفة
grove	bostān (m)	بستان
forest clearing	ezālet el ɣābāt (f)	إزالة الغابات
thicket	agama (f)	أجمة
scrubland	arāḍy el ʃogayrāt (pl)	أراضي الشجيرات
footpath (troddenpath)	mamarr (m)	ممرّ
gully	wādy ḍaye' (m)	وادي ضيّق
tree	ʃagara (f)	شجرة
leaf	wara'a (f)	ورقة
leaves (foliage)	wara' (m)	ورق
fall of leaves	tasā'oṭ el awrā' (m)	تساقط الأوراق
to fall (ab. leaves)	saqaṭ	سقط
top (of the tree)	ra's (m)	رأس
branch	ɣoṣn (m)	غصن
bough	ɣoṣn ra'īsy (m)	غصن رئيسي
bud (on shrub, tree)	bor'om (m)	برعم
needle (of pine tree)	ʃawka (f)	شوكة
pine cone	kūz el ṣnowbar (m)	كوز الصنوبر
hollow (in a tree)	gofe (m)	جوف
nest	'eʃ (m)	عشّ
burrow (animal hole)	goḥr (m)	جحر
trunk	gez' (m)	جذع
root	gezr (m)	جذر

bark	leḥā' (m)	لحاء
moss	ṭaḥlab (m)	طحلب
to uproot (remove trees or tree stumps)	eqtala'	إقتلع
to chop down	'aṭṭa'	قطّع
to deforest (vt)	azāl el ɣabāt	أزال الغابات
tree stump	gez' el ʃagara (m)	جذع الشجرة
campfire	nār moχayem (m)	نار مخيّم
forest fire	ḥarī' ɣāba (m)	حريق غابة
to extinguish (vt)	ṭaffa	طفّى
forest ranger	ḥāres el ɣāba (m)	حارس الغابة
protection	ḥemāya (f)	حماية
to protect (~ nature)	ḥama	حمى
poacher	sāre' el ṣeyd (m)	سارق الصيد
steel trap	maṣyada (f)	مصيدة
to gather, to pick (vt)	gamma'	جمّع
to lose one's way	tāh	تاه

205. Natural resources

natural resources	sarawāt ṭabi'iya (pl)	ثروات طبيعيّة
minerals	ma'āden (pl)	معادن
deposits	rawāseb (pl)	رواسب
field (e.g., oilfield)	ḥaql (m)	حقل
to mine (extract)	estaχrag	إستخرج
mining (extraction)	esteχrāg (m)	إستخراج
ore	χām (m)	خام
mine (e.g., for coal)	mangam (m)	منجم
shaft (mine ~)	mangam (m)	منجم
miner	'āmel mangam (m)	عامل منجم
gas (natural ~)	ɣāz (m)	غاز
gas pipeline	χaṭṭ anabīb ɣāz (m)	خطّ أنابيب غاز
oil (petroleum)	nafṭ (m)	نفط
oil pipeline	anabīb el nafṭ (pl)	أنابيب النفط
oil well	bīr el nafṭ (m)	بير النفط
derrick (tower)	ḥaffāra (f)	حفّارة
tanker	nāqelet betrūl (f)	ناقلة بترول
sand	raml (m)	رمل
limestone	ḥagar el kals (m)	حجر الكلس
gravel	ḥaṣa (m)	حصى
peat	χaθ faḥm nabāty (m)	خث فحم نباتي
clay	ṭīn (m)	طين

coal	faḥm (m)	فحم
iron (ore)	ḥadīd (m)	حديد
gold	dahab (m)	ذهب
silver	faḍḍa (f)	فضّة
nickel	nikel (m)	نيكل
copper	neḥās (m)	نحاس
zinc	zink (m)	زنك
manganese	manganīz (m)	منجنيز
mercury	ze'baq (m)	زئبق
lead	roṣāṣ (m)	رصاص
mineral	ma'dan (m)	معدن
crystal	kristāl (m)	كريستال
marble	roχām (m)	رخام
uranium	yuranuim (m)	يورانيوم

The Earth. Part 2

206. Weather

weather	ṭa's (m)	طقس
weather forecast	naʃra gawiya (f)	نشرة جوية
temperature	ḥarāra (f)	حرارة
thermometer	termometr (m)	ترمومتر
barometer	barometr (m)	بارومتر
humid (adj)	roṭob	رطب
humidity	roṭūba (f)	رطوبة
heat (extreme ~)	ḥarāra (f)	حرارة
hot (torrid)	ḥarr	حارّ
it's hot	el gaww ḥarr	الجَو حرّ
it's warm	el gaww dafa	الجَو دفا
warm (moderately hot)	dāfe'	دافئ
it's cold	el gaww bāred	الجَو بارد
cold (adj)	bāred	بارد
sun	ʃams (f)	شمس
to shine (vi)	nawwar	نوَر
sunny (day)	moʃmes	مشمس
to come up (vi)	ʃara'	شرق
to set (vi)	ɣarab	غرب
cloud	saḥāba (f)	سحابة
cloudy (adj)	meɣayem	مغيَم
rain cloud	saḥābet maṭar (f)	سحابة مطر
somber (gloomy)	meɣayem	مغيَم
rain	maṭar (m)	مطر
it's raining	el donia betmaṭṭar	الدنيا بتمطَر
rainy (~ day, weather)	momṭer	ممطر
to drizzle (vi)	maṭṭaret razāz	مطَرت رذاذ
pouring rain	maṭar monhamer (f)	مطر منهمر
downpour	maṭar ɣazīr (m)	مطر غزير
heavy (e.g., ~ rain)	ʃedīd	شديد
puddle	berka (f)	بركة
to get wet (in rain)	ettbal	إتْبل
fog (mist)	ʃabbūra (f)	شبَورة
foggy	fih ʃabbūra	فيه شبَورة

snow	talg (m)	ثلج
it's snowing	fih talg	فيه ثلج

207. Severe weather. Natural disasters

thunderstorm	ʻāṣefa raʻdiya (f)	عاصفة رعدية
lightning (~ strike)	bar' (m)	برق
to flash (vi)	baraq	برق
thunder	raʻd (m)	رعد
to thunder (vi)	dawa	دوى
it's thundering	el samā' dawat raʻd (f)	السماء دوّت رعد
hail	maṭar bard (m)	مطر برد
it's hailing	maṭṭaret bard	مطّرت برد
to flood (vt)	ɣamar	غمر
flood, inundation	fayaḍān (m)	فيضان
earthquake	zelzāl (m)	زلزال
tremor, quake	hazza arḍiya (f)	هزّة أرضية
epicenter	markaz el zelzāl (m)	مركز الزلزال
eruption	sawarān (m)	ثوَران
lava	ḥomam borkāniya (pl)	حمم بركانية
twister, tornado	eʻṣār (m)	إعصار
typhoon	tyfūn (m)	طوفان
hurricane	eʻṣār (m)	إعصار
storm	ʻāṣefa (f)	عاصفة
tsunami	tsunāmy (m)	تسونامي
cyclone	eʻṣār (m)	إعصار
bad weather	ṭa's saye' (m)	طقس سيء
fire (accident)	ḥarī' (m)	حريق
disaster	karsa (f)	كارثة
meteorite	nayzek (m)	نيَزك
avalanche	enheyār talgy (m)	إنهيار ثلجي
snowslide	enheyār talgy (m)	إنهيار ثلجي
blizzard	ʻāṣefa talgiya (f)	عاصفة ثلجيّة
snowstorm	ʻāṣefa talgiya (f)	عاصفة ثلجيّة

208. Noises. Sounds

silence (quiet)	ṣamt (m)	صمت
sound	ṣote (m)	صوت

noise	dawʃa (f)	دوشة
to make noise	ʻamal dawʃa	عمل دوشة
noisy (adj)	mozʻeg	مزعج
loudly (to speak, etc.)	beṣote ʻāly	بصوت عالي
loud (voice, etc.)	ʻāly	عالي
constant (e.g., ~ noise)	mostamerr	مستمِر
cry, shout (n)	ṣarχa (f)	صرخة
to cry, to shout (vi)	ṣarraχ	صرّخ
whisper	hamsa (f)	همسة
to whisper (vi, vt)	hamas	همس
barking (dog's ~)	nebāḥ (m)	نباح
to bark (vi)	nabaḥ	نبح
groan (of pain, etc.)	anīn (m)	أنين
to groan (vi)	ann	أنّ
cough	koḥḥa (f)	كحّة
to cough (vi)	kaḥḥ	كحّ
whistle	taṣfīr (m)	تصفير
to whistle (vi)	ṣaffar	صفّر
knock (at the door)	ṭar', da'' (m)	طرق, دقّ
to knock (at the door)	da''	دقّ
to crack (vi)	far'aʻ	فرقع
crack (cracking sound)	far'aʻa (f)	فرقعة
siren	sarīna (f)	سرينة
whistle (factory ~, etc.)	ṣafīr (m)	صفير
to whistle (ab. train)	ṣaffar	صفّر
honk (car horn sound)	tazmīr (m)	تزمير
to honk (vi)	zammar	زمّر

209. Winter

winter (n)	ʃetā' (m)	شتاء
winter (as adj)	ʃetwy	شتوي
in winter	fel ʃetā'	في الشتاء
snow	talg (m)	ثلج
it's snowing	fih talg	فيه ثلج
snowfall	tasā'oṭ el tolūg (m)	تساقط الثلوج
snowdrift	rokma talgiya (f)	ركمة ثلجية
snowflake	nadfet talg (f)	ندفة ثلج
snowball	koret talg (f)	كرة ثلج
snowman	rāgel men el talg (m)	راجل من الثلج
icicle	'eṭʻet galīd (f)	قطعة جليد

December	desember (m)	ديسمبر
January	yanāyer (m)	يناير
February	febrāyer (m)	فبراير
frost (severe ~, freezing cold)	ṣaqee' (m)	صقيع
frosty (weather, air)	ṣā'e'	صاقع
below zero (adv)	taḥt el ṣefr	تحت الصفر
first frost	ṣaqee' (m)	صقيع
hoarfrost	ṣaqee' motagammed (m)	صقيع متجمّد
cold (cold weather)	bard (m)	برد
it's cold	el gaww bāred	الجوّ بارد
fur coat	balṭo farww (m)	بالطو فروّ
mittens	gwanty men ɣeyr aṣābe' (m)	جوانتي من غير أصابع
to get sick	mereḍ	مرض
cold (illness)	zokām (m)	زكام
to catch a cold	gālo bard	جاله برد
ice	galīd (m)	جليد
black ice	ɣaṭā' galīdy 'lal arḍ (m)	غطاء جليدي على الأرض
to freeze over (ab. river, etc.)	etgammed	إتجمّد
ice floe	roqāqet galīd (f)	رقاقة جليد
skis	zallagāt (pl)	زلّاجات
skier	motazaḥleq 'alal galīd (m)	متزحلق على الجليد
to ski (vi)	tazallag	تزلّج
to skate (vi)	tazallag	تزلّج

Fauna

210. Mammals. Predators

predator	moftares (m)	مفترس
tiger	nemr (m)	نمر
lion	asad (m)	أسد
wolf	ze'b (m)	ذئب
fox	ta'lab (m)	ثعلب
jaguar	nemr amrīky (m)	نمر أمريكي
leopard	fahd (m)	فهد
cheetah	fahd ṣayād (m)	فهد صيّاد
black panther	nemr aswad (m)	نمر أسوّد
puma	asad el gebāl (m)	أسد الجبال
snow leopard	nemr el tolūg (m)	نمر الثلوج
lynx	waʃaq (m)	وشق
coyote	qayūṭ (m)	قيوط
jackal	ebn 'āwy (m)	ابن آوى
hyena	ḍeb' (m)	ضبع

211. Wild animals

animal	ḥayawān (m)	حيوان
beast (animal)	waḥʃ (m)	وحش
squirrel	sengāb (m)	سنجاب
hedgehog	qonfoz (m)	قنفذ
hare	arnab barry (m)	أرنب برّي
rabbit	arnab (m)	أرنب
badger	ɣarīr (m)	غرير
raccoon	rakūn (m)	راكون
hamster	hamster (m)	هامستر
marmot	marmoṭ (m)	مرموط
mole	χold (m)	خلد
mouse	fār (m)	فأر
rat	gerz (m)	جرذ
bat	χoffāʃ (m)	خفّاش
ermine	qāqem (m)	قاقِم
sable	sammūr (m)	سمّور

marten	fara'īāt (m)	فرائيات
weasel	ebn 'ers (m)	ابن عرس
mink	mink (m)	منك
beaver	qondos (m)	قندس
otter	ta'lab maya (m)	ثعلب الميّة
horse	ḥoṣān (m)	حصان
moose	eyl el mūz (m)	أيّل الموظ
deer	ayl (m)	أيل
camel	gamal (m)	جمل
bison	bison (m)	بيسون
aurochs	byson orobby (m)	بيسون أوروبي
buffalo	gamūs (m)	جاموس
zebra	ḥomār waḥʃy (m)	حمار وحشي
antelope	ẓaby (m)	ظبي
roe deer	yaḥmūr orobby (m)	يحمورأوروبيّ
fallow deer	eyl asmar orobby (m)	أيّل أسمر أوروبي
chamois	ʃamwah (f)	شاموراه
wild boar	χenzīr barry (m)	خنزير برّي
whale	ḥūt (m)	حوت
seal	foqma (f)	فقمة
walrus	el kab' (m)	الكبع
fur seal	foqmet el farā' (f)	فقمة الفراء
dolphin	dolfīn (m)	دولفين
bear	dobb (m)	دبّ
polar bear	dobb 'oṭṭby (m)	دبّ قطبي
panda	banda (m)	باندا
monkey	'erd (m)	قرد
chimpanzee	ʃimbanzy (m)	شيمبانزي
orangutan	orangutan (m)	أورنغوتان
gorilla	ɣorella (f)	غوريلا
macaque	'erd el makāk (m)	قرد المكاك
gibbon	gibbon (m)	جيبون
elephant	fīl (m)	فيل
rhinoceros	χartīt (m)	خرتيت
giraffe	zarāfa (f)	زرافة
hippopotamus	faras el nahr (m)	فرس النهر
kangaroo	kangarū (m)	كانجارو
koala (bear)	el koala (m)	الكوالا
mongoose	nems (m)	نمس
chinchilla	ʃenʃīla (f)	شنشيلة
skunk	ẓerbān (m)	ظربان
porcupine	nīṣ (m)	نيص

212. Domestic animals

cat	ʾoṭṭa (f)	قطّة
tomcat	ʾoṭṭ (m)	قطّ
dog	kalb (m)	كلب
horse	ḥoṣān (m)	حصان
stallion (male horse)	χeyl faḥl (m)	خيل فحل
mare	faras (f)	فرس
cow	baʾara (f)	بقرة
bull	sore (m)	ثور
ox	sore (m)	ثور
sheep (ewe)	χarūf (f)	خروف
ram	kebʃ (m)	كبش
goat	meʿza (f)	معزة
billy goat, he-goat	māʿez zakar (m)	ماعز ذكر
donkey	ḥomār (m)	حمار
mule	baɣl (m)	بغل
pig, hog	χenzīr (m)	خنزير
piglet	χannūṣ (m)	خنّوص
rabbit	arnab (m)	أرنب
hen (chicken)	farχa (f)	فرخة
rooster	dīk (m)	ديك
duck	baṭṭa (f)	بطّة
drake	dakar el baṭṭ (m)	ذكر البط
goose	wezza (f)	وزّة
tom turkey, gobbler	dīk rūmy (m)	ديك رومي
turkey (hen)	dīk rūmy (m)	ديك رومي
domestic animals	ḥayawānāt dawāgen (pl)	حيوانات دواجن
tame (e.g., ~ hamster)	alīf	أليف
to tame (vt)	rawweḍ	روّض
to breed (vt)	rabba	ربّى
farm	mazraʿa (f)	مزرعة
poultry	dawāgen (pl)	دواجن
cattle	māʃeya (f)	ماشية
herd (cattle)	qaṭeeʿ (m)	قطيع
stable	esṭabl χeyl (m)	إسطبل خيل
pigpen	ḥazīret χanazīr (f)	حظيرة الخنازير
cowshed	zerībet el baʾar (f)	زريبة البقر
rabbit hutch	qan el arāneb (m)	قن الأرانب
hen house	qan el ferāχ (m)	قن الفراخ

213. Dogs. Dog breeds

dog	kalb (m)	كلب
sheepdog	kalb rā'y (m)	كلب رعي
German shepherd	kalb rā'y almāny (m)	كلب راعي ألمانيَ
poodle	būdle (m)	بودل
dachshund	daʃhund (m)	داشهند
bulldog	bulldog (m)	بولدوج
boxer	bokser (m)	بوكسر
mastiff	mastiff (m)	ماستيف
Rottweiler	rottfeyler (m)	روت فايلر
Doberman	doberman (m)	دوبرمان
basset	basset (m)	باسيت
bobtail	bobtayl (m)	بوبتيل
Dalmatian	delmāṭy (m)	دلماطي
cocker spaniel	kokker spaniel (m)	كوكر سبانييل
Newfoundland	nyu faundland (m)	نيوفاوندلاند
Saint Bernard	sant bernard (m)	سانت بيرنارد
husky	hasky (m)	هاسكي
Chow Chow	tʃaw tʃaw (m)	تشاوتشاو
spitz	esbitz (m)	إسبتز
pug	bug (m)	بج

214. Sounds made by animals

barking (n)	nebāḥ (m)	نباح
to bark (vi)	nabaḥ	نبِح
to meow (vi)	mawmaw	موْمَو
to purr (vi)	χarχar	خرخر
to moo (vi)	χār	خار
to bellow (bull)	χār	خار
to growl (vi)	damdam	دمدم
howl (n)	'awā' (m)	عواء
to howl (vi)	'awa	عوى
to whine (vi)	ann	أنّ
to bleat (sheep)	ma'ma'	مأمأ
to oink, to grunt (pig)	qaba'	قبع
to squeal (vi)	qaba'	قبع
to croak (vi)	na''	نقّ
to buzz (insect)	ṭann	طنّ
to chirp (crickets, grasshopper)	'ar'ar	عرعر

215. Young animals

cub	ḥayawān ṣaɣīr (m)	حيوان صغير
kitten	'oṭṭa saɣīra (f)	قطّة صغيرة
baby mouse	fār ṣaɣīr (m)	فار صغير
puppy	garww (m)	جرو
leveret	χarna' (m)	خرنق
baby rabbit	arnab saɣīr (m)	أرنب صغير
wolf cub	garmūza (m)	جرموزا
fox cub	hagras (m)	هجرس
bear cub	daysam (m)	ديسم
lion cub	ʃebl el asad (m)	شبل الأسد
tiger cub	farz (m)	فرز
elephant calf	daɣfal (m)	دغفل
piglet	χannūṣ (m)	خنّوص
calf (young cow, bull)	'egl (m)	عجل
kid (young goat)	gady (m)	جدي
lamb	ḥaml (m)	حمل
fawn (young deer)	el raʃa (m)	الرشا
young camel	ṣaɣīr el gamal (m)	صغير الجمل
snakelet (baby snake)	ḥerbeʃ (m)	حربش
froglet (baby frog)	ḍeffḍa' saɣīr (m)	ضفدع صغير
baby bird	farχ (m)	فرخ
chick (of chicken)	katkūt (m)	كتكوت
duckling	baṭṭa ṣaɣīra (f)	بطّة صغيرة

216. Birds

bird	ṭā'er (m)	طائر
pigeon	ḥamāma (f)	حمامة
sparrow	'aṣfūr dawri (m)	عصفور دوري
tit (great tit)	qarqaf (m)	قرقف
magpie	'a''a' (m)	عقعق
raven	ɣorāb aswad (m)	غراب أسود
crow	ɣorāb (m)	غراب
jackdaw	zāɣ zar'y (m)	زاغ زرعي
rook	ɣorāb el qeyẓ (m)	غراب القيظ
duck	baṭṭa (f)	بطّة
goose	wezza (f)	وزّة
pheasant	tadarrog (m)	تدرج
eagle	'eqāb (m)	عقاب
hawk	el bāz (m)	الباز

falcon	ṣa’r (m)	صقر
vulture	nesr (m)	نسر
condor (Andean ~)	kondor (m)	كندور
swan	el temm (m)	التَم
crane	karkiya (m)	كركية
stork	loqloq (m)	لقلق
parrot	babaɣā’ (m)	ببغاء
hummingbird	ṭannān (m)	طنّان
peacock	ṭawūs (m)	طاووس
ostrich	na‘āma (f)	نعامة
heron	belʃone (m)	بلشون
flamingo	flamingo (m)	فلامينجو
pelican	bag‘a (f)	بجعة
nightingale	‘andalīb (m)	عندليب
swallow	el sonūnū (m)	السنونو
thrush	somnet el ḥoqūl (m)	سمنة الحقول
song thrush	somna moɣarreda (m)	سمنة مغرِدة
blackbird	ʃaḥrūr aswad (m)	شحرور أسود
swift	semmāma (m)	سمّامة
lark	qabra (f)	قبرة
quail	semmān (m)	سمّان
woodpecker	na’ār el χaʃab (m)	نقار الخشب
cuckoo	weqwāq (m)	وقواق
owl	būma (f)	بومة
eagle owl	būm orāsy (m)	بوم أوراسي
wood grouse	dīk el χalang (m)	ديك الخلنج
black grouse	ṭyhūg aswad (m)	طيهوج أسود
partridge	el ḥagal (m)	الحجل
starling	zerzūr (m)	زرزور
canary	kanāry (m)	كناري
hazel grouse	ṭyhūg el bondo’ (m)	طيهوج البندق
chaffinch	ʃarʃūr (m)	شرشور
bullfinch	deɣnāʃ (m)	دغناش
seagull	nawras (m)	نورس
albatross	el qoṭros (m)	القطرس
penguin	beṭrīq (m)	بطريق

217. Birds. Singing and sounds

to sing (vi)	ɣanna	غنّى
to call (animal, bird)	nāda	نادى

to crow (rooster)	ṣāḥ	صاح
cock-a-doodle-doo	kokokūko	كوكوكوكو
to cluck (hen)	kāky	كاكي
to caw (vi)	na'aq	نعق
to quack (duck)	baṭbaṭ	بطبط
to cheep (vi)	ṣawṣaw	صوّصو
to chirp, to twitter	za'za'	زقزق

218. Fish. Marine animals

bream	abramīs (m)	أبراميس
carp	ʃabbūṭ (m)	شبّوط
perch	farχ (m)	فرخ
catfish	'armūṭ (m)	قرموط
pike	karāky (m)	كراكي
salmon	salamon (m)	سلمون
sturgeon	ḥafʃ (m)	حفش
herring	renga (f)	رنجة
Atlantic salmon	salamon aṭlasy (m)	سلمون أطلسي
mackerel	makerel (m)	ماكريل
flatfish	samak mefalṭah (f)	سمك مفلطح
zander, pike perch	samak sandar (m)	سمك سندر
cod	el qadd (m)	القد
tuna	tuna (f)	تونة
trout	salamon mera''aṭ (m)	سلمون مرقّط
eel	ḥankalīs (m)	حنكليس
electric ray	ra'ād (m)	رعاد
moray eel	moraya (f)	موراية
piranha	bīrana (f)	بيرانا
shark	'erʃ (m)	قرش
dolphin	dolfīn (m)	دولفين
whale	ḥūt (m)	حوت
crab	kaboria (m)	كابوريا
jellyfish	'andīl el baḥr (m)	قنديل البحر
octopus	aχṭabūṭ (m)	أخطبوط
starfish	negmet el baḥr (f)	نجمة البحر
sea urchin	qonfoz el baḥr (m)	قنفذ البحر
seahorse	ḥoṣān el baḥr (m)	حصان البحر
oyster	maḥār (m)	محار
shrimp	gammbary (m)	جمّبري
lobster	estakoza (f)	استكوزا
spiny lobster	estakoza (m)	استاكوزا

219. Amphibians. Reptiles

snake	teʿbān (m)	ثعبان
venomous (snake)	sām	سام
viper	afʿa (f)	أفعى
cobra	kobra (m)	كوبرا
python	teʿbān byton (m)	ثعبان بايثون
boa	bawāʾ el ʿaṣera (f)	بواء العاصرة
grass snake	teʿbān el ʿoʃb (m)	ثعبان العشب
rattle snake	afʿa megalgela (f)	أفعى مجلجلة
anaconda	anakonda (f)	أناكوندا
lizard	seḥliya (f)	سحليّة
iguana	eɣwana (f)	إغوانة
monitor lizard	warl (m)	ورل
salamander	salamander (m)	سلمندر
chameleon	ḥerbāya (f)	حرباية
scorpion	ʿaʾrab (m)	عقرب
turtle	solḥefah (f)	سلحفاة
frog	ḍeffḍaʿ (m)	ضفدع
toad	ḍeffḍaʿ el ṭeyn (m)	ضفدع الطين
crocodile	temsāḥ (m)	تمساح

220. Insects

insect, bug	ḥaʃara (f)	حشرة
butterfly	farāʃa (f)	فراشة
ant	namla (f)	نملة
fly	debbāna (f)	دبّانة
mosquito	namūsa (f)	ناموسة
beetle	χonfesa (f)	خنفسة
wasp	dabbūr (m)	دبّور
bee	naḥla (f)	نحلة
bumblebee	naḥla ṭannāna (f)	نحلة طنّانة
gadfly (botfly)	naʿra (f)	نعرة
spider	ʿankabūt (m)	عنكبوت
spiderweb	nasīg ʿankabūt (m)	نسيج عنكبوت
dragonfly	yaʿsūb (m)	يعسوب
grasshopper	garād (m)	جراد
moth (night butterfly)	ʿetta (f)	عثّة
cockroach	ṣarṣūr (m)	صرصور
tick	qarāda (f)	قرادة

flea	barɣūt (m)	برغوث
midge	ba'ūḍa (f)	بعوضة
locust	garād (m)	جراد
snail	ḥalazōn (m)	حلزون
cricket	ṣarṣūr el ḥaql (m)	صرصور الحقل
lightning bug	yarā'a (f)	يراعة
ladybug	χonfesa mena'ṭṭa (f)	خنفسة منقّطة
cockchafer	χonfesa motlefa lel nabāt (f)	خنفسة متّلفة للنبات
leech	'alaqa (f)	علقة
caterpillar	yasrū' (m)	يسروع
earthworm	dūda (f)	دودة
larva	yaraqa (f)	يرقة

221. Animals. Body parts

beak	monqār (m)	منقار
wings	agneḥa (pl)	أجنحة
foot (of bird)	regl (f)	رجل
feathers (plumage)	rīʃ (m)	ريش
feather	rīʃa (f)	ريشة
crest	'orf el dīk (m)	عرف الديك
gills	χāyaʃīm (pl)	خياشيم
spawn	beyḍ el samak (pl)	بيض السمك
larva	yaraqa (f)	يرقة
fin	za'nafa (f)	زعنفة
scales (of fish, reptile)	ḥarāfeʃ (pl)	حرافش
fang (canine)	nāb (m)	ناب
paw (e.g., cat's ~)	yad (f)	يد
muzzle (snout)	χaṭm (m)	خطم
mouth (of cat, dog)	bo' (m)	بوء
tail	deyl (m)	ذيل
whiskers	ʃawāreb (pl)	شوارب
hoof	ḥāfer (m)	حافر
horn	'arn (m)	قرن
carapace	der' (m)	درع
shell (of mollusk)	maḥāra (f)	محارة
eggshell	'eʃret beyḍa (f)	قشرة بيضة
animal's hair (pelage)	ʃa'r (m)	شعر
pelt (hide)	geld (m)	جلد

222. Actions of animals

to fly (vi)	ṭār	طار
to fly in circles	ḥallaq	حلّق
to fly away	ṭār	طار
to flap (~ the wings)	rafraf	رفرف
to peck (vi)	na'ar	نقر
to sit on eggs	'a'ad 'alal beyḍ	قعد على البيض
to hatch out (vi)	fa'as	فقس
to build a nest	bana 'esʃa	بنى عشّة
to slither, to crawl	zaḥaf	زحف
to sting, to bite (insect)	lasa'	لسع
to bite (ab. animal)	'aḍḍ	عضّ
to sniff (vt)	taʃammam	تشمّم
to bark (vi)	nabaḥ	نبح
to hiss (snake)	has-hes	هسهس
to scare (vt)	χawwef	خوّف
to attack (vt)	hagam	هجم
to gnaw (bone, etc.)	'araḍ	قرض
to scratch (with claws)	χarbeʃ	خربش
to hide (vi)	estaχabba	إستخبّى
to play (kittens, etc.)	le'eb	لعب
to hunt (vi, vt)	eṣṭād	إصطاد
to hibernate (vi)	kān di sobār el ʃetā'	كان في سبات الشتاء
to go extinct	enqaraḍ	إنقرض

223. Animals. Habitats

habitat	mawṭen (m)	موّطن
migration	hegra (f)	هجرة
mountain	gabal (m)	جبل
reef	ʃo'āb (pl)	شعاب
cliff	garf (m)	جرف
forest	ɣāba (f)	غابة
jungle	adɣāl (pl)	أدغال
savanna	savanna (f)	سافانّا
tundra	tundra (f)	تندرا
steppe	barāry (pl)	براري
desert	ṣaḥra' (f)	صحراء
oasis	wāḥa (f)	واحة
sea	baḥr (m)	بحر

lake	boḥeyra (f)	بحيرة
ocean	moḥīṭ (m)	محيط
swamp (marshland)	mostanqa' (m)	مستنقع
freshwater (adj)	maya 'azba	ميّة عذبة
pond	berka (f)	بركة
river	nahr (m)	نهر
den (bear's ~)	wekr (m)	وكر
nest	'eʃ (m)	عشّ
hollow (in a tree)	gofe (m)	جوف
burrow (animal hole)	goḥr (m)	جحر
anthill	'eʃ naml (m)	عش نمل

224. Animal care

zoo	ḥadīqet el ḥayawān (f)	حديقة حيوان
nature preserve	maḥmiya ṭabe'iya (f)	محمية طبيعية
breeder (cattery, kennel, etc.)	morabby (m)	مربّي
open-air cage	'afaṣ fel hawā' el ṭal' (m)	قفص في الهواء الطلق
cage	'afaṣ (m)	قفص
doghouse (kennel)	beyt el kalb (m)	بيت الكلب
dovecot	borg el ḥamām (m)	برج الحمام
aquarium (fish tank)	ḥoḍe samak (m)	حوض سمك
dolphinarium	ḥoḍe dolfīn (m)	حوض دولفين
to breed (animals)	rabba	ربّي
brood, litter	zorriya (f)	ذريّة
to tame (vt)	rawweḍ	روّض
to train (animals)	darrab	درّب
feed (fodder, etc.)	'alaf (m)	علف
to feed (vt)	akkel	أكّل
pet store	maḥal ḥayawanāt (m)	محل حيوانات
muzzle (for dog)	kamāma (f)	كمامة
collar (e.g., dog ~)	ṭo'e (m)	طوق
name (of animal)	esm (m)	اسم
pedigree (of dog)	selselet el nasab (f)	سلسلة النسب

225. Animals. Miscellaneous

pack (wolves)	qaṭee' (m)	قطيع
flock (birds)	serb (m)	سرب
shoal, school (fish)	serb (m)	سرب
herd (horses)	qaṭee' (m)	قطيع

male (n)	dakar (m)	ذكر
female (n)	onsa (f)	أنثى
hungry (adj)	ge'ān	جعان
wild (adj)	barry	برّي
dangerous (adj)	χaṭīr	خطير

226. Horses

horse	ḥoṣān (m)	حصان
breed (race)	solāla (f)	سلالة
foal	mahr (m)	مهر
mare	faras (f)	فرس
mustang	mustān (m)	موستان
pony	ḥoṣān qazam (m)	حصان قزم
draft horse	ḥoṣān el na'l (m)	حصان النقل
mane	'orf (m)	عرف
tail	deyl (m)	ذيل
hoof	ḥāfer (m)	حافر
horseshoe	na'l (m)	نعل
to shoe (vt)	na''al	نعّل
blacksmith	ḥaddād (m)	حدّاد
saddle	serg (m)	سرج
stirrup	rekāb (m)	ركاب
bridle	legām (m)	لجام
reins	'anān (m)	عنان
whip (for riding)	korbāg (m)	كرباج
rider	fāres (m)	فارس
to saddle up (vt)	asrag	أسرج
to mount a horse	rekeb ḥoṣān	ركب حصان
gallop	ramāḥa (f)	رماحة
to gallop (vi)	gery bel ḥoṣān	جري بالحصان
trot (n)	harwala (f)	هروَلة
at a trot (adv)	harwel	هروَل
to go at a trot	harwel	هروَل
racehorse	ḥoṣān sebā' (m)	حصان سباق
horse racing	sebā' el χeyl (m)	سباق الخيل
stable	esṭabl χeyl (m)	إسطبل خيل
to feed (vt)	akkel	أكّل
hay	'asʃ (m)	قشّ
to water (animals)	sa'a	سقى

to wash (horse)	naḍḍaf	نظّف
horse-drawn cart	'arabet χayl (f)	عربة خيل
to graze (vi)	erta'a	إرتعى
to neigh (vi)	ṣahal	صهل
to kick (about horse)	rafas	رفس

Flora

227. Trees

tree	ʃagara (f)	شجرة
deciduous (adj)	nafḍiya	نفضيّة
coniferous (adj)	ṣonoberiya	صنوبرية
evergreen (adj)	dā'emet el χoḍra	دائمة الخضرة
apple tree	ʃagaret toffāḥ (f)	شجرة تفّاح
pear tree	ʃagaret komettra (f)	شجرة كمثّرى
cherry tree	ʃagaret karaz (f)	شجرة كرز
plum tree	ʃagaret bar'ū' (f)	شجرة برقوق
birch	batola (f)	بتولا
oak	ballūṭ (f)	بلّوط
linden tree	zayzafūn (f)	زيزفون
aspen	ḥūr rāgef	حور راجف
maple	qayqab (f)	قيقب
spruce	rateng (f)	راتينج
pine	ṣonober (f)	صنوبر
larch	arziya (f)	أرزية
fir tree	tanūb (f)	تنوب
cedar	el orz (f)	الأرز
poplar	ḥūr (f)	حور
rowan	ɣobayrā' (f)	غبيراء
willow	ṣefsāf (f)	صفصاف
alder	gār el mā' (m)	جار الماء
beech	el zān (f)	الزان
elm	derdar (f)	دردار
ash (tree)	marān (f)	مران
chestnut	kastanā' (f)	كستناء
magnolia	maɣnolia (f)	ماغنوليا
palm tree	naχla (f)	نخلة
cypress	el soro (f)	السرو
mangrove	mangrūf (f)	مانجروف
baobab	baobab (f)	باوباب
eucalyptus	eukalyptus (f)	أوكالبتوس
sequoia	sequoia (f)	سيكويا

228. Shrubs

bush	ʃogeyra (f)	شجيرة
shrub	ʃogayrāt (pl)	شجيرات
grapevine	karma (f)	كرمة
vineyard	karam (m)	كرم
raspberry bush	zar'et tūt el 'alī' el aḥmar (f)	زرعة توت العليق الأحمر
redcurrant bush	keʃmeʃ aḥmar (m)	كشمش أحمر
gooseberry bush	'enab el sa'lab (m)	عنب الثعلب
acacia	aqaqia (f)	أقاقيا
barberry	berbarīs (m)	برباريس
jasmine	yasmīn (m)	ياسمين
juniper	'ar'ar (m)	عرعر
rosebush	ʃogeyret ward (f)	شجيرة ورد
dog rose	ward el seyāg (pl)	ورد السياج

229. Mushrooms

mushroom	feṭr (f)	فطر
edible mushroom	feṭr ṣāleḥ lel akl (m)	فطر صالح للأكل
poisonous mushroom	feṭr sām (m)	فطر سام
cap (of mushroom)	ṭarbūʃ el feṭr (m)	طربوش الفطر
stipe (of mushroom)	sāq el feṭr (m)	ساق الفطر
cep (Boletus edulis)	feṭr boleṭe ma'kūl (m)	فطر بوليط مأكول
orange-cap boletus	feṭr aḥmar (m)	فطر أحمر
birch bolete	feṭr boleṭe (m)	فطر بوليط
chanterelle	feṭr el ʃanterel (m)	فطر الشانتريل
russula	feṭr russula (m)	فطر روسولا
morel	feṭr el ɣoʃna (m)	فطر الغوشنة
fly agaric	feṭr amanīt el ṭā'er (m)	فطر أمانيت الطائر
death cap	feṭr amanīt falusyāny el sām (m)	فطر أمانيت فالوسياني السام

230. Fruits. Berries

fruit	tamra (f)	تمرة
fruits	tamr (m)	تمر
apple	toffāḥa (f)	تفّاحة
pear	komettra (f)	كمّثرى
plum	bar'ū' (m)	برقوق
strawberry (garden ~)	farawla (f)	فراولة

cherry	karaz (m)	كرز
grape	'enab (m)	عنب
raspberry	tūt el 'alī' el aḥmar (m)	توت العليق الأحمر
blackcurrant	keʃmeʃ aswad (m)	كشمش أسود
redcurrant	keʃmeʃ aḥmar (m)	كشمش أحمر
gooseberry	'enab el sa'lab (m)	عنب الثعلب
cranberry	'enabiya ḥāda el χebā' (m)	عنبية حادة الخباء
orange	bortoqāl (m)	برتقال
mandarin	yosfy (m)	يوسفي
pineapple	ananās (m)	أناناس
banana	moze (m)	موز
date	tamr (m)	تمر
lemon	lymūn (m)	ليمون
apricot	meʃmeʃ (f)	مشمش
peach	χawχa (f)	خوخة
kiwi	kiwi (m)	كيوي
grapefruit	grabe frūt (m)	جريب فروت
berry	tūt (m)	توت
berries	tūt (pl)	توت
cowberry	'enab el sore (m)	عنب الثور
wild strawberry	farawla barriya (f)	فراولة برّيّة
bilberry	'enab al aḥrāg (m)	عنب الأحراج

231. Flowers. Plants

flower	zahra (f)	زهرة
bouquet (of flowers)	bokeyh (f)	بوكيه
rose (flower)	warda (f)	وردة
tulip	tolīb (f)	توليب
carnation	'oronfol (m)	قرنفل
gladiolus	el dalbūs (f)	الدَلْبُوث
cornflower	qanṭeryūn 'anbary (m)	قنطريون عنبري
harebell	garīs mostadīr el awrā' (m)	جريس مستدير الأوراق
dandelion	handabā' (f)	هندباء
camomile	kamomile (f)	كاموميل
aloe	el alowa (m)	الألوّة
cactus	ṣabbār (m)	صبّار
rubber plant, ficus	faykas (m)	فيكس
lily	zanbaq (f)	زنبق
geranium	ɣarnūqy (f)	غرنوقي
hyacinth	el lavender (f)	اللافندر
mimosa	mimoza (f)	ميموزا

narcissus	nerges (f)	نرجس
nasturtium	abo χangar (f)	أبو خنجر
orchid	orkid (f)	أوركيد
peony	fawnia (f)	فاوانيا
violet	el banafseg (f)	البنفسج
pansy	bansy (f)	بانسي
forget-me-not	'āzān el fa'r (pl)	آذان الفأر
daisy	aqwaḥān (f)	أقحوان
poppy	el χoʃχāʃ (f)	الخشخاش
hemp	qanb (m)	قنب
mint	ne'nā' (m)	نعناع
lily of the valley	zanbaq el wādy (f)	زنبق الوادي
snowdrop	zahrat el laban (f)	زهرة اللبن
nettle	'arrāṣ (m)	قرّاص
sorrel	ḥammāḍ bostāny (m)	حمّاض بستاني
water lily	niloferiya (f)	نيلوفرية
fern	sarχas (m)	سرخس
lichen	aʃna (f)	أشنة
greenhouse (tropical ~)	ṣoba (f)	صوبة
lawn	'oʃb aχḍar (m)	عشب أخضر
flowerbed	geneynet zohūr (f)	جنينة زهور
plant	nabāt (m)	نبات
grass	'oʃb (m)	عشب
blade of grass	'oʃba (f)	عشبة
leaf	wara'a (f)	ورقة
petal	wara'et el zahra (f)	ورقة الزهرة
stem	sāq (f)	ساق
tuber	darna (f)	درنة
young plant (shoot)	nabta saɣīra (f)	نبتة صغيرة
thorn	ʃawka (f)	شوكة
to blossom (vi)	fattaḥet	فتّحت
to fade, to wither	debel	ذبل
smell (odor)	rīḥa (f)	ريحة
to cut (flowers)	'aṭa'	قطع
to pick (a flower)	'aṭaf	قطف

232. Cereals, grains

grain	ḥobūb (pl)	حبوب
cereal crops	maḥaṣīl el ḥubūb (pl)	محاصيل الحبوب

ear (of barley, etc.)	sonbola (f)	سنبلة
wheat	'amḥ (m)	قمح
rye	ʃelm mazrūʿ (m)	شيلم مزروع
oats	ʃofān (m)	شوفان
millet	el deχn (m)	الدخن
barley	ʃeʿīr (m)	شعير
corn	dora (f)	ذرة
rice	rozz (m)	رز
buckwheat	ḥanṭa soda' (f)	حنطة سوداء
pea plant	besella (f)	بسلّة
kidney bean	faṣolya (f)	فاصوليا
soy	fūl el ṣoya (m)	فول الصويا
lentil	ʿads (m)	عدس
beans (pulse crops)	fūl (m)	فول

233. Vegetables. Greens

vegetables	χoḍār (pl)	خضار
greens	χoḍrawāt waraqiya (pl)	خضروات ورقية
tomato	ṭamāṭem (f)	طماطم
cucumber	χeyār (m)	خيار
carrot	gazar (m)	جزر
potato	baṭāṭes (f)	بطاطس
onion	baṣal (m)	بصل
garlic	tūm (m)	ثوم
cabbage	koronb (m)	كرنب
cauliflower	'arnabīṭ (m)	قرنبيط
Brussels sprouts	koronb broksel (m)	كرنب بروكسل
broccoli	brūkuli (m)	بروكلي
beetroot	bangar (m)	بنجر
eggplant	bātengān (m)	باذنجان
zucchini	kōsa (f)	كوسة
pumpkin	qarʿ ʿasaly (m)	قرع عسلي
turnip	left (m)	لفت
parsley	ba'dūnes (m)	بقدونس
dill	ʃabat (m)	شبت
lettuce	χass (m)	خسّ
celery	karfas (m)	كرفس
asparagus	helione (m)	هليون
spinach	sabāneχ (m)	سبانخ
pea	besella (f)	بسلّة
beans	fūl (m)	فول
corn (maize)	dora (f)	ذرة

kidney bean	faṣolya (f)	فاصوليا
pepper	felfel (m)	فلفل
radish	fegl (m)	فجل
artichoke	χarʃūf (m)	خرشوف

REGIONAL GEOGRAPHY

Countries. Nationalities

234. Western Europe

Europe	orobba (f)	أوروبا
European Union	el etteḥād el orobby (m)	الإتّحاد الأوروبّي
European (n)	orobby (m)	أوروبّي
European (adj)	orobby	أوروبّي
Austria	el nemsa (f)	النمسا
Austrian (masc.)	nemsāwy (m)	نمساوي
Austrian (fem.)	nemsāwiya (f)	نمساويّة
Austrian (adj)	nemsāwy	نمساوي
Great Britain	briṭaniya el 'ozma (f)	بريطانيا العظمى
England	engeltera (f)	إنجلّترا
British (masc.)	briṭāny (m)	بريطاني
British (fem.)	briṭaniya (f)	بريطانيّة
English, British (adj)	englīzy	إنجليزي
Belgium	balʒīka (f)	بلجيكا
Belgian (masc.)	balʒīky (m)	بلجيكي
Belgian (fem.)	balʒīkiya (f)	بلجيكيّة
Belgian (adj)	balʒīky	بلجيكي
Germany	almānya (f)	ألمانيا
German (masc.)	almāny (m)	ألماني
German (fem.)	almaniya (f)	ألمانيّة
German (adj)	almāniya	ألمانية
Netherlands	holanda (f)	هولندا
Holland	holanda (f)	هولندا
Dutch (masc.)	holandy (m)	هولندي
Dutch (fem.)	holandiya (f)	هولنديّة
Dutch (adj)	holandy	هولندي
Greece	el yunān (f)	اليونان
Greek (masc.)	yunāny (m)	يوناني
Greek (fem.)	yunaniya (f)	يونانيّة
Greek (adj)	yunāny	يوناني
Denmark	el denmark (f)	الدنمارك
Dane (masc.)	denmarky (m)	دنماركي

Dane (fem.)	denmarkiya (f)	دانماركيّة
Danish (adj)	denemarky	دانماركي
Ireland	irelanda (f)	أيرلندا
Irish (masc.)	irelandy (m)	أيرلندي
Irish (fem.)	irelandiya (f)	أيرلنديّة
Irish (adj)	irelandy	أيرلندي
Iceland	'āyslanda (f)	آيسلندا
Icelander (masc.)	'āyslandy (m)	آيسلندي
Icelander (fem.)	'āyslandiya (f)	آيسلنديّة
Icelandic (adj)	'āyslandy	آيسلندي
Spain	asbānya (f)	إسبانيا
Spaniard (masc.)	asbāny (m)	إسباني
Spaniard (fem.)	asbaniya (f)	إسبانية
Spanish (adj)	asbāny	إسباني
Italy	eṭālia (f)	إيطاليا
Italian (masc.)	eṭāly (m)	إيطالي
Italian (fem.)	eṭaliya (f)	إيطالية
Italian (adj)	eṭāly	إيطالي
Cyprus	'obroṣ (f)	قبرص
Cypriot (masc.)	'obroṣy (m)	قبرصي
Cypriot (fem.)	'obroṣiya (f)	قبرصية
Cypriot (adj)	'obroṣy	قبرصي
Malta	malṭa (f)	مالطا
Maltese (masc.)	malṭy (m)	مالطي
Maltese (fem.)	malṭiya (f)	مالطيّة
Maltese (adj)	malṭy	مالطي
Norway	el nerwīg (f)	النرويج
Norwegian (masc.)	nerwīgy (m)	نرويجي
Norwegian (fem.)	nerwīgiya (f)	نرويجية
Norwegian (adj)	nerwīgy	نرويجي
Portugal	el bortoɣāl (f)	البرتغال
Portuguese (masc.)	bortoɣāly (m)	برتغالي
Portuguese (fem.)	bortoɣaliya (f)	برتغاليّة
Portuguese (adj)	bortoɣāly	برتغالي
Finland	finlanda (f)	فنلّندا
Finn (masc.)	finlandy (m)	فنلّندي
Finn (fem.)	finlandiya (f)	فنلّنديّة
Finnish (adj)	finlandy	فنلّندي
France	faransa (f)	فرنسا
French (masc.)	faransāwy (m)	فرنساوي
French (fem.)	faransawiya (f)	فرنساويّة
French (adj)	faransāwy	فرنساوي

Sweden	el sweyd (f)	السويد
Swede (masc.)	sweydy (m)	سويدي
Swede (fem.)	sweydiya (f)	سويدية
Swedish (adj)	sweydy	سويدي
Switzerland	swesra (f)	سويسرا
Swiss (masc.)	swesry (m)	سويسري
Swiss (fem.)	swesriya (f)	سويسرية
Swiss (adj)	swesry	سويسري
Scotland	oskotlanda (f)	اسكتلندا
Scottish (masc.)	oskotlandy (m)	اسكتلندي
Scottish (fem.)	oskotlandiya (f)	اسكتلندية
Scottish (adj)	oskotlandy	اسكتلندي
Vatican	el vatikān (m)	الفاتيكان
Liechtenstein	liʃtenʃtayn (m)	ليشتنشتاين
Luxembourg	luksemburg (f)	لوكسمبورج
Monaco	monako (f)	موناكو

235. Central and Eastern Europe

Albania	albānia (f)	ألبانيا
Albanian (masc.)	albāny (m)	ألباني
Albanian (fem.)	albaniya (f)	ألبانية
Albanian (adj)	albāny	ألباني
Bulgaria	bolɣāria (f)	بلغاريا
Bulgarian (masc.)	bolɣāry (m)	بلغاري
Bulgarian (fem.)	bolɣariya (f)	بلغارية
Bulgarian (adj)	bolɣāry	بلغاري
Hungary	el magar (f)	المجر
Hungarian (masc.)	magary (m)	مجري
Hungarian (fem.)	magariya (f)	مجرية
Hungarian (adj)	magary	مجري
Latvia	latvia (f)	لاتفيا
Latvian (masc.)	latvy (m)	لاتفي
Latvian (fem.)	latviya (f)	لاتفية
Latvian (adj)	latvy	لاتفي
Lithuania	litwānia (f)	ليتوانيا
Lithuanian (masc.)	litwāny (m)	لتواني
Lithuanian (fem.)	litwaniya (f)	لتوانية
Lithuanian (adj)	litwāny	لتواني
Poland	bolanda (f)	بولندا
Pole (masc.)	bolandy (m)	بولندي
Pole (fem.)	bolandiya (f)	بولندية

Polish (adj)	bolanndy	بولنّدي
Romania	romānia (f)	رومانيا
Romanian (masc.)	romāny (m)	روماني
Romanian (fem.)	romaniya (f)	رومانية
Romanian (adj)	romāny	روماني
Serbia	ṣerbia (f)	صربيا
Serbian (masc.)	ṣerby (m)	صربي
Serbian (fem.)	ṣerbiya (f)	صربية
Serbian (adj)	ṣarby	صربي
Slovakia	slovākia (f)	سلوفاكيا
Slovak (masc.)	slovāky (m)	سلوفاكي
Slovak (fem.)	slovakiya (f)	سلوفاكية
Slovak (adj)	slovāky	سلوفاكي
Croatia	kroātya (f)	كرواتيا
Croatian (masc.)	kroāty (m)	كرواتي
Croatian (fem.)	kroatiya (f)	كرواتية
Croatian (adj)	kroāty	كرواتي
Czech Republic	gomhoriya el tʃīk (f)	جمهورية التشيك
Czech (masc.)	tʃīky (m)	تشيكي
Czech (fem.)	tʃīkiya (f)	تشيكية
Czech (adj)	tʃīky	تشيكي
Estonia	estūnia (f)	إستونيا
Estonian (masc.)	estūny (m)	إستوني
Estonian (fem.)	estuniya (f)	إستونية
Estonian (adj)	estūny	إستوني
Bosnia and Herzegovina	el bosna wel harsek (f)	البوسنة والهرسك
Macedonia (Republic of ~)	maqdūnia (f)	مقدونيا
Slovenia	slovenia (f)	سلوفينيا
Montenegro	el gabal el aswad (m)	الجبل الأسوّد

236. Former USSR countries

Azerbaijan	azrabiʒān (m)	أذربيجان
Azerbaijani (masc.)	azrabiʒāny (m)	أذربيجاني
Azerbaijani (fem.)	azrabiʒaniya (f)	أذربيجانية
Azerbaijani, Azeri (adj)	azrabiʒāny	أذربيجاني
Armenia	armīnia (f)	أرمينيا
Armenian (masc.)	armīny (m)	أرميني
Armenian (fem.)	arminiya (f)	أرمينية
Armenian (adj)	armīny	أرميني
Belarus	belarūsia (f)	بيلاروسيا
Belarusian (masc.)	belarūsy (m)	بيلاروسي

Belarusian (fem.)	belarūsiya (f)	بيلاروسيّة
Belarusian (adj)	belarūsy	بيلاروسي
Georgia	ʒorʒia (f)	جورجيا
Georgian (masc.)	ʒorʒy (m)	جورجي
Georgian (fem.)	ʒorʒiya (f)	جورجية
Georgian (adj)	ʒorʒy	جورجي
Kazakhstan	kazaχistān (f)	كازاخستان
Kazakh (masc.)	kazaχistāny (m)	كازاخستاني
Kazakh (fem.)	kazaχistaniya (f)	كازاخستانية
Kazakh (adj)	kazaχistāny	كازاخستاني
Kirghizia	qirɣizestān (f)	قيرغيزستان
Kirghiz (masc.)	qirɣizestāny (m)	قيرغيزستاني
Kirghiz (fem.)	qirɣizestaniya (f)	قيرغيزستانية
Kirghiz (adj)	qirɣizestāny	قيرغيزستاني
Moldova, Moldavia	moldāvia (f)	مولدافيا
Moldavian (masc.)	moldāvy (m)	مولدافي
Moldavian (fem.)	moldaviya (f)	مولدافية
Moldavian (adj)	moldāvy	مولدافي
Russia	rūsya (f)	روسيا
Russian (masc.)	rūsy (m)	روسي
Russian (fem.)	rusiya (f)	روسية
Russian (adj)	rūsy	روسي
Tajikistan	ṭaʒīkistan (f)	طاجيكستان
Tajik (masc.)	ṭaʒīky (m)	طاجيكي
Tajik (fem.)	ṭaʒikiya (f)	طاجيكية
Tajik (adj)	ṭaʒīky	طاجيكي
Turkmenistan	turkmānistān (f)	تركمانستان
Turkmen (masc.)	turkmāny (m)	تركماني
Turkmen (fem.)	turkmaniya (f)	تركمانية
Turkmenian (adj)	turkmāny	تركماني
Uzbekistan	uzbakistān (f)	أوزبكستان
Uzbek (masc.)	uzbaky (m)	أوزبكي
Uzbek (fem.)	uzbakiya (f)	أوزبكية
Uzbek (adj)	uzbaky	أوزبكي
Ukraine	okrānia (f)	أوكرانيا
Ukrainian (masc.)	okrāny (m)	أوكراني
Ukrainian (fem.)	okraniya (f)	أوكرانية
Ukrainian (adj)	okrāny	أوكراني

237. Asia

Asia	asya (f)	آسيا
Asian (adj)	ʾāsyawy	آسيوي

Vietnam	vietnām (f)	فيتنام
Vietnamese (masc.)	vietnāmy (m)	فيتنامي
Vietnamese (fem.)	vietnāmiya (f)	فيتناميّة
Vietnamese (adj)	vietnāmy	فيتنامي
India	el hend (f)	الهند
Indian (masc.)	hendy (m)	هندي
Indian (fem.)	hendiya (f)	هنديّة
Indian (adj)	hendy	هندي
Israel	isra'īl (f)	إسرائيل
Israeli (masc.)	isra'īly (m)	إسرائيلي
Israeli (fem.)	isra'iliya (f)	إسرائيليّة
Israeli (adj)	israīly	إسرائيلي
Jew (n)	yahūdy (m)	يهودي
Jewess (n)	yahudiya (f)	يهوديّة
Jewish (adj)	yahūdy	يهودي
China	el ṣīn (f)	الصين
Chinese (masc.)	ṣīny (m)	صيني
Chinese (fem.)	ṣīniya (f)	صينيّة
Chinese (adj)	ṣīny	صيني
Korean (masc.)	kūry (m)	كوري
Korean (fem.)	kuriya (f)	كوريّة
Korean (adj)	kūry	كوري
Lebanon	lebnān (f)	لبنان
Lebanese (masc.)	lebnāny (m)	لبناني
Lebanese (fem.)	lebnāniya (f)	لبنانيّة
Lebanese (adj)	lebnāny	لبناني
Mongolia	manɣūlia (f)	منغوليا
Mongolian (masc.)	manɣūly (m)	منغولي
Mongolian (fem.)	manɣuliya (f)	منغوليّة
Mongolian (adj)	manɣūly	منغولي
Malaysia	malīzya (f)	ماليزيا
Malaysian (masc.)	malīzy (m)	ماليزي
Malaysian (fem.)	maliziya (f)	ماليزيّة
Malaysian (adj)	malīzy	ماليزي
Pakistan	bakistān (f)	باكستان
Pakistani (masc.)	bakistāny (m)	باكستاني
Pakistani (fem.)	bakistaniya (f)	باكستانيّة
Pakistani (adj)	bakistāny	باكستاني
Saudi Arabia	el so'odiya (f)	السعوديّة
Arab (masc.)	'araby (m)	عربي
Arab (fem.)	'arabiya (f)	عربيّة
Arab, Arabic (adj)	'araby	عربي

Thailand	tayland (f)	تايلاند
Thai (masc.)	taylandy (m)	تايلاندي
Thai (fem.)	taylandiya (f)	تايلانديّة
Thai (adj)	taylandy	تايلاندي
Taiwan	taywān (f)	تايوان
Taiwanese (masc.)	taywāny (m)	تايواني
Taiwanese (fem.)	taywaniya (f)	تايوانية
Taiwanese (adj)	taywāny	تايواني
Turkey	turkia (f)	تركيا
Turk (masc.)	turky (m)	تركي
Turk (fem.)	turkiya (f)	تركيّة
Turkish (adj)	turky	تركي
Japan	el yabān (f)	اليابان
Japanese (masc.)	yabāny (m)	ياباني
Japanese (fem.)	yabaniya (f)	يابانيّة
Japanese (adj)	yabāny	ياباني
Afghanistan	afɣanistan (f)	أفغانستان
Bangladesh	bangladeʃ (f)	بنجلاديش
Indonesia	indonisya (f)	إندونيسيا
Jordan	el ordon (m)	الأردن
Iraq	el ʿerāq (m)	العراق
Iran	iran (f)	إيران
Cambodia	kambodya (f)	كمبوديا
Kuwait	el kuweyt (f)	الكويت
Laos	laos (f)	لاوس
Myanmar	myanmar (f)	ميانمار
Nepal	nebāl (f)	نيبال
United Arab Emirates	el emārāt el ʿarabiya el mottaḥeda (pl)	الإمارات العربية المتّحدة
Syria	soria (f)	سوريا
Palestine	felesṭīn (f)	فلسطين
South Korea	korea el ganūbiya (f)	كوريا الجنوبيّة
North Korea	korea el ʃamāliya (f)	كوريا الشماليّة

238. North America

United States of America	el welayāt el mottaḥda el amrīkiya (pl)	الولايات المتّحدة الأمريكيّة
American (masc.)	amrīky (m)	أمريكي
American (fem.)	amrīkiya (f)	أمريكيّة
American (adj)	amrīky	أمريكي
Canada	kanada (f)	كندا
Canadian (masc.)	kanady (m)	كندي

| Canadian (fem.) | kanadiya (f) | كنديّة |
| Canadian (adj) | kanady | كندي |

Mexico	el maksīk (f)	المكسيك
Mexican (masc.)	maksīky (m)	مكسيكي
Mexican (fem.)	maksīkiya (f)	مكسيكيّة
Mexican (adj)	maksīky	مكسيكي

239. Central and South America

Argentina	arʒantīn (f)	الأرجنتين
Argentinian (masc.)	arʒantīny (m)	أرجنتيني
Argentinian (fem.)	arʒantiniya (f)	أرجنتينيّة
Argentinian (adj)	arʒantīny	أرجنتيني

Brazil	el barazīl (f)	البرازيل
Brazilian (masc.)	barazīly (m)	برازيلي
Brazilian (fem.)	baraziliya (f)	برازيليّة
Brazilian (adj)	barazīly	برازيلي

Colombia	kolombia (f)	كولومبيا
Colombian (masc.)	kolomby (m)	كولومبي
Colombian (fem.)	kolombiya (f)	كولومبيّة
Colombian (adj)	kolomby	كولومبي

Cuba	kūba (f)	كوبا
Cuban (masc.)	kūby (m)	كوبي
Cuban (fem.)	kūbiya (f)	كوبيّة
Cuban (adj)	kūby	كوبي

Chile	tʃīly (f)	تشيلي
Chilean (masc.)	tʃīly (m)	تشيلي
Chilean (fem.)	tʃīliya (f)	تشيليّة
Chilean (adj)	tʃīly	تشيلي

| Bolivia | bolivia (f) | بوليفيا |
| Venezuela | venzweyla (f) | فنزويلا |

| Paraguay | baraguay (f) | باراجواي |
| Peru | beru (f) | بيرو |

Suriname	surinam (f)	سورينام
Uruguay	uruguay (f)	أوروجواي
Ecuador	el equador (f)	الإكوادور

The Bahamas	gozor el bahāmas (pl)	جزر البهاماس
Haiti	haïti (f)	هايتي
Dominican Republic	gomhoriya el dominikan (f)	جمهوريّة الدومينيكان
Panama	banama (f)	بنما
Jamaica	ʒamayka (f)	جامايكا

240. Africa

Egypt	maṣr (f)	مصر
Egyptian (masc.)	maṣry (m)	مصري
Egyptian (fem.)	maṣriya (f)	مصريّة
Egyptian (adj)	maṣry	مصري
Morocco	el maɣreb (m)	المغرب
Moroccan (masc.)	maɣreby (m)	مغربي
Moroccan (fem.)	maɣrebiya (f)	مغربية
Moroccan (adj)	maɣreby	مغربي
Tunisia	tunis (f)	تونس
Tunisian (masc.)	tunsy (m)	تونسي
Tunisian (fem.)	tunesiya (f)	تونسية
Tunisian (adj)	tunsy	تونسي
Ghana	ɣana (f)	غانا
Zanzibar	zanʒibār (f)	زنجبار
Kenya	kenya (f)	كينيا
Libya	libya (f)	ليبيا
Madagascar	madaɣaʃkar (f)	مدغشقر
Namibia	namibia (f)	ناميبيا
Senegal	el senɣāl (f)	السنغال
Tanzania	tanznia (f)	تنزانيا
South Africa	afreqia el ganūbiya (f)	أفريقيا الجنوبيّة
African (masc.)	afrīqy (m)	أفريقي
African (fem.)	afriqiya (f)	أفريقية
African (adj)	afrīqy	أفريقي

241. Australia. Oceania

Australia	ostorālya (f)	أستراليا
Australian (masc.)	ostorāly (m)	أسترالي
Australian (fem.)	ostoraleya (f)	أستراليّة
Australian (adj)	ostorāly	أسترالي
New Zealand	nyu zelanda (f)	نيوزيلندا
New Zealander (masc.)	nyu zelandy (m)	نيوزيلندي
New Zealander (fem.)	nyu zelandiya (f)	نيوزيلنديّة
New Zealand (as adj)	nyu zelandy	نيوزيلندي
Tasmania	tasmania (f)	تاسمانيا
French Polynesia	bolenezia el faransiya (f)	بولينزيا الفرنسيّة

242. Cities

Amsterdam	amesterdam (f)	امستردام
Ankara	ankara (f)	أنقرة
Athens	atīna (f)	أثينا
Baghdad	baɣdād (f)	بغداد
Bangkok	bangkok (f)	بانكوك
Barcelona	barʃelona (f)	برشلونة
Beijing	bekīn (f)	بيكين
Beirut	beyrut (f)	بيروت
Berlin	berlin (f)	برلين
Mumbai (Bombay)	bombay (f)	بومباى
Bonn	bonn (f)	بون
Bordeaux	bordu (f)	بوردو
Bratislava	bratislava (f)	براتيسلافا
Brussels	broksel (f)	بروكسل
Bucharest	buχarest (f)	بوخارست
Budapest	budabest (f)	بودابست
Cairo	el qahera (f)	القاهرة
Kolkata (Calcutta)	kalkutta (f)	كلكتا
Chicago	ʃikāgo (f)	شيكاجو
Copenhagen	kobenhāgen (f)	كوبنهاجن
Dar-es-Salaam	dar el salām (f)	دار السلام
Delhi	delhi (f)	دلهي
Dubai	dubaī (f)	دبي
Dublin	dablin (f)	دبلن
Düsseldorf	dusseldorf (f)	دوسلدورف
Florence	florensa (f)	فلورنسا
Frankfurt	frankfurt (f)	فرانكفورت
Geneva	ʒenive (f)	جنيف
The Hague	lahāy (f)	لاهاى
Hamburg	hamburg (m)	هامبورج
Hanoi	hanoy (f)	هانوى
Havana	havana (f)	هافانا
Helsinki	helsinki (f)	هلسنكي
Hiroshima	hiroʃīma (f)	هيروشيما
Hong Kong	hong kong (f)	هونج كونج
Istanbul	isṭanbul (f)	إسطنبول
Jerusalem	el qods (f)	القدس
Kyiv	kyiv (f)	كييف
Kuala Lumpur	kuala lumpur (f)	كوالالمبور
Lisbon	laʃbūna (f)	لشبونة
London	london (f)	لندن
Los Angeles	los anʒeles (f)	لوس أنجلوس

Lyons	lyon (f)	ليون
Madrid	madrīd (f)	مدريد
Marseille	marsilia (f)	مرسيليا
Mexico City	madīnet meksiko (f)	مدينة مكسيكو
Miami	mayami (f)	ميامي
Montreal	montreal (f)	مونتريال
Moscow	moskū (f)	موسكو
Munich	muniχ (f)	ميونخ
Nairobi	nayrobi (f)	نيروبي
Naples	naboli (f)	نابولي
New York	nyu york (f)	نيويورك
Nice	nīs (f)	نيس
Oslo	oslo (f)	أوسلو
Ottawa	ottawa (f)	أوتاوا
Paris	baris (f)	باريس
Prague	braɣ (f)	براغ
Rio de Janeiro	rio de ʒaneyro (f)	ريو دي جانيرو
Rome	roma (f)	روما
Saint Petersburg	sant betersburɣ (f)	سانت بطرسبرغ
Seoul	seūl (f)	سيول
Shanghai	ʃanghay (f)	شنجهاي
Singapore	sinɣafūra (f)	سنغافورة
Stockholm	stokχolm (f)	ستوكهولم
Sydney	sydney (f)	سيدني
Taipei	taybey (f)	تايبيه
Tokyo	ṭokyo (f)	طوكيو
Toronto	toronto (f)	تورونتو
Venice	venesya (f)	فينيسيا
Vienna	vienna (f)	فيينا
Warsaw	warsaw (f)	وارسو
Washington	waʃinṭon (f)	واشنطن

243. Politics. Government. Part 1

politics	seyāsa (f)	سياسة
political (adj)	seyāsy	سياسي
politician	seyāsy (m)	سياسي
state (country)	dawla (f)	دولة
citizen	mowāṭen (m)	مواطن
citizenship	mewaṭna (f)	مواطنة
national emblem	ʃeʿār waṭany (m)	شعار وطني
national anthem	naʃīd waṭany (m)	نشيد وطني
government	ḥokūma (f)	حكومة

head of state	ra'sel dawla (m)	رأس الدولة
parliament	barlamān (m)	برلمان
party	ḥezb (m)	حزب
capitalism	ra'smaliya (f)	رأسماليّة
capitalist (adj)	ra'smāly	رأسمالي
socialism	eʃterakiya (f)	إشتراكيّة
socialist (adj)	eʃterāky	إشتراكي
communism	ʃeyū'iya (f)	شيوعيّة
communist (adj)	ʃeyū'y	شيوعي
communist (n)	ʃeyū'y (m)	شيوعي
democracy	dīmoqraṭiya (f)	ديموقراطيّة
democrat	demoqrāṭy (m)	ديموقراطي
democratic (adj)	demoqrāṭy	ديموقراطي
Democratic party	el ḥezb el demokrāṭy (m)	الحزب الديموقراطي
liberal (n)	librāly (m)	ليبيرالي
liberal (adj)	librāly	ليبيرالي
conservative (n)	moḥāfeẓ (m)	محافظ
conservative (adj)	moḥāfeẓ	محافظ
republic (n)	gomhoriya (f)	جمهورية
republican (n)	gomhūry (m)	جمهوري
Republican party	el ḥezb el gomhūry (m)	الحزب الجمهوري
elections	entaχabāt (pl)	إنتخابات
to elect (vt)	entaχab	إنتخب
elector, voter	nāχeb (m)	ناخب
election campaign	ḥamla enteχabiya (f)	حملة إنتخابيّة
voting (n)	taṣwīt (m)	تصويت
to vote (vi)	ṣawwat	صوّت
suffrage, right to vote	ḥa' el enteχāb (m)	حق الإنتخاب
candidate	morasʃaḥ (m)	مرشّح
to be a candidate	rasʃaḥ nafsoh	رشّح نفسه
campaign	ḥamla (f)	حملة
opposition (as adj)	mo'āreḍ	معارض
opposition (n)	mo'arḍa (f)	معارضة
visit	zeyāra (f)	زيارة
official visit	zeyāra rasmiya (f)	زيارة رسميّة
international (adj)	dawly	دوّلي
negotiations	mofawḍāt (pl)	مفاوضات
to negotiate (vi)	tafāwaḍ	تفاوض

244. Politics. Government. Part 2

society	mogtamaʿ (m)	مجتمع
constitution	dostūr (m)	دستور
power (political control)	solṭa (f)	سلطة
corruption	fasād (m)	فساد
law (justice)	qanūn (m)	قانون
legal (legitimate)	qanūny	قانوني
justice (fairness)	ʿadāla (f)	عدالة
just (fair)	ʿādel	عادل
committee	lagna (f)	لجنة
bill (draft law)	maʃrūʿ qanūn (m)	مشروع قانون
budget	mowazna (f)	موازنة
policy	seyāsa (f)	سياسة
reform	eṣlāḥ (m)	إصلاح
radical (adj)	oṣūly	أصولي
power (strength, force)	ʾowwa (f)	قوّة
powerful (adj)	ʾawy	قوي
supporter	moʾayed (m)	مؤيد
influence	taʾsīr (m)	تأثير
regime (e.g., military ~)	nezām ḥokm (m)	نظام حكم
conflict	χelāf (m)	خلاف
conspiracy (plot)	moʾamra (f)	مؤامرة
provocation	estefzāz (m)	إستفزاز
to overthrow (regime, etc.)	asqaṭ	أسقط
overthrow (of government)	esqāṭ (m)	إسقاط
revolution	sawra (f)	ثورة
coup d'état	enqelāb (m)	إنقلاب
military coup	enqelāb ʿaskary (m)	إنقلاب عسكري
crisis	azma (f)	أزمة
economic recession	rokūd eqteṣādy (m)	ركود إقتصادي
demonstrator (protester)	motaẓāher (m)	متظاهر
demonstration	mozahra (f)	مظاهرة
martial law	ḥokm ʿorfy (m)	حكم عرفي
military base	qaʿeda ʿaskariya (f)	قاعدة عسكريّة
stability	esteqrār (m)	إستقرار
stable (adj)	mostaqerr	مستقرّ
exploitation	esteɣlāl (m)	إستغلال
to exploit (workers)	estaɣall	إستغلّ
racism	ʿonṣoriya (f)	عنصريّة
racist	ʿonṣory (m)	عنصري

fascism	faʃiya (f)	فاشيّة
fascist	fāʃy (m)	فاشي

245. Countries. Miscellaneous

foreigner	agnaby (m)	أجنبي
foreign (adj)	agnaby	أجنبي
abroad (in a foreign country)	fel χāreg	في الخارج
emigrant	mohāger (m)	مهاجر
emigration	hegra (f)	هجرة
to emigrate (vi)	hāgar	هاجر
the West	el ɣarb (m)	الغرب
the East	el ʃar' (m)	الشرق
the Far East	el ʃar' el aqṣa (m)	الشرق الأقصى
civilization	ḥaḍāra (f)	حضارة
humanity (mankind)	el baʃariya (f)	البشريّة
the world (earth)	el ʿālam (m)	العالم
peace	salām (m)	سلام
worldwide (adj)	ʿālamy	عالمي
homeland	waṭan (m)	وطن
people (population)	ʃaʿb (m)	شعب
population	sokkān (pl)	سكّان
people (a lot of ~)	nās (pl)	ناس
nation (people)	omma (f)	أمّة
generation	gīl (m)	جيل
territory (area)	arḍ (f)	أرض
region	mante'a (f)	منطقة
state (part of a country)	welāya (f)	ولاية
tradition	ta'līd (m)	تقليد
custom (tradition)	ʿāda (f)	عادة
ecology	ʿelm el bī'a (m)	علم البيئة
Indian (Native American)	hendy aḥmar (m)	هندي أحمر
Gypsy (masc.)	ɣagary (m)	غجري
Gypsy (fem.)	ɣagariya (f)	غجريّة
Gypsy (adj)	ɣagary	غجري
empire	embraṭoriya (f)	إمبراطورية
colony	mostaʿmara (f)	مستعمرة
slavery	ʿobūdiya (f)	عبودية
invasion	ɣazw (m)	غزو
famine	magāʿa (f)	مجاعة

246. Major religious groups. Confessions

religion	dīn (m)	دين
religious (adj)	dīny	ديني
faith, belief	emān (m)	إيمان
to believe (in God)	aman	أمن
believer	mo'men (m)	مؤمن
atheism	el elḥād (m)	الإلحاد
atheist	molḥed (m)	ملحد
Christianity	el masīḥiya (f)	المسيحيّة
Christian (n)	mesīḥy (m)	مسيحي
Christian (adj)	mesīḥy	مسيحي
Catholicism	el kasolekiya (f)	الكاثوليكيّة
Catholic (n)	kasolīky (m)	كاثوليكي
Catholic (adj)	kasolīky	كاثوليكي
Protestantism	brotestantiya (f)	بروتستانتية
Protestant Church	el kenīsa el brotestantiya (f)	الكنيسة البروتستانتية
Protestant (n)	brotestanty (m)	بروتستانتي
Orthodoxy	orsozeksiya (f)	الأرثوذكسيّة
Orthodox Church	el kenīsa el orsozeksiya (f)	الكنيسة الأرثوذكسيّة
Orthodox (n)	arsazoksy (m)	أرثوذكسي
Presbyterianism	maʃīχiya (f)	مشيخية
Presbyterian Church	el kenīsa el maʃīχiya (f)	الكنيسة المشيخية
Presbyterian (n)	maʃīχiya (f)	مشيخية
Lutheranism	el luseriya (f)	اللوثرية
Lutheran (n)	luterriya (m)	لوثرية
Baptist Church	el kenīsa el me'medaniya (f)	الكنيسة المعمدانية
Baptist (n)	me'medāny (m)	معمداني
Anglican Church	el kenīsa el anʒlekaniya (f)	الكنيسة الإنجليكانية
Anglican (n)	enʒelikāny (m)	أنجليكاني
Mormonism	el moromoniya (f)	المورمونية
Mormon (n)	mesīḥy mormōn (m)	مسيحي مرمون
Judaism	el yahūdiya (f)	اليهودية
Jew (n)	yahūdy (m)	يهودي
Buddhism	el būziya (f)	البوذية
Buddhist (n)	būzy (m)	بوذي
Hinduism	el hindūsiya (f)	الهندوسية
Hindu (n)	hendūsy (m)	هندوسي

Islam	el islām (m)	الإسلام
Muslim (n)	muslim (m)	مسلم
Muslim (adj)	islāmy	إسلامي
Shiah Islam	el mazhab el ʃee'y (m)	المذهب الشيعي
Shiite (n)	ʃee'y (m)	شيعي
Sunni Islam	el mazhab el sunny (m)	المذهب السنّي
Sunnite (n)	sunni (m)	سنّي

247. Religions. Priests

priest	kāhen (m)	كاهن
the Pope	el bāba (m)	البابا
monk, friar	rāheb (m)	راهب
nun	rāheba (f)	راهبة
pastor	'essīs (m)	قسّيس
abbot	ra'īs el deyr (m)	رئيس الدير
vicar (parish priest)	viqār (m)	فيقار
bishop	asqof (m)	أسقف
cardinal	kardinal (m)	كاردينال
preacher	mobasʃer (m)	مبشّر
preaching	tabʃīr (f)	تبشير
parishioners	ra'yet el abraʃiya (f)	رعية الأبرشية
believer	mo'men (m)	مؤمن
atheist	molḥed (m)	ملحد

248. Faith. Christianity. Islam

Adam	'ādam (m)	آدم
Eve	ḥawwā' (f)	حوّاء
God	allah (m)	الله
the Lord	el rabb (m)	الربّ
the Almighty	el qadīr (m)	القدير
sin	zanb (m)	ذنب
to sin (vi)	aznab	أذنب
sinner (masc.)	mozneb (m)	مذنب
sinner (fem.)	mozneba (f)	مذنبة
hell	el gaḥīm (f)	الجحيم
paradise	el ganna (f)	الجنّة
Jesus	yasū' (m)	يسوع
Jesus Christ	yasū' el masīḥ (m)	يسوع المسيح

the Holy Spirit	el rūḥ el qods (m)	الروح القدس
the Savior	el masīḥ (m)	المسيح
the Virgin Mary	maryem el ʿazrāʾ (f)	مريم العذراء
the Devil	el ʃayṭān (m)	الشيطان
devil's (adj)	ʃeyṭāny	شيطاني
Satan	el ʃayṭān (m)	الشيطان
satanic (adj)	ʃeyṭāny	شيطاني
angel	malāk (m)	ملاك
guardian angel	malāk ḥāres (m)	ملاك حارس
angelic (adj)	malāʾeky	ملائكي
apostle	rasūl (m)	رسول
archangel	el malāk el raʾīsy (m)	الملاك الرئيسي
the Antichrist	el masīḥ el daggāl (m)	المسيح الدجّال
Church	el kenīsa (f)	الكنيسة
Bible	el ketāb el moqaddas (m)	الكتاب المقدّس
biblical (adj)	tawrāty	توراتي
Old Testament	el ʿaḥd el ʾadīm (m)	العهد القديم
New Testament	el ʿaḥd el gedīd (m)	العهد الجديد
Gospel	engīl (m)	إنجيل
Holy Scripture	el ketāb el moqaddas (m)	الكتاب المقدّس
Heaven	el ganna (f)	الجنّة
Commandment	waṣiya (f)	وصيّة
prophet	naby (m)	نبي
prophecy	nobūʾa (f)	نبوءة
Allah	allah (m)	الله
Mohammed	moḥammed (m)	محمّد
the Koran	el qorʾān (m)	القرآن
mosque	masged (m)	مسجد
mullah	mullah (m)	ملا
prayer	ṣalāh (f)	صلاة
to pray (vi, vt)	ṣalla	صلّى
pilgrimage	ḥagg (m)	حج
pilgrim	ḥagg (m)	حاج
Mecca	makka el mokarrama (f)	مكة المكرّمة
church	kenīsa (f)	كنيسة
temple	maʿbad (m)	معبد
cathedral	katedraʾiya (f)	كاتدرائية
Gothic (adj)	qūṭy	قوطي
synagogue	kenīs (m)	كنيس
mosque	masged (m)	مسجد
chapel	kenīsa saɣīra (f)	كنيسة صغيرة
abbey	deyr (m)	دير

convent	deyr (m)	دير
monastery	deyr (m)	دير
bell (church ~s)	garas (m)	جرس
bell tower	borg el garas (m)	برج الجرس
to ring (ab. bells)	da''	دق
cross	ṣalīb (m)	صليب
cupola (roof)	'obba (f)	قبّة
icon	ramz (m)	رمز
soul	nafs (f)	نفس
fate (destiny)	maṣīr (m)	مصير
evil (n)	ʃarr (m)	شرّ
good (n)	χeyr (m)	خير
vampire	maṣṣāṣ demā' (m)	مصّاص دماء
witch (evil ~)	sāḥera (f)	ساحرة
demon	ʃeṭān (m)	شيطان
spirit	roḥe (m)	روح
redemption (giving us ~)	takfīr (m)	تكفير
to redeem (vt)	kaffar 'an	كفّر عن
church service, mass	qedās (m)	قداس
to say mass	'ām be χedma dīniya	قام بخدمة دينية
confession	e'terāf (m)	إعتراف
to confess (vi)	e'taraf	إعترف
saint (n)	qeddīs (m)	قدّيس
sacred (holy)	moqaddas (m)	مقدّس
holy water	maya moqaddesa (f)	ماية مقدّسة
ritual (n)	ʃa'ā'er (pl)	شعائر
ritual (adj)	ʃa'ā'ery	شعائري
sacrifice	zabīḥa (f)	ذبيحة
superstition	χorāfa (f)	خرافة
superstitious (adj)	mo'men bel χorafāt (m)	مؤمن بالخرافات
afterlife	aχra (f)	الآخرة
eternal life	ḥayat el abadiya (f)	حياة الأبدية

MISCELLANEOUS

249. Various useful words

background (green ~)	χalefiya (f)	خلفية
balance (of situation)	tawāzon (m)	توازن
barrier (obstacle)	ḥāgez (m)	حاجز
base (basis)	asās (m)	أساس
beginning	bedāya (f)	بداية
category	fe'a (f)	فئة
cause (reason)	sabab (m)	سبب
choice	eχteyār (m)	إختيار
coincidence	ṣodfa (f)	صدّفة
comfortable (~ chair)	morīḥ	مريح
comparison	moqarna (f)	مقارنة
compensation	ta'wīḍ (m)	تعويض
degree (extent, amount)	daraga (f)	درجة
development	tanmeya (f)	تنمية
difference	far' (m)	فرق
effect (e.g., of drugs)	ta'sīr (m)	تأثير
effort (exertion)	mag-hūd (m)	مجهود
element	'onṣor (m)	عنصر
end (finish)	nehāya (f)	نهاية
example (illustration)	mesāl (m)	مثال
fact	ḥa'ī'a (f)	حقيقة
frequent (adj)	motakarrer (m)	متكرّر
growth (development)	nomoww (m)	نموّ
help	mosa'da (f)	مساعدة
ideal	mesāl (m)	مثال
kind (sort, type)	nū' (m)	نوع
labyrinth	matāha (f)	متاهة
mistake, error	χaṭa' (m)	خطأ
moment	laḥza (f)	لحظة
object (thing)	mawḍū' (m)	موضوع
obstacle	'aqaba (f)	عقبة
original (original copy)	aṣl (m)	أصل
part (~ of sth)	goz' (m)	جزء
particle, small part	goz' (m)	جزء
pause (break)	estrāḥa (f)	إستراحة

position	mawqef (m)	موقف
principle	mabda' (m)	مبدأ
problem	moʃkela (f)	مشكلة
process	'amaliya (f)	عمليّة
progress	ta'addom (m)	تقدّم
property (quality)	χaṣṣa (f)	خاصّة
reaction	radd fe'l (m)	ردّ فعل
risk	moχaṭra (f)	مخاطرة
secret	serr (m)	سرّ
series	selsela (f)	سلسلة
shape (outer form)	ʃakl (m)	شكل
situation	ḥāla (f), waḍ' (m)	حالة, وضع
solution	ḥall (m)	حلّ
standard (adj)	'ādy -qeyāsy	عادي, قياسي
standard (level of quality)	'eyās (m)	قياس
stop (pause)	estrāḥa (f)	إستراحة
style	oslūb (m)	أسلوب
system	nezām (m)	نظام
table (chart)	gadwal (m)	جدول
tempo, rate	eqā' (m)	إيقاع
term (word, expression)	moṣṭalaḥ (m)	مصطلح
thing (object, item)	ḥāga (f)	حاجة
truth (e.g., moment of ~)	ḥa'ī'a (f)	حقيقة
turn (please wait your ~)	dore (m)	دور
type (sort, kind)	nū' (m)	نوع
urgent (adj)	mesta'gel	مستعجل
urgently (adv)	be ʃakl 'āgel	بشكل عاجل
utility (usefulness)	manf'a (f)	منفعة
variant (alternative)	ʃakl moχtalef (m)	شكل مختلف
way (means, method)	ṭarī'a (f)	طريقة
zone	mante'a (f)	منطقة

250. Modifiers. Adjectives. Part 1

additional (adj)	eḍāfy	إضافي
ancient (~ civilization)	'adīm	قديم
artificial (adj)	ṣenā'y	صناعي
back, rear (adj)	χalfy	خلفي
bad (adj)	weḥeʃ	وحش
beautiful (~ palace)	gamīl	جميل
beautiful (person)	gamīl	جميل
big (in size)	kebīr	كبير

bitter (taste)	morr	مرّ
blind (sightless)	a'ma	أعمى
calm, quiet (adj)	hady	هادئ
careless (negligent)	mohmel	مهمل
caring (~ father)	mohtamm	مهتمّ
central (adj)	markazy	مركزي
cheap (low-priced)	reχīṣ	رخيص
cheerful (adj)	farḥān	فرحان
children's (adj)	lel aṭfāl	للأطفال
civil (~ law)	madany	مدني
clandestine (secret)	serry	سرّي
clean (free from dirt)	neḍīf	نظيف
clear (explanation, etc.)	wāḍeḥ	واضح
clever (smart)	zaky	ذكي
close (near in space)	'arīb	قريب
closed (adj)	ma'fūl	مقفول
cloudless (sky)	ṣāfy	صافي
cold (drink, weather)	bāred	بارد
compatible (adj)	motawāfaq	متوافق
contented (satisfied)	rāḍy	راضي
continuous (uninterrupted)	motawāṣal	متواصل
cool (weather)	mon'eʃ	منعش
dangerous (adj)	χaṭīr	خطير
dark (room)	ḍalma	ظلمة
dead (not alive)	mayet	ميّت
dense (fog, smoke)	kasīf	كثيف
destitute (extremely poor)	mo'dam	معدم
different (not the same)	moχtalef	مختلف
difficult (decision)	ṣa'b	صعب
difficult (problem, task)	ṣa'b	صعب
dim, faint (light)	bāhet	باهت
dirty (not clean)	weseχ	وسخ
distant (in space)	be'īd	بعيد
dry (clothes, etc.)	nāʃef	ناشف
easy (not difficult)	sahl	سهل
empty (glass, room)	χāly	خالي
even (e.g., ~ surface)	mosaṭṭaḥ	مسطّح
exact (amount)	maẓbūṭ	مظبوط
excellent (adj)	momtāz	ممتاز
excessive (adj)	mofreṭ	مفرط
expensive (adj)	ɣāly	غالي
exterior (adj)	χāregy	خارجي
far (the ~ East)	be'īd	بعيد

fast (quick)	saree'	سريع
fatty (food)	dasem	دسم
fertile (land, soil)	χeṣb	خصب
flat (~ panel display)	mosaṭṭaḥ	مسطّح
foreign (adj)	agnaby	أجنبي
fragile (china, glass)	qābel lel kasr	قابل للكسر
free (at no cost)	be balāʃ	ببلاش
free (unrestricted)	ḥorr	حرّ
fresh (~ water)	'azb	عذب
fresh (e.g., ~ bread)	ṭāza	طازة
frozen (food)	mogammad	مجمّد
full (completely filled)	malyān	مليان
gloomy (house, forecast)	moẓlem	مظلم
good (book, etc.)	kewayes	كويّس
good, kind (kindhearted)	ṭayeb	طيّب
grateful (adj)	ʃāker	شاكر
happy (adj)	sa'īd	سعيد
hard (not soft)	gāmed	جامد
heavy (in weight)	te'īl	ثقيل
hostile (adj)	meʃ weddy	مش ودّي
hot (adj)	soχn	سخن
huge (adj)	ḍaχm	ضخم
humid (adj)	roṭob	رطب
hungry (adj)	ge'ān	جعان
ill (sick, unwell)	'ayān	عيّان
immobile (adj)	sābet	ثابت
important (adj)	mohemm	مهمّ
impossible (adj)	mostaḥīl	مستحيل
incomprehensible	meʃ wāḍeḥ	مش واضح
indispensable (adj)	ḍarūry	ضروري
inexperienced (adj)	'alīl el χebra	قليل الخبرة
insignificant (adj)	meʃ mohemm	مش مهمّ
interior (adj)	dāχely	داخلي
joint (~ decision)	moʃtarak	مشترك
last (e.g., ~ week)	māḍy	ماضي
last (final)	'āχer	آخر
left (e.g., ~ side)	el ʃemāl	الشمال
legal (legitimate)	qanūny	قانوني
light (in weight)	χafīf	خفيف
light (pale color)	fāteḥ	فاتح
limited (adj)	maḥdūd	محدود
liquid (fluid)	sā'el	سائل
long (e.g., ~ hair)	ṭawīl	طويل

loud (voice, etc.)	ʿāly	عالي
low (voice)	wāṭy	واطي

251. Modifiers. Adjectives. Part 2

main (principal)	raʾīsy	رئيسي
matt, matte	maṭfy	مطفي
meticulous (job)	motqan	متقن
mysterious (adj)	ɣāmeḍ	غامض
narrow (street, etc.)	ḍayeʾ	ضيّق
native (~ country)	aṣly	أصلي
nearby (adj)	ʾarīb	قريب
nearsighted (adj)	ʾaṣīr el naẓar	قصير النظر
needed (necessary)	lāzem	لازم
negative (~ response)	salby	سلبي
neighboring (adj)	mogāwer	مجاور
nervous (adj)	ʿaṣaby	عصبي
new (adj)	gedīd	جديد
next (e.g., ~ week)	elly gayī	اللي جاي
nice (kind)	laṭīf	لطيف
nice (voice)	laṭīf	لطيف
normal (adj)	ʿādy	عادي
not big (adj)	meʃ kebīr	مش كبير
not difficult (adj)	meʃ ṣaʿb	مش صعب
obligatory (adj)	ḍarūry	ضروري
old (house)	ʾadīm	قديم
open (adj)	maftūḥ	مفتوح
opposite (adj)	moqābel	مقابل
ordinary (usual)	ʿādy	عادي
original (unusual)	aṣly	أصلي
past (recent)	elly fāt	اللي فات
permanent (adj)	dāʾem	دائم
personal (adj)	ʃaχṣy	شخصي
polite (adj)	moʾaddab	مؤدّب
poor (not rich)	faʾīr	فقير
possible (adj)	momken	ممكن
present (current)	ḥāḍer	حاضر
previous (adj)	elly fāt	اللي فات
principal (main)	asāsy	أساسي
private (~ jet)	χāṣṣa	خاصّة
probable (adj)	moḥtamal	محتمل
prolonged (e.g., ~ applause)	momtad	ممتد

public (open to all)	ʿām	عام
punctual (person)	daqīq	دقيق
quiet (tranquil)	hady	هادئ
rare (adj)	nāder	نادر
raw (uncooked)	nayī	نيّ
right (not left)	el yemīn	اليمين
right, correct (adj)	ṣaḥīḥ	صحيح
ripe (fruit)	mestewy	مستوّي
risky (adj)	mogāzef	مجازف
sad (~ look)	zaʿlān	زعلان
sad (depressing)	zaʿlān	زعلان
safe (not dangerous)	ʾāmen	آمن
salty (food)	māleḥ	مالح
satisfied (customer)	rāḍy	راضي
second hand (adj)	mostaʿmal	مستعمل
shallow (water)	ḍaḥl	ضحل
sharp (blade, etc.)	ḥād	حاد
short (in length)	ʾaṣīr	قصير
short, short-lived (adj)	ʾaṣīr	قصير
significant (notable)	mohemm	مهمّ
similar (adj)	ʃabīh	شبيه
simple (easy)	basīṭ	بسيط
skinny	rofayaʿ	رفيّع
small (in size)	ṣoɣeyyir	صغيّر
smooth (surface)	amlas	أملس
soft (~ toys)	nāʿem	ناعم
solid (~ wall)	matīn	متين
sour (flavor, taste)	ḥāmeḍ	حامض
spacious (house, etc.)	wāseʿ	واسع
special (adj)	χāṣṣ	خاصّ
straight (line, road)	mostaqīm	مستقيم
strong (person)	ʾawy	قوّي
stupid (foolish)	ɣaby	غبي
suitable (e.g., ~ for drinking)	monāseb	مناسب
sunny (day)	moʃmes	مشمس
superb, perfect (adj)	momtāz	ممتاز
swarthy (adj)	asmar	أسمر
sweet (sugary)	mesakkar	مسكّر
tan (adj)	asmar	أسمر
tasty (delicious)	ṭaʿmo ḥelw	طعمه حلو
tender (affectionate)	ḥanūn	حنون
the highest (adj)	aʿla	أعلى
the most important	ahamm	أهمّ

the nearest	a''rab	أقرب
the same, equal (adj)	momāsel	مماثل
thick (e.g., ~ fog)	kasīf	كثيف
thick (wall, slice)	teχīn	تخين
thin (person)	rofaya'	رفيّع
tight (~ shoes)	ḍaye'	ضيّق
tired (exhausted)	ta'bān	تعبان
tiring (adj)	mot'eb	متعب
transparent (adj)	ʃaffāf	شفّاف
unclear (adj)	meʃ wāḍeḥ	مش واضح
unique (exceptional)	farīd	فريد
various (adj)	moχtalef	مختلف
warm (moderately hot)	dāfe'	دافئ
wet (e.g., ~ clothes)	mablūl	مبلول
whole (entire, complete)	koll el nās	كلّ
wide (e.g., ~ road)	wāse'	واسع
young (adj)	ʃāb	شاب

MAIN 500 VERBS

252. Verbs A-C

to accompany (vt)	rāfaq	رافق
to accuse (vt)	ettaham	إتّهم
to acknowledge (admit)	e'taraf	إعترف
to act (take action)	'amal	عمل
to add (supplement)	aḍāf	أضاف
to address (speak to)	χāṭab	خاطب
to admire (vi)	o'gab be	أعجب بـ
to advertise (vt)	a'lan	أعلن
to advise (vt)	naṣaḥ	نصح
to affirm (assert)	aṣarr	أصرّ
to agree (say yes)	ettafa'	إتّفق
to aim (to point a weapon)	ṣawwab 'ala ...	صوّب على ...
to allow (sb to do sth)	samaḥ	سمح
to amputate (vt)	batr	بتر
to answer (vi, vt)	gāwab	جاوب
to apologize (vi)	e'tazar	إعتذر
to appear (come into view)	ẓahar	ظهر
to applaud (vi, vt)	ṣaffa'	صفّق
to appoint (assign)	'ayen	عيّن
to approach (come closer)	'arrab	قرّب
to arrive (ab. train)	weṣel	وصل
to ask (~ sb to do sth)	ṭalab	طلب
to aspire to ...	sa'a	سعى
to assist (help)	sā'ed	ساعد
to attack (mil.)	hagam	هجم
to attain (objectives)	balaɣ	بلغ
to avenge (get revenge)	entaqam	إنتقم
to avoid (danger, task)	tagannab	تجنّب
to award (give medal to)	manaḥ	منح
to battle (vi)	qātal	قاتل
to be (vi)	kān	كان
to be a cause of ...	sabbeb	سبّب
to be afraid	χāf	خاف
to be angry (with ...)	ettḍāye'	إتّضايق

to be at war	ḥārab	حارب
to be based (on ...)	estanad ʿala	إستند على
to be bored	zeheʾ	زهق
to be convinced	eqtanaʿ	إقتنع
to be enough	kaffa	كفّى
to be envious	ḥasad	حسد
to be indignant	estāʾ	إستاء
to be interested in ...	ehtamm be	إهتمّ بـ
to be lost in thought	saraḥ	سرح
to be lying (~ on the table)	kān mawgūd	كان موّجود
to be needed	maṭlūb	مطلوب
to be perplexed (puzzled)	eḥtār	إحتار
to be preserved	ḥafaẓ	حفظ
to be required	maṭlūb	مطلوب
to be surprised	etfāgeʾ	إتفاجئ
to be worried	ʾeleʾ	قلق
to beat (to hit)	ḍarab	ضرب
to become (e.g., ~ old)	baʾa	بقى
to behave (vi)	taṣarraf	تصرّف
to believe (think)	eʿtaqad	إعتقد
to belong to ...	χaṣṣ	خصّ
to berth (moor)	rasa	رسا
to blind (other drivers)	ʿama	عمي
to blow (wind)	habb	هبّ
to blush (vi)	eḥmarr	إحمرّ
to boast (vi)	tabāha	تباهى
to borrow (money)	estalaf	إستلف
to break (branch, toy, etc.)	kasar	كسر
to breathe (vi)	ettnaffes	إتّنفّس
to bring (sth)	gāb	جاب
to burn (paper, logs)	ḥaraʾ	حرق
to buy (purchase)	eʃtara	إشترى
to call (~ for help)	estaɣās	إستغاث
to call (yell for sb)	nāda	نادى
to calm down (vt)	ṭamʾan	طمأن
can (v aux)	ʾeder	قدر
to cancel (call off)	alɣa	ألغى
to cast off (of a boat or ship)	aqlaʿ	أقلع
to catch (e.g., ~ a ball)	mesek	مسك
to change (~ one's opinion)	ɣayar	غيّر
to change (exchange)	ṣarraff	صرّف
to charm (vt)	fatan	فتن
to choose (select)	eχtār	إختار

to chop off (with an ax)	'aṭṭa'	قطّع
to clean (e.g., kettle from scale)	naḍḍaf	نظّف
to clean (shoes, etc.)	naḍḍaf	نظّف
to clean up (tidy)	ratteb	رتّب
to close (vt)	'afal	قفل
to comb one's hair	masʃaṭ	مشّط
to come down (the stairs)	nezel	نزل
to come out (book)	ṣadar	صدر
to compare (vt)	qāran	قارن
to compensate (vt)	'awwaḍ	عوّض
to compete (vi)	nāfes	نافس
to compile (~ a list)	gamma'	جمّع
to complain (vi, vt)	ʃaka	شكا
to complicate (vt)	'a''ad	عقّد
to compose (music, etc.)	laḥḥan	لحّن
to compromise (reputation)	sawwa' som'etoh	سوّء سمعته
to concentrate (vi)	rakkez	ركّز
to confess (criminal)	e'taraf	إعترف
to confuse (mix up)	etlaχbaṭ	إتلخبط
to congratulate (vt)	hanna	هنّأ
to consult (doctor, expert)	estaʃār ...	إستشار...
to continue (~ to do sth)	estamar	إستمر
to control (vt)	et-ḥakkem	إتحكّم
to convince (vt)	aqna'	أقنع
to cooperate (vi)	ta'āwan	تعاون
to coordinate (vt)	nassaq	نسّق
to correct (an error)	ṣaḥḥaḥ	صحّح
to cost (vt)	kallef	كلّف
to count (money, etc.)	'add	عدّ
to count on ...	e'tamad 'ala ...	إعتمد على...
to crack (ceiling, wall)	etʃa''e'	إتشقّق
to create (vt)	'amal	عمل
to crush, to squash (~ a bug)	fa''aṣ	فعّص
to cry (weep)	baka	بكى
to cut off (with a knife)	'aṭṭa'	قطّع

253. Verbs D-G

to dare (~ to do sth)	etḥadda	إتّحدّى
to date from ...	tarīχo	تاريخه

to deceive (vi, vt)	χada‘	خدع
to decide (~ to do sth)	’arrar	قرّر
to decorate (tree, street)	zayen	زيّن
to dedicate (book, etc.)	karras	كرّس
to defend (a country, etc.)	dāfa‘	دافع
to defend oneself	dāfa‘ ‘an nafsoh	دافع عن نفسه
to demand (request firmly)	ṭāleb	طالب
to denounce (vt)	estankar	إستنكر
to deny (vt)	ankar	أنكر
to depend on …	e‘tamad ‘ala …	إعتمد على...
to deprive (vt)	ḥaram men	حرم من
to deserve (vt)	estaḥaqq	إستحقّ
to design (machine, etc.)	ṣammam	صمّم
to desire (want, wish)	kān ‘āyez	كان عايز
to despise (vt)	eḥtaqar	إحتقر
to destroy (documents, etc.)	atlaf	أتلف
to differ (from sth)	eχtalaf	إختلف
to dig (tunnel, etc.)	ḥafar	حفر
to direct (point the way)	waggeh	وجّه
to disappear (vi)	eχtafa	إختفى
to discover (new land, etc.)	ektaʃaf	إكتشف
to discuss (vt)	nā’eʃ	ناقش
to distribute (leaflets, etc.)	wazza‘	وزّع
to disturb (vt)	az‘ag	أزعج
to dive (vi)	ɣāṣ	غاص
to divide (math)	’asam	قسم
to do (vt)	‘amal	عمل
to do the laundry	ɣasal el malābes	غسل الملابس
to double (increase)	ḍā‘af	ضاعف
to doubt (have doubts)	ʃakk fe	شكّ في
to draw a conclusion	estantag	إستنتج
to dream (daydream)	ḥelem	حلم
to dream (in sleep)	ḥelem	حلم
to drink (vi, vt)	ʃereb	شرب
to drive a car	sā’ ‘arabiya	ساق عربية
to drive away (scare away)	χawwef	خوّف
to drop (let fall)	wa’’a‘	وقّع
to drown (ab. person)	ɣere’	غرق
to dry (clothes, hair)	gaffaf	جفّف
to eat (vi, vt)	akal	أكل
to eavesdrop (vi)	tanaṣṣat	تنصّت

to emit (diffuse - odor, etc.)	fāḥ	فاح
to enjoy oneself	estamtaʿ	إستمتع
to enter (on the list)	saggel	سجّل
to enter (room, house, etc.)	daχal	دخل
to entertain (amuse)	salla	سلّى
to equip (fit out)	gahhez	جهّز
to examine (proposal)	baḥs fi	بحث في
to exchange (sth)	tabādal	تبادل
to excuse (forgive)	ʿazar	عذر
to exist (vi)	kān mawgūd	كان موجود
to expect (anticipate)	tawaqqaʿ	توقّع
to expect (foresee)	tanabbaʾ	تنبّأ
to expel (from school, etc.)	faṣal	فصل
to explain (vt)	ʃaraḥ	شرح
to express (vt)	ʿabbar	عبّر
to extinguish (a fire)	ṭaffa	طفّي
to fall in love (with ...)	ḥabb	حبّ
to feed (provide food)	akkel	أكّل
to fight (against the enemy)	qātal	قاتل
to fight (vi)	etχāneʾ	إتخانق
to fill (glass, bottle)	mala	ملأ
to find (~ lost items)	laʾa	لقى
to finish (vt)	χallaṣ	خلّص
to fish (angle)	eṣṭād samak	إصطاد سمك
to fit (ab. dress, etc.)	nāseb	ناسب
to flatter (vt)	gāmal	جامل
to fly (bird, plane)	ṭār	طار
to follow ... (come after)	tatabbaʿ	تتبّع
to forbid (vt)	manaʿ	منع
to force (compel)	agbar	أجبر
to forget (vi, vt)	nesy	نسي
to forgive (pardon)	ʿafa	عفا
to form (constitute)	ʃakkal	شكّل
to get dirty (vi)	ettwassaχ	إتّوسّخ
to get infected (with ...)	etʿada	إتعدى
to get irritated	enzaʿag	إنزعج
to get married	ettgawwez	إتّجوز
to get rid of ...	ettχallaṣ min ...	إتّخلّص من...
to get tired	teʿeb	تعب
to get up (arise from bed)	ʾām	قام

to give (vt)	edda	أدّى
to give a bath (to bath)	ḥammem	حمّم
to give a hug, to hug (vt)	ḥaḍan	حضن
to give in (yield to)	estaslam	إستسلم
to glimpse (vt)	lamaḥ	لمح
to go (by car, etc.)	rāḥ	راح
to go (on foot)	meʃy	مشى
to go for a swim	sebeḥ	سبح
to go out (for dinner, etc.)	χarag	خرج
to go to bed (go to sleep)	nām	نام
to greet (vt)	sallem ʿala	سلّم على
to grow (plants)	anbat	أنبت
to guarantee (vt)	ḍaman	ضمن
to guess (the answer)	χammen	خمّن

254. Verbs H-M

to hand out (distribute)	wazzaʿ ʿala	وزّع على
to hang (curtains, etc.)	ʿallaʾ	علّق
to have (vt)	malak	ملك
to have a try	ḥāwel	حاول
to have breakfast	feṭer	فطر
to have dinner	etʿasʃa	إتعشّى
to have lunch	etɣadda	إتغدّى
to head (group, etc.)	raʾs	رأس
to hear (vt)	semeʿ	سمع
to heat (vt)	sakχan	سخّن
to help (vt)	sāʿed	ساعد
to hide (vt)	χabba	خبّأ
to hire (e.g., ~ a boat)	aggar	أجّر
to hire (staff)	waẓẓaf	وظّف
to hope (vi, vt)	tamanna	تمنّى
to hunt (for food, sport)	eṣṭād	إصطاد
to hurry (vi)	estaʿgel	إستعجل
to imagine (to picture)	taṣawwar	تصوّر
to imitate (vt)	ʾalled	قلّد
to implore (vt)	etwassel	إتوسّل
to import (vt)	estawrad	إستورّد
to increase (vi)	ezdād	إزداد
to increase (vt)	zawwed	زوّد
to infect (vt)	ʿada	عدى
to influence (vt)	assar fi	أثّر في
to inform (e.g., ~ the police about)	ʾāl le	قال لـ

to inform (vt)	ʾāl ly	قال لي
to inherit (vt)	waras	ورث
to inquire (about ...)	estafsar	إستفسر
to insert (put in)	dakχal	دخّل
to insinuate (imply)	lammaḥ	لمّح
to insist (vi, vt)	aṣarr	أصرّ
to inspire (vt)	alham	ألهم
to instruct (teach)	ʿallem	علّم
to insult (offend)	ahān	أهان
to interest (vt)	hamm	همّ
to intervene (vi)	etdakχal	إتدخل
to introduce (sb to sb)	ʿarraf	عرّف
to invent (machine, etc.)	eχtaraʿ	إخترع
to invite (vt)	ʿazam	عزم
to iron (clothes)	kawa	كوّى
to irritate (annoy)	estafazz	إستفزّ
to isolate (vt)	ʿazal	عزل
to join (political party, etc.)	enḍamm le	إنضمّ لـ
to joke (be kidding)	hazzar	هزّر
to keep (old letters, etc.)	eḥtafaẓ	إحتفظ
to keep silent	seket	سكت
to kill (vt)	ʾatal	قتل
to knock (at the door)	daʾʾ	دقّ
to know (sb)	ʿeref	عرف
to know (sth)	ʿeref	عرف
to laugh (vi)	ḍeḥek	ضحك
to launch (start up)	aṭlaq	أطلق
to leave (~ for Mexico)	sāb	ساب
to leave (forget sth)	sāb	ساب
to leave (spouse)	sāb	ساب
to liberate (city, etc.)	ḥarrar	حرّر
to lie (~ on the floor)	raʾad	رقد
to lie (tell untruth)	kedeb	كذب
to light (campfire, etc.)	wallaʿ	ولّع
to light up (illuminate)	nawwar	نوّر
to like (I like ...)	ʿagab	عجب
to limit (vt)	ḥadded	حدّد
to listen (vi)	semeʿ	سمع
to live (~ in France)	seken	سكن
to live (exist)	ʿāʃ	عاش
to load (gun)	ʿammar	عمّر
to load (vehicle, etc.)	ʃaḥn	شحن
to look (I'm just ~ing)	baṣṣ	بصّ
to look for ... (search)	dawwar ʿala	دوّر على

to look like (resemble)	kān yeʃbeh	كان يشبه
to lose (umbrella, etc.)	ḍaya'	ضيّع
to love (e.g., ~ dancing)	ḥabb	حبّ
to love (sb)	ḥabb	حبّ
to lower (blind, head)	nazzel	نزّل
to make (~ dinner)	ḥaḍḍar	حضّر
to make a mistake	ɣeleṭ	غلط
to make angry	narfez	نرفز
to make easier	sahhal	سهّل
to make multiple copies	ṣawwar	صوّر
to make the acquaintance	ta'arraf	تعرّف
to make use (of ...)	estanfa'	إستنفع
to manage, to run	adār	أدار
to mark (make a mark)	'allem	علّم
to mean (signify)	'aṣad	قصد
to memorize (vt)	ḥafaẓ	حفظ
to mention (talk about)	zakar	ذكر
to miss (school, etc.)	ɣāb	غاب
to mix (combine, blend)	χalaṭ	خلط
to mock (make fun of)	saχar	سخر
to move (to shift)	ḥarrak	حرّك
to multiply (math)	ḍarab	ضرب
must (v aux)	kān lāzem	كان لازم

255. Verbs N-R

to name, to call (vt)	samma	سمّى
to negotiate (vi)	tafāwaḍ	تفاوض
to note (write down)	katab molaḥẓa	كتب ملاحظة
to notice (see)	lāḥaẓ	لاحظ
to obey (vi, vt)	ṭā'	طاع
to object (vi, vt)	e'tarad	إعترض
to observe (see)	rāqab	راقب
to offend (vt)	ahān	أهان
to omit (word, phrase)	ḥazaf	حذف
to open (vt)	fataḥ	فتح
to order (in restaurant)	ṭalab	طلب
to order (mil.)	amar	أمر
to organize (concert, party)	nazzam	نظّم
to overestimate (vt)	bāleɣ fel ta'dīr	بالغ في التقدير
to own (possess)	malak	ملك
to participate (vi)	ʃārek	شارك
to pass through (by car, etc.)	marr be	مرّ بـ

to pay (vi, vt)	dafaʿ	دفع
to peep, spy on	etgasses ʿala	إتجسس على
to penetrate (vt)	dakχal	دخَل
to permit (vt)	samaḥ	سمح
to pick (flowers)	ʾaṭaf	قطف
to place (put, set)	ḥaṭṭ	حطّ
to plan (~ to do sth)	χaṭṭeṭ	خطّط
to play (actor)	massel	مثّل
to play (children)	leʿeb	لعب
to point (~ the way)	ʃāwer	شاور
to pour (liquid)	ṣabb	صبّ
to pray (vi, vt)	ṣalla	صلّى
to prefer (vt)	faḍḍal	فضّل
to prepare (~ a plan)	ḥaḍḍar	حضّر
to present (sb to sb)	ʾaddem	قدّم
to preserve (peace, life)	ḥafaẓ	حفظ
to prevail (vt)	ɣalab	غلب
to progress (move forward)	taʾaddam	تقدّم
to promise (vt)	waʿad	وعد
to pronounce (vt)	naṭaʾ	نطق
to propose (vt)	ʿaraḍ	عرض
to protect (e.g., ~ nature)	ḥama	حمى
to protest (vi)	eḥtagg	إحتجّ
to prove (vt)	asbat	أثبت
to provoke (vt)	estafazz	إستفزّ
to pull (~ the rope)	ʃadd	شدّ
to punish (vt)	ʿāqab	عاقب
to push (~ the door)	zaʾʾ	زقّ
to put away (vt)	ʃāl	شال
to put in order	nazzam	نظّم
to put, to place	ḥaṭṭ	حطّ
to quote (cite)	estaʃ-hed	إستشهد
to reach (arrive at)	weṣel	وصل
to read (vi, vt)	ʾara	قرأ
to realize (a dream)	ḥaʾʾaʾ	حقّق
to recognize (identify sb)	mayez	ميّز
to recommend (vt)	naṣaḥ	نصح
to recover (~ from flu)	ʃefy	شفي
to redo (do again)	ʿād	عاد
to reduce (speed, etc.)	ʾallel	قلّل
to refuse (~ sb)	rafaḍ	رفض
to regret (be sorry)	nedem	ندم

to reinforce (vt)	ʻazzez	عزّز
to remember (Do you ~ me?)	eftakar	إفتكر
to remember (I can't ~ her name)	eftakar	إفتكر
to remind of ...	fakkar be ...	فكّر بـ...
to remove (~ a stain)	ʃāl	شال
to remove (~ an obstacle)	ʃāl, azāl	شال, أزال
to rent (sth from sb)	est'gar	إستأجر
to repair (mend)	ṣallaḥ	صلّح
to repeat (say again)	karrar	كرّر
to report (make a report)	'addem taqrīr	قدّم تقرير
to reproach (vt)	lām	لام
to reserve, to book	ḥagaz	حجز
to restrain (hold back)	manaʻ nafso	منع نفسه
to return (come back)	regeʻ	رجع
to risk, to take a risk	χāṭar	خاطر
to rub out (erase)	masaḥ	مسح
to run (move fast)	gery	جري
to rush (hurry sb)	estaʻgel	إستعجل

256. Verbs S-W

to satisfy (please)	rāḍa	راضى
to save (rescue)	anqaz	أنقذ
to say (~ thank you)	'āl	قال
to scold (vt)	wabbeχ	وبّخ
to scratch (with claws)	χarbeʃ	خربش
to select (to pick)	eχtār	إختار
to sell (goods)	bāʻ	باع
to send (a letter)	arsal	أرسل
to send back (vt)	aʻād	أعاد
to sense (~ danger)	ḥass be	حسّ بـ
to sentence (vt)	ḥakam	حكم
to serve (in restaurant)	χaddem	خدّم
to settle (a conflict)	sawwa	سوّى
to shake (vt)	ragg	رجّ
to shave (vi)	ḥala'	حلق
to shine (gleam)	lemʻ	لمع
to shiver (with cold)	ertaʻaʃ	إرتعش
to shoot (vi)	ḍarab bel nār	ضرب بالنار
to shout (vi)	ṣarraχ	صرّخ

to show (to display)	'arad̩	عرض
to shudder (vi)	erta'aʃ	ارتعش
to sigh (vi)	tanahhad	تنهّد
to sign (document)	waqqa'	وقّع
to signify (mean)	dallel	دلّل
to simplify (vt)	bassat̩	بسّط
to sin (vi)	aznab	أذنب
to sit (be sitting)	'a'ad	قعد
to sit down (vi)	'a'ad	قعد
to smell (emit an odor)	fāḥ	فاح
to smell (inhale the odor)	ʃamm	شمّ
to smile (vi)	ebtasam	إبتسم
to snap (vi, ab. rope)	et'at̩a'	إتقطع
to solve (problem)	ḥall	حلّ
to sow (seed, crop)	bezr	بذر
to spill (liquid)	dala'	دلق
to spill out, scatter (flour, etc.)	sa'at̩	سقط
to spit (vi)	taff	تفّ
to stand (toothache, cold)	etthammel	إتّحمّل
to start (begin)	bada'	بدأ
to steal (money, etc.)	sara'	سرق
to stop (for pause, etc.)	wa''af	وقّف
to stop (please ~ calling me)	bat̩t̩al	بطّل
to stop talking	seket	سكت
to stroke (caress)	masaḥ 'ala	مسح على
to study (vt)	daras	درس
to suffer (feel pain)	'āna	عانى
to support (cause, idea)	ayed	أيّد
to suppose (assume)	eftarad̩	إفترض
to surface (ab. submarine)	ertafa' le sat̩-ḥ el maya	إرتفع لسطح الميّة
to surprise (amaze)	fāga'	فاجئ
to suspect (vt)	eʃtabah fi	إشتبه في
to swim (vi)	'ām, sabaḥ	عام, سبح
to take (get hold of)	aχad	أخذ
to take a bath	estaḥamma	إستحمّى
to take a rest	ertāḥ	إرتاح
to take away (e.g., about waiter)	rāḥ be	راح بـ
to take off (airplane)	aqla'	أقلع
to take off (painting, curtains, etc.)	ʃāl	شال

to take pictures	ṣawwar	صوّر
to talk to ...	kallem ...	كلّم...
to teach (give lessons)	darres	درّس
to tear off, to rip off (vt)	ʾaṭaʿ	قطع
to tell (story, joke)	ḥaka	حكى
to thank (vt)	ʃakar	شكر
to think (believe)	eʿtaqad	إعتقد
to think (vi, vt)	fakkar	فكّر
to threaten (vt)	hadded	هدّد
to throw (stone, etc.)	rama	رمى
to tie to ...	rabaṭ be ...	ربط بـ...
to tie up (prisoner)	rabaṭ	ربط
to tire (make tired)	taʿab	تعّب
to touch (one's arm, etc.)	lamas	لمس
to tower (over ...)	ertafaʿ	إرتفع
to train (animals)	darrab	درّب
to train (sb)	darrab	درّب
to train (vi)	etdarrab	إتدرّب
to transform (vt)	ḥawwel	حوّل
to translate (vt)	targem	ترجم
to treat (illness)	ʿālag	عالج
to trust (vt)	wasaq	وثق
to try (attempt)	ḥāwel	حاول
to turn (e.g., ~ left)	ḥād	حاد
to turn away (vi)	aʿraḍ ʿan	أعرض عن
to turn off (the light)	ṭaffa	طفّى
to turn on (computer, etc.)	fataḥ, ʃagɣal	فتح, شغّل
to turn over (stone, etc.)	ʾalab	قلب
to underestimate (vt)	estaχaff	إستخفّ
to underline (vt)	ḥaṭṭ χaṭṭ taḥt	حطّ خطّ تحت
to understand (vt)	fehem	فهم
to undertake (vt)	ʾām be	قام بـ
to unite (vt)	waḥḥed	وحّد
to untie (vt)	fakk	فكّ
to use (phrase, word)	estaχdam	إستخدم
to vaccinate (vt)	laqqaḥ	لقّح
to vote (vi)	ṣawwat	صوّت
to wait (vt)	estanna	إستنّى
to wake (sb)	ṣaḥḥa	صحّى
to want (wish, desire)	ʿāyez	عايز
to warn (of the danger)	ḥazzar	حذّر
to wash (clean)	ɣasal	غسل

to water (plants)	sa'a	سقى
to wave (the hand)	ʃāwer	شاور
to weigh (have weight)	wazan	وزن
to work (vi)	eʃtaɣal	إشتغل
to worry (make anxious)	a'la'	أقلق
to worry (vi)	'ala'	قلق
to wrap (parcel, etc.)	laff	لفّ
to wrestle (sport)	ṣāra'	صارع
to write (vt)	katab	كتب
to write down	katab	كتب

Printed in Great Britain
by Amazon

62455618R00159